D1612344

Frontispiece. *A selection of typical relief-moulded Lowestoft porcelains of Hughes type, see page 54. Tea caddy 4⁹⁄₁₀ ins. high (see also Plate 67). c.1760-8.* Author's Collection.

LOWESTOFT PORCELAINS

Geoffrey A. Godden
F.R.S.A.

Antique Collector's Club

ISBN 0 907462 64 2

First published in 1969 by Herbert Jenkins Ltd., London
This edition published 1985
for the Antique Collectors' Club
by the Antique Collectors' Club Ltd.

British Library CIP Data
Godden, Geoffrey A.
Lowestoft porcelains.— Rev. ed.
1. Lowestoft porcelain
I. Title
738.2'7 NK4399.L7

Printed in England by the Antique Collectors' Club, Church Street,
Woodbridge, Suffolk

TO A.J.B. KIDDELL
— a friend of all collectors, much missed.

By the same author

Victorian Porcelain
Encyclopaedia of British Pottery and Porcelain Marks
An Illustrated Encyclopaedia of British Pottery and Porcelain
The Handbook of British Pottery and Porcelain Marks
Minton Pottery and Porcelain of the First Period
Caughley and Worcester Porcelain, 1775-1800
Coalport and Coalbrookdale Porcelains
Stevengraphs and other Victorian Silk Pictures
Jewitt's Ceramic Art of Great Britain 1800-1900 (Revised and re-illustrated edition, 1972)
The Illustrated Guide to Lowestoft Porcelain
The Illustrated Guide to Mason's Patent Ironstone China
The Illustrated Guide to Ridgway Porcelains
British Porcelain, an Illustrated Guide
British Pottery, an Illustrated Guide
Godden's Guide to English Porcelain
Oriental Export Market Porcelain and its influence on European wares
Godden's Guide to Mason's China and the Ironstone Wares
Chamberlain — Worcester Porcelain 1788-1852
Staffordshire Porcelain
English China
Ridgway Porcelains — Revised edition

CONTENTS

ANTIQUE COLLECTORS' CLUB

The Antique Collectors' Club was formed in 1966 and now has a five figure membership spread throughout the world. It publishes the only independently run monthly antiques magazine *Antique Collecting* which caters for those collectors who are interested in widening their knowledge of antiques, both by greater awareness of quality and by discussion of the factors which influence the price that is likely to be asked. The Antique Collectors' Club pioneered the provision of information on prices for collectors and the magazine still leads in the provision of detailed articles on a variety of subjects.

It was in response to the enormous demand for information on "what to pay" that the price guide series was introduced in 1968 with the first edition of *The Price Guide to Antique Furniture* (completely revised, 1978), a book which broke new ground by illustrating the more common types of antique furniture, the sort that collectors could buy in shops and at auctions rather than the rare museum pieces which had previously been used (and still to a large extent are used) to make up the limited amount of illustrations in books published by commercial publishers. Many other price guides have followed, all copiously illustrated, and greatly appreciated by collectors for the valuable information they contain, quite apart from prices. The Antique Collectors' Club also publishes other books on antiques, including horology and art reference works, and a full book list is available.

Club membership, which is open to all collectors, costs £11.50 per annum. Members receive free of charge *Antique Collecting,* the Club's magazine (published every month except August), which contains well-illustrated articles dealing with the practical aspects of collecting not normally dealt with by magazines. Prices, features of value, investment potential, fakes and forgeries are all given prominence in the magazine.

Among other facilities available to members are private buying and selling facilities, the longest list of "For Sales" of any antiques magazine, an annual ceramics conference and the opportunity to meet other collectors at their local antique collectors' clubs. There are nearly eighty in Britain and so far a dozen overseas. Members may also buy the Club's publications at special pre-publication prices.

As its motto implies, the Club is an amateur organisation designed to help collectors get the most out of their hobby: it is informal and friendly and gives enormous enjoyment to all concerned.

For Collectors — By Collectors — About Collecting

The Antique Collectors' Club, 5 Church Street, Woodbridge, Suffolk

COLOUR PLATES

Author's Preface
to the
1969 Edition

Although, as editor of this new series of *Illustrated Guides,* I could have chosen any one of several subjects to launch the project, the present choice was not merely arbitrary, for the truth is that Lowestoft china is my first love. It was Lowestoft that started me collecting during my school days, and, although I have admittedly expanded my interests considerably since, it has never ceased to give me pleasure.

The Lowestoft porcelains are in many respects unique for, from 1757 to about 1773, no overglaze enamelled decoration was employed, [see page 25] all patterns being in underglaze blue. In the main, the factory catered for local needs, supplying useful, rather than ornamental, objects, and a fine range of special presentation pieces was decorated to order, showing local scenes or commemorating weddings and births. The charming, circular, birth tablets [Plates 227, 229 and 234] are unique, and record the names and dates of birth of local children. The well-known Trifle pieces [Colour Plate 11, Plates 224-5, 233 and 239], mugs, inkpots and similar objects painted for sale to visitors to Lowestoft and other East Anglian resorts or villages, were the forerunners of a vast market catering for the natural instinct to buy mementoes of places visited, though none of the later equivalents has the charm of these original Lowestoft 'Trifles'.

Even the simple standard designs, whether in underglaze blue or in the later overglaze enamels, have a naïve charm that is quite delightful and perfectly appropriate to the relatively soft, friendly body, so that even the later pieces have a primitive appearance quite different from that of some of the more sophisticated English porcelains of the same period.

Although prices have risen considerably in the past few years, it is still possible to buy standard Lowestoft patterns quite cheaply and, while the key, inscribed and dated, pieces rightly command a high price at auction, the knowledgeable collector stands a good chance of discovering bargains in unexpected places. The — possibly unique — plate illustrated in Plate 85, was recently displayed in a Brighton shop for several weeks with a price tag of under fifteen pounds; when subsequently sold at Sotheby's it changed hands at six hundred pounds! I hope that this example will not influence people to collect Lowestoft for the financial reward only, but that they will be attracted by the natural, unpretentious charm of the wares made in this small East Coast factory.

Geoffrey A. Godden

1969

ACKNOWLEDGEMENTS

Firstly, I wish to acknowledge the generous help that I have received over many years from the late Mr. A.J.B. Kiddell of Messrs. Sotheby's. It is not only right but also fitting that this book on Lowestoft porcelain should be dedicated to this friend of all collectors.

I am also indebted to many fellow collectors for much assistance and advice and also for supplying photographs of pieces in their own collections. These enthusiasts include: Norman Baker, Mr. and Mrs. Peter Bennett, A.W. Denny, Mr. and Mrs. John Howell, Mr. and Mrs. E. Hutchinson, E.E. Levine, George J. Levine, Henry Levine, J.H. Nurse, Miss Paul, S. Spero, C. Staal, N. Turner, Dr. B. Watney and H.C. Wolton.

Appreciation is also due to many Trade friends for their ready co-operation and particularly for supplying illustrations. These include T.C.S. Brooke of Wroxham; E. Hutchinson, 'Chanctonbury Gallery', Washington, Sussex; E.D. Levine, The Antique Gallery, Cromer; Henry Levine, Norwich; Simon Spero, 'China Choice', London; J. and E.D. Vandekar, London; W.W. Warner (Antiques) Ltd., Brasted; and Winifred Williams (Antiques), London. Other trade photographs have been supplied by Messrs. Godden of Worthing, Ltd. Many other illustrations depict articles which have been sold through Messrs. Sotheby and Co. The credit to all the above firms, given in the relevant captions, are courtesy credits only, acknowledging the source of the illustration, and the reader should understand that many articles are not still in that ownership.

Many other illustrations have been supplied by the Directors, or Curators, of public museums. I should like to thank the following for their able and willing attention to my many requests: L.M. Bickerton, Curator, Worthing Museum and Art Gallery; Miss P.M. Butler, Curator, Ipswich Museums and Art Galleries; R.J. Charleston, Keeper, Dept. of Ceramics, Victoria and Albert Museum; A.A.C. Hedges, Curator, Great Yarmouth Museums; W. James, Borough Librarian, Lowestoft Libraries; D. Piper, Director, Fitzwilliam Museum, Cambridge; H. Sandon, Curator, Worcester Royal Porcelain Co., Ltd.; Miss Sheenah Smith, Asst. Keeper of Art, Castle Museum, Norwich (Director — Francis W. Cheetham, B.A., F.M.A.); Hugh Tait, Asst. Keeper, Dept. of British and Medieval Antiquities, British Museum. [Several of these persons have now retired from the posts here quoted.] Other illustrations originate from the County Museum, Truro, and from the Ceylon Tea Centre, London. Recent finds of 'wasters' on the factory side are reproduced by permission of the officers of the Lowestoft Archaeological and Local History Society, and the ownership of earlier finds are acknowledged under the relevant illustrations. The records of former sale prices, quoted in Appendix II, have, in the main, been gleaned from Messrs. Sotheby's and Messrs. Christie's printed catalogues. These and other Auctioneers are acknowledged in the heading to each sale.

To the list of helpers to the original edition I must add my gratitude to the following for their generous help in the preparation of this revised edition and for some of the new illustrations — Mrs. Elizabeth Adams, Mrs. Sheila Davis, C.C. Silburn, Christopher Spencer and Simon Spero.

Plate 1. *Nineteenth century photograph of the Lowestoft factory buildings, as they appeared in the 1890s. Many moulds and factory 'wasters' were found under a floor.* Reproduced from F.A. Crisp's 'Lowestoft China Factory', (1907).

Introduction to Revised Edition

It has given me particular pleasure to sanction this revised edition of my 1969 book *The Illustrated Guide to Lowestoft Porcelain,* for it was the first work in the then Herbert Jenkins series of *Illustrated Guides* dealing with various aspects of British ceramics. As editor of the series, I prepared this book partly as a guide to my other authors and also because Lowestoft was my 'first love'.

I was lucky in that I was collecting, in a modest way, whilst still at school in the mid- and late 1940s. I see that my earliest purchases cost two shillings (10p), five shillings (25p), one pound five shillings (£1.25p) and so on. These purchases gave me pleasure and interest then, as they, and subsequent buys, have over the last forty years. My only regret is that I did not buy more in the 1940s and 1950s, but more of this financial aspect later.

The 1969 first edition was out of print in 1976 and new copies have therefore been unobtainable for some nine years. A straight reprint would therefore have filled a great need, especially for new collectors. However, it seemed advantageous to seize the opportunity and to revise the original text, to add to it where appropriate and to include new illustrations. Although now issued as a revised edition, this present book could reasonably be regarded as a new work and of interest and help to all collectors.

Quite obviously much research has been carried on since 1969, some interesting discoveries have been made and some specialist books and Papers published. I shall in this Introduction briefly draw attention to the new situation as we understand it today.

Whilst we still do not know the exact date of the factory's establishment or rather when the first successful products were sold to the public, our old tentative establishment date of 1757 has in part been substantiated by the discovery by Mrs. Elizabeth Adams of an insurance policy dated January 27th, 1756, taken out by Obed Aldred, 'Bricklayer', not Philip Walker or Luson (page 41). This important policy mentions a 'stock of stoneware' (not porcelain), four warehouses and a 'Kilnhouse adjoining'. A single kiln is adequate to fire stonewares — especially once-fired saltglaze stonewares — but the production of porcelain would require two kilns — one for the first, high (biscuit) firing and the second for the glazed porcelain which was fired at a lower temperature. Abel Bly's first-hand account of the porcelain factory as he remembered it, mentioned two kilns — see page 45 — as does a 1765 insurance cover.

Mr. John Howell in his excellent E.C.C. Paper 'Early Lowestoft' published in the *Transactions of the English Ceramic Circle,* Vol. II, part 2 (1982) has suggested that the 'stock of Stone Ware' mentioned in the January 1756 policy need not have been domestic useful wares but that it could well have been tiles, bricks and such ceramic building materials. To support this contention we have the fact that the policy was in Obed Aldred's name and he was a bricklayer by trade. Mr. Howell's theory also links with Philip Walker's advertisement relating to the sale of pantiles and roofing tiles at Gunton, see page 42.

The policy is mentioned by Mrs. Adams in her E.C.C. Paper 'The Bow Insurances and Related Matters', *Transactions of the English Ceramic Circle,* Vol. 9, part 1 (1973) and in *The Northern Ceramic Society Newsletter* number 28 of December, 1977.

Mrs. Elizabeth Adam's researches amongst the Sun Insurance Company's eighteenth century policies have also brought to light a further partner in the Lowestoft Porcelain Works. According to a 1765 policy we should add Robert Williams to the list of partners given by me on page 42. Mrs. Adams also discovered a 1766 policy for 'Robert Williams of Yarmouth, pipemaker'.

On the other hand Robert Browne, a partner who collectors have considered to be a key figure, reputedly the factory chemist and manager, may not have been so important or talented in the early days for Christopher Spencer and John Howell have independently discovered documents wherein he is described as a Smith or workman; and, on the marriage licence of his daughter, Ann, Robert Browne more fully described himself as a 'Blacksmith' (see *Early Lowestoft* by C. Spencer, page 14). However, one should bear firmly in mind that when John Stevenson was apprenticed on June 12th, 1760, it was to 'Robert Browne of Lowestoft Porcelain maker'. A Mr. Browne appears in the Bow wages records as receiving 18/- a week in the important 1757-8 period.

Mr. Spencer and Sheenah Smith have both suggested that the partner who Edmund Gillinwater listed in 1790 as John Rickman was in fact one James Richmond.

Moving from the partners to the products we still have the all-important advertisement which I quote on page 43. This announcement dated January 26th, 1760, appeared in the *Ipswich Journal* and also in the *Norwich Mercury,* gives the then trading style 'Walker & Co.' and seems to be the first notice to dealers that a new type of 'Porcelain or China Ware' would be available from Lady Day — March 25th, 1760. The new wares were described only as 'a great variety of neat Blue and White China or Porcelain at the Manufactory in this Town'.

The great tantalising problems which concern many dedicated collectors are what was being offered in March 1760 and what experimental wares were produced before the partners were confident that they had an acceptable product. Also for how long had these pre-1760 experiments been carried on? In other words what, if any, Lowestoft porcelains were produced in the late 1750s?

From 1761 onwards we are on reasonably firm ground for we have a succession of dated, presentation pieces — see Appendix I, also we have various moulded wares which include in the design the date, or rather year, when the master mould or basic design was first worked, see page 54, and items of the type shown in Plates 53 to 63.

But to complicate matters we have at least two basic types of Lowestoft porcelain which pre-date the 1761 examples.

Firstly, we have the most attractive early porcelains which normally have a poor translucency, some bubbling of the body and a rather bubbled hazy glaze — faults which in no way detract from the primitive appeal of this rare class which is decorated in a characteristic manner. Very typical examples are shown in Plates 32 to 37 and in Colour Plates 1 and 5. The mass of 'wasters' found on the factory site in 1902 include a relatively high percentage of this class, some 'wasters' having as yet no link with known, perfect, examples. The difficulties experienced seem understandably to have concerned the firing. Many of the early 'wasters' are fire stained or have over-fired, very bubbled or run glaze. A small selection of such early 'wasters' from my own collection is shown in Plate 29. Further early 'wasters' are featured in Sheenah Smith's *Lowestoft Porcelain in Norwich Castle Museum* Vol. I and in Christopher Spencer's *Early Lowestoft*.

It is now generally agreed that these pieces were produced in the 1757-9 experimental period but the rare cane handle here shown as Plate 2 belongs to this class and I pose the question could the management have produced such an object in its earliest experimental days? One may also ponder how experimental is the delightful and perfect spoon tray shown in Colour Plate 5. A piece which Christopher Spencer states is his 'favourite piece of English porcelain. The elegant fluted shuttle shape is

Plate 2. *A rare, possibly unique, early Lowestoft cane handle, painted in underglaze blue in a characteristic style. 1¾ ins. high. c.1758-60.* Author's Collection.

Plate 3. *A very rare and early Lowestoft cream or milk jug painted with a typical mock-Oriental scene in underglaze blue. Painter's number '3'. 3¼ ins. high. c.1758-60.* Private Collection. (Photograph Geoffrey Godden, Chinaman).

complemented by the superb decoration of water birds and flowering plants. The decoration gives a feeling of movement and one can almost sense an impression of sound issuing from the beaks of the craning birds as they call to their acrobatic colleague overhead.' Mr. Spencer dates this piece c.1758-9. He is probably correct in this dating but surely, on the evidence of this and some other pieces, this period can hardly be called experimental. Obviously some very good pieces were being produced, were put on market and successfully sold to the buying public for we have them available today. The 'First Period' perhaps rather than the experimental period would be a more fitting description for these pieces tentatively dated 1757 to 1759.

It must be stated that rare as these early pieces are they are quite distinctive, being of unique form and style of decoration, not showing any dependency on the contemporary Bow porcelains. That is apart from the high proportion of bone ash in the body mix, an analysis of which I publish on page 53. The pre-1760 body often displays a pinkish surface tinge and pieces can show a likeness to tin-glaze Delft-like earthenwares. My original description when I likened the body to glazed pipe clay has been generally accepted. In general the early underglaze blue is rather pale in contrast to that used in the early 1760s. It is also rather grey in comparison with the brighter and darker later tints.

Following these very early porcelains with their pale often greyish blue under a bubbled glaze, we have a small class with an entirely different appearance. The glaze is

Plate 4. *A superb early Lowestoft mug painted in underglaze blue, note the early handle form. Painter's number '2' on inside of footrim. 6ins. high. c.1760.* Author's Collection.

Colour Plate 1. *A selection of blue and white Lowestoft porcelains. Left to right: a typical relief-moulded sauce boat, a rare tall vase, a typical toy coffee cup and saucer and a very rare early leaf-shape dish. Vase 8ins. high. c.1758-75.* Photograph Godden of Worthing Ltd.

Plate 5. *The front and reverse side of a splendid Lowestoft cylindrical mug, with a slightly flared base. Painted in underglaze blue in a very typical style. Painter's number '3'. c.1761-2.* Author's Collection.

wet looking, almost oily, devoid of bubbles and the blue is brighter and darker. Such wares, on account of their rarity, were seemingly only produced for a brief period. Typical examples are illustrated in Plates 42, 43 and 44.

We then come to the reasonably standard pieces of a very compact, dense, heavy body with a good glaze but not of the wet looking variety just described. The dated 1761-plus wares belong to this and later classes, indicating that the previous type predate 1761 or, to be more exact, predate 1762.

Much interest has been rightly shown in the often delightful and charming relief-moulded Lowestoft porcelains with underglaze blue landscape subjects panels (see Frontispiece). Recent research on these wares is contained in Christopher Spencer's 1981 book *Early Lowestoft* and in John Howell's English Ceramic Circle's Paper of the same title (*Transactions,* Vol. II, part 2, 1982). I have noted, on page 56, Mr. Howell's bombshell that James Hughes described himself as a 'painter' rather than a modeller or designer as I would have wished, for Hughes' name is traditionally linked with those moulded wares which sometimes bear the initials 'I.H.' and a year date incorporated in the moulding. In addition to the recent publications just mentioned, Sheenah Smith's *Lowestoft Porcelain in Norwich Castle Museum* contains very helpful drawings and illustrations.

I cannot resist including in this Introduction new illustrations of a rare early c.1759-60 Hughes type teapot (Plate 6), two so dainty little cream (?) boats (Plate 9), two upright silver shape milk or cream jugs (Plate 7) the right hand example being very

ERRATUM

Page 21, 3rd line:
for 1890s *read* 1980s.

Colour Plate 2. *A perhaps unique small teapot hand painted and inscribed in underglaze blue (see page 238). 4ins. high, c.1785. Sold in 1887 for £2, in 1933 for £34 and in 1948 for £84. Probable value in the 1890s over £1,000.*

Plate 6. *An exceedingly rare and early relief-moulded teapot of Hughes type (see page 54). Indistinct painter's number inside footrim. 5½ ins. high. c.1760-2.* Photograph C.C. Silburn, Esq.

Plate 7. *Two typical Lowestoft relief-moulded cream or milk jugs of Hughes type (see page 20). The example on the right a near copy of a Worcester shape is the rarer. 3½ ins. high. c.1762-5.* Author's Collection.

Colour Plate 2. *A perhaps unique small teapot hand painted and inscribed in underglaze blue (see page 238). 4ins. high, c.1785. Sold in 1887 for £2, in 1933 for £34 and in 1948 for £84. Probable value in the 1890s over £1,000.*

Plate 6. *An exceedingly rare and early relief-moulded teapot of Hughes type (see page 54). Indistinct painter's number inside footrim. 5½ ins. high. c.1760-2.* Photograph C.C. Silburn, Esq.

Plate 7. *Two typical Lowestoft relief-moulded cream or milk jugs of Hughes type (see page 20). The example on the right a near copy of a Worcester shape is the rarer. 3½ ins. high. c.1762-5.* Author's Collection.

Plate 8. *A rare large size tea (or chocolate) cup and saucer, relief moulded with an unusual floral design — the cup moulding being similar to an early Worcester design. Diameter of saucer 6⅛ ins. c.1762-75.* Author's Collection.

Plate 9. *Two typically charming small size Lowestoft relief-moulded 'boats'. Note the underglaze blue dashes by the handle joints. Painter's mark 'X' and '3' (lower example). 4ins. long.* Author's Collection.

Plate 10. *A rare relief-moulded Lowestoft sauce boat, painted in underglaze blue. Note, the relief-moulded birds each side of the main panel. 7¾ ins. long. c.1765.* Author's Collection.

Plate 11. *A simple moulded oval butter (?) tureen and cover. The cover ribbing is also known running across the cover (see Plate 52). Painter's number '8' on footrim. 5ins. long. c.1765.* Author's Collection.

Plate 12. *A rare ribbed creamer and an equally unusual coffee cup or can. 2½ ins. high. c.1765.* Godden of Worthing Ltd.

closely copied from a standard Worcester model, and a rare cup and saucer (Plate 8). This handled cup is of an unusually large size, a breakfast cup perhaps.

I am happy also to include two new illustrations (Plates 11 & 12) of the attractive closely ribbed porcelains which are usually decorated only with simple border designs.

Attention should also be drawn to John Howell's important E.C.C. Paper 'Transfer-printed Lowestoft Porcelain' as published in the *Transactions of the English Ceramic Circle,* Vol. 7, part 3 (1970). The Lowestoft printing is always in underglaze blue and, although not of outstanding quality, it often has a naïve charm lacking in

Plate 13. *A surprisingly rare Lowestoft printed design in underglaze blue. The so-called 'Tea Party' design. Diameter of saucer 4¾ ins. c.1775.* Author's Collection.

printed wares from other factories. Admittedly some Lowestoft printed wares are mere copies of popular and therefore saleable Worcester productions, but other designs are unique to the Lowestoft factory. Some of these designs are also surprisingly rare. Mr. Howell in 1969 knew of only one saucer of the Chinese tea party design. I here show a second example, in Plate 13.

The Lowestoft blue printed wares of the approximate period 1768-90 comprise a surprisingly large number of shapes, apart from the standard tea and coffee wares. I here show in Plates 14-16 a rare spittoon and an unusual ribbed coffee pot, the latter with particularly rare blue prints, and an oval Hughes-type butter bowl, a type rarely found with printed decoration (Plate 16). John Howell's E.C.C. Paper illustrated many other prints and forms which occur with blue printed decoration.

A type of blue printed (and blue painted) Lowestoft not mentioned by Mr. Howell is the generally unsatisfactory pieces which have the printed design overpainted with red and green enamel colours, sometimes with slight gilding. The set of three mugs shown in Plate 17 is of this unlovely type. Perhaps stale stock was enamelled up in this manner to make it more saleable, but it must be remembered that such combinations of blue and white and enamelling occur on perfectly genuine Chinese and Japanese porcelains, as well as on some Bow, Liverpool and Worcester designs. Such contemporary factory decoration should not be confused with the later 'clobbering' of old porcelains to suit the taste of some later collectors. The inscribed and dated 1775 example listed as item D82 A, on page 227 is also of this type.

One of the most important developments since the publication of the first volume of this book in 1969 has been the realisation that the overglaze enamel designs were

Plate 14. *A rare Lowestoft handled spittoon, printed in underglaze blue with a copy of a stock Worcester print. Printed open crescent mark. 4½ins. high. c.1775.* Geoffrey Godden, Chinaman.

Plate 15. *An unusual Lowestoft fluted coffee pot and cover, printed in underglaze blue. 10ins. high. c.1775-80.* Godden of Worthing Ltd.

Plate 16. *A relief-moulded oval butter pot, the reserve panels decorated with underglaze blue floral sprays. 6½ins. long. c.1775-80.* Geoffrey Godden, Chinaman.

Plate 17. *A set of three Lowestoft blue printed mugs. The flower prints occur on the earliest dated printed example known (1771). With these mugs the blue prints have added enamel decoration. 5 ½ to 3 ¼ ins. high. c.1775-80.* Author's Collection.

Plate 18. *An early example of overglaze enamelled decoration on a Lowestoft globular teapot. The Oriental-style pattern is typical. 5 ½ ins. high. c.1768-70.* Sotheby's.

Plate 19. *A rare and early Lowestoft enamelled teapot with characteristic open flower knob. 4 ⅞ ins. high. c.1768-70.* Victoria and Albert Museum (C.189.1924) (Crown Copyright).

introduced prior to 1774. Once again collectors are indebted to the clear mind of collector John Howell. His thoughts on the subject are published in his E.C.C. Paper 'Some Notes on the Introduction of Polychrome Decoration at Lowestoft' (*Transactions of the English Ceramic Circle,* vol. 9, part 3, 1975).

Mr. Howell rightly draws attention to the fact that as early as 1763 the Lowestoft management had a London dealer acting, at least, as stockist of their wares, for as I state on page 44 *Mortimer's London Directory* of 1763 contains an entry for William Mathews, Leostoffe (sic) China Warehouse, Addle Street, Aldermanbury. This London outlet — small as it may have been — must have suggested that designs other than blue and white were in demand. Of course, there is a small class of overglaze decoration which clearly pre-dates 1770. This is the so-called black pencilled ware, such as the 1766 dated mug which I illustrate as Plate 83. The feeding cup shown in Plate 113 could also be of this period. In general this class of decoration is in the style of some Chinese export market porcelains which can be quite early, c.1740 onwards.

Enamelled Lowestoft teapots of the type I now show as Plates 18 and 19 can reasonably be linked with blue and white pieces of the 1768-70 period. This particular open flower knob and the rather low domed cover are typical of this rather rare form which seemingly was only made for a short period. This open flower type knob is interestingly seen on a Hughes-type covered sugar bowl shown in Plate 74, an example confidently dated to the mid-1760s. It occurs again on the splendid Tulip painter coffee pot shown in Plate 148, an example of c.1770. This flower knob is quite different from the rather solid later example which is normally mounted on a dumpy hump — see Plates 127, 129, 141, 142, 202 and 204. The style of decoration on these two teapots is typical of the Lowestoft factory's earliest essays in overglaze painting but of course they represent standard motifs popular at all English factories of the period.

The milk (or cream) jug on the right of Plate 20 would be of the same 1768 period —

Plate 20. *Four Lowestoft sparrow beak jugs, bearing different styles of overglaze enamel decoration. That on the right is the earliest c.1768-70. 3½ to 3¼ ins. high. c.1768-90.* Author's Collection.

Plate 21. *Two early Lowestoft enamelled coffee cups. Note the early handle form and compare with Plate 20 right. c.1768-70.* Author's Collection.

Plate 22. *A Lowestoft teabowl and saucer bearing a most unusual Oriental style overglaze design, perhaps copied direct from a Chinese example. Diameter of saucer 4¾ ins. c.1775.* Author's Collection.

note the handle form with the thumb rest. Incidentally, the jug shown second from the left is of a rare form with a simple loop handle and is an early example from the hand of the Tulip painter (see page 180). Dated pieces by this painter commence in 1774.

I now agree that Lowestoft overglaze enamel decoration definitely predates 1774 and that it can be as early as 1767 or 1768. I refer the reader to John Howell's E.C.C. Paper for a full summary of the facts and close my brief résumé of it with two further illustrations of interesting and rare pieces. A very rare cup (note handle form) decorated with a popular and much copied Oriental deer hunting pattern and a most unusual teabowl and saucer, the design of which may well have been copied from a Chinese example, are shown in Plates 21 and 22. Remember the great competition in the market was not so much the other English porcelain manufacturers but the masses of Chinese hard-paste porcelains which were being shipped into London in vast quantities. For this aspect of the trade the reader is referred to my book *Oriental Export Market Porcelain.*

By the way, I regard such recent statements as 'A London warehouse was opened in 1763, thus indicating a rapid growth in the factory's output' to be open to question.

Evidently there was one dealer — amongst almost hundreds plying their trade in London — who included a supply of Lowestoft porcelain. It seems unlikely to me that he owned a 'warehouse' of Lowestoft porcelain as the modern reader may interpret the 1763 newspaper announcement. I am an enthusiastic collector of Lowestoft but I cannot believe that the 1763 products made much impact in London, being rivalled not only by the flood of Chinese true porcelains but also by the Worcester, Derby and Chelsea porcelains.

In the 1969 edition I expressed some doubt on a class of figure models which matched in their basic form examples which were obviously of Lowestoft make. However, the problem examples were of a different body and glaze, were often on other bases and were decorated in a different style.

However, in 1983 I purchased such a putto which matched one of a pair of the

Plate 23. *Two Lowestoft putti figures showing the two basic types. The earliest is on the left, see page 143. 5ins. c.1768-80.* Author's Collection.

accepted type and, on comparing the two examples, I find myself reasonably convinced that they are both Lowestoft but of different periods. The problem class with a harder body and glaze and thin applied leaves are, I believe, of the 1768-72 period and the others some ten or more years later. Both types are rare and exceedingly few Lowestoft figures are at present known. I show my two types, side by side, in Plate 23.

Sheenah Smith in her 1975 catalogue of the blue and white Lowestoft porcelain in the Castle Museum at Norwich gave a brief account of an interesting document which had just been brought to her attention by Mrs. Marian Bell. This was the *Journal of Maximilien de Lazowski,* secretary to the Duc de Lioncourt, which is an account written in French, of a tour around Norfolk and Suffolk in 1784. Helpfully for Lowestoft collectors he then visited the factory and recorded interesting information which is not available from any other known source.

The Journal was written up by Miss Smith in an article 'Lazowski and Lowestoft Porcelain' published in *The Connoisseur* magazine of February 1977. The reader is referred to this article but, in essence, Lazowski recorded in 1784 that the Lowestoft factory then employed ninety to a hundred workers (a surprisingly high number). He also noted that the two kilns were fired with coal, not wood, and that the firing of the biscuit (unglazed) wares lasted for twenty-eight hours with a further three days allowed for cooling.

Lazowski recorded some wage rates — adult skilled workers earned 14/- (60p) a week, some painters were paid £1.1s.0d or £1.10s.6d (£1.52) and the children were given 7/- or 8/- a week (35p or 40p). He also reported that the Lowestoft blue and white was cheap, citing three pence (under two new pence) a cup or gilt cup at six pence (2½ new pence). Rather unhelpful information without the knowledge of the quality of the decoration. Mr. Spencer has endeavoured to estimate the original cost of the standard lines, see his book *Early Lowestoft,* page 50.

A great surprise to me was this informed Continental traveller's reference to the large export market enjoyed by the Lowestoft management. He even wrote that about half the total production was sent to Holland and, from there, some was shipped to France. The Dutch were, of course, like the English and to a lesser degree the French, great importers of Chinese porcelains. This may account for the large number of Oriental inspired or Oriental style designs found on Lowestoft porcelain — the management was catering for its markets. That, by the way, is why they continued for over forty years! In connection with the Dutch trade I would mention that the trio of teabowl, saucer and large cup shown in Plate 24 was purchased in Holland in recent years. The large, shallow, handled cup is a rarity and may have been introduced for the Continental customers. The Staffordshire factory records contain many references to Dutch size cups, indicating that this market had special requirements in regard to form or size.

I should also like to take this opportunity to qualify my beliefs on the date of closure of the factory. In the original book I stated with confidence that this took place in 1799 and not, as hitherto had been thought, in 1802 or 1803.

We have still not discovered any firm evidence, such as a closing down sale or a dissolution of partnership notice, so we have to consider the available facts to arrive at a conclusion. My then new 1799 theory was based on two points. Firstly, our lengthy list of dated Lowestoft porcelains ceased with a February 1799 birth tablet. Moreover, some later pieces decorated in the Lowestoft manner perhaps by former factory artists, were of an earthenware body, as if a supply of porcelain blanks was not longer available.

Plate 24. *A Lowestoft blue and white trio, the design being a copy of a stock Worcester design. Note the painter's number inside the footrim of the upturned teabowl, also the rare handled coffee (?) cup shape and the typical handle dashes. Diameter of saucer 5⅜ins. c.1780.* Godden of Worthing Ltd.

Secondly, as told on page 174, I discovered that many former Lowestoft hands, even complete families, were taken on by the Chamberlain management in Worcester in the latter part of 1799. The fact that many key workers had left by October 1799 suggests that production had ceased if it had not already done so.

However, research on relevant Wills suggests that a slightly later closure is at least possible. Philip Walker's Will, dated June 5th, 1802, refers in the past tense to the late porcelain manufactory, so it was evidently closed by June 1802. The Manor Court Records also show that the factory buildings were transferred in July and November 1802, but this 1802 change of ownership does not necessarily prove that the factory had only just closed. It takes time to clear premises, find a new tenant and complete a sale.

The most telling information is contained in Thomas Walker's Will dated January 28th, 1786 (Suffolk Record Office, Ipswich, IC.AAI. 208.26) and proved on April 2nd, 1788. In 1786 it was there stated that the Lowestoft porcelain concern was planned to continue for a further sixteen years from October 1785 and then cease. Taken at face value it could be stated that the factory closed in October 1801.

However, it is difficult to see how a person in January 1786 could dictate what other partners would do under various circumstances fifteen or sixteen years later. The Will obviously stated the then planned intention and the exact date given most probably relates to the duration of the lease on the property or the duration of any partnership agreement. Obviously, if circumstances dictate, a concern can be closed before a lease or partnership agreement runs out. The management were unlikely to have continued if they found themselves trading at a loss in the late 1790s.

I have on page 47 quoted the remarks of Robert Browne's son:

> I have heard my father (the factory manager) say that they discontinued the works principally because they could not produce the ware so cheaply as the Staffordshire potters, and that they were getting old and wished to retire from the business. . . .

This can hardly have been foreseen by Thomas Walker (Philip's father) in 1786 or by any of the then partners. I believe the Will in effect states only the last possible date for a planned closure and could take no account of the later trading position or feeling of the elderly partners.

Until post-1799 dated specimens are reported or records of a closing down sale are discovered, I, taking account of the movement of the many factory workers away from Lowestoft in the autumn of 1799, remain of the opinion (and it is no more) that the Lowestoft porcelain factory was purely an eighteenth century enterprise, and ceased production towards the end of 1799.

I would, however, be pleased to be proved wrong should firm evidence be forthcoming in the future. In the meantime, I believe the available information and documentation is given and listed in Sheenah Smith's excellent catalogue of the blue and white Lowestoft at the Castle Museum, Norwich.

I have already stated that the later products of the 1790s seem exceedingly rare. Some typical forms are shown in Plates 217-20 and 231-2, and such teawares are decorated in a very sparse manner, as were all inexpensive wares from other factories of the 1790s but probably the last shapes have not hitherto been featured in any book on Lowestoft porcelain. In part this is because they are so rare and I am only able now to show a teabowl and saucer and an odd saucer, together with an unglazed factory 'waster'.

I refer to the spiral fluted or 'shankered' wares here shown in Plate 25. As most

Plate 25. *Very scarce late Lowestoft spiral fluted teawares (shown with an unglazed factory waster) decorated in a typical restrained style of the late 1790s. Diameter of saucers 4 ¾ ins. c.1795-9.* Author's Collection.

readers will know most English factories of at least the 1795-1800 period were producing similar teawares, but the Lowestoft pieces in a typical soft body and glaze are the rarest of all. It certainly seems that the management, whilst endeavouring to compete with the Chamberlain-Worcester and Flight-Worcester porcelains, did so on the lowest level instead of going their own way or finding new markets for their products. They could hardly have hoped to find success in such simply decorated teasets which the market expected to buy for £1.50, or £2 for a complete service. On the evidence of the scarcity of the late wares the factory was gradually wound down. This may well be why we have not found evidence of a closing down sale. There was little or

Plate 26. *A selection of representative pieces from a Redgrave-type (page 105) two bird pattern tea and coffee service. Note, the characteristic Lowestoft teapot stand and spoon tray shapes. Coffee pot 9¾ ins. high — see also Colour Plate 7. c.1775-80.* Author's Collection.

nothing worthy of sale after many (or all) of the workers left for Worcester in the autumn of 1799.

In this updating section many readers may well require comments on post-1969 prices. As may be expected, prices have risen considerably as more and more discerning collectors seek the smaller numbers of available examples. You will see that I have added new sale reports (entries 205 to 274) to Appendix II although only the latest sales are really relevant as each brings new and usually even higher prices. It is of considerable interest that several pieces illustrated in this book were included in the sale of the late Henry Levine's collection at Norwich in November 1982. Also this sale can be related to other more standard wares of the general type illustrated in this book.

In regard to the reasonably standard teawares (not the scarce inscribed or dated pieces or rare forms) it can be stated on the evidence of this November 1982 sale that the prices given for the attractive so-called sparrow beak creamers of the type shown in Plate 20, left, were £130 and £140. When the formal Chinese Export Market type enamelled patterns were replaced by more natural floral sprays by the Tulip painter (as Plate 20 second from left) the price rose to £340. It should be stated that this non-London firm of auctioneers did not charge a buyer's premium, so the prices quoted reflect the true cost to the buyer. On the other hand, many purchases were made by members of the Trade who would obviously expect to resell the items at a higher price. A middle period blue and white creamer also fetched £130 while an attractive early example made £290. A rare transfer-printed 'Tea party' creamer made £220, this design is here shown as Plate 13.

I have here used the auctioneer's description 'creamer' for these upright sparrow beak jugs, although I regard them as milk jugs especially when they have inexpensive styles of decoration. Creamers — quite rare objects — I feel are the squat containers of various types, as Plates 120, 138 and 150.

The selection of Redgrave-type teawares shown in Plate 146 showed how the unusual forms commanded high prices. Obviously each tea service originally comprised up to a dozen teabowls and saucers, but only one teapot and one creamer. It may not be so obvious that seemingly only some services were sold complete with a spoon tray or with a tea canister. Also, it would appear that not all teapots were sold with a matching stand. Furthermore, most of the less expensive tea services did not include a covered sugar bowl, but had instead an open bowl smaller in size than the wide large waste bowl. The two saucer-shape bread and butter plates are surprisingly rarely found in Lowestoft services.

Having read these comments you will better understand the following prices which relate to the pieces illustrated in Plate 146:

The cracked teapot fetched	£240
The matching teapot stand (of a standard Lowestoft form)	£370
The two spoon trays	£290
	and £270
The tea canister (lacking a cover)	£310
The small, fluted, bowl	£140
The sparrow beak creamer	£110
A larger creamer	£140

It must be understood that Mr. Levine's 'service' was a made-up one, gathered together over the years. Some of the shapes did not match, for example, the fluted bowl

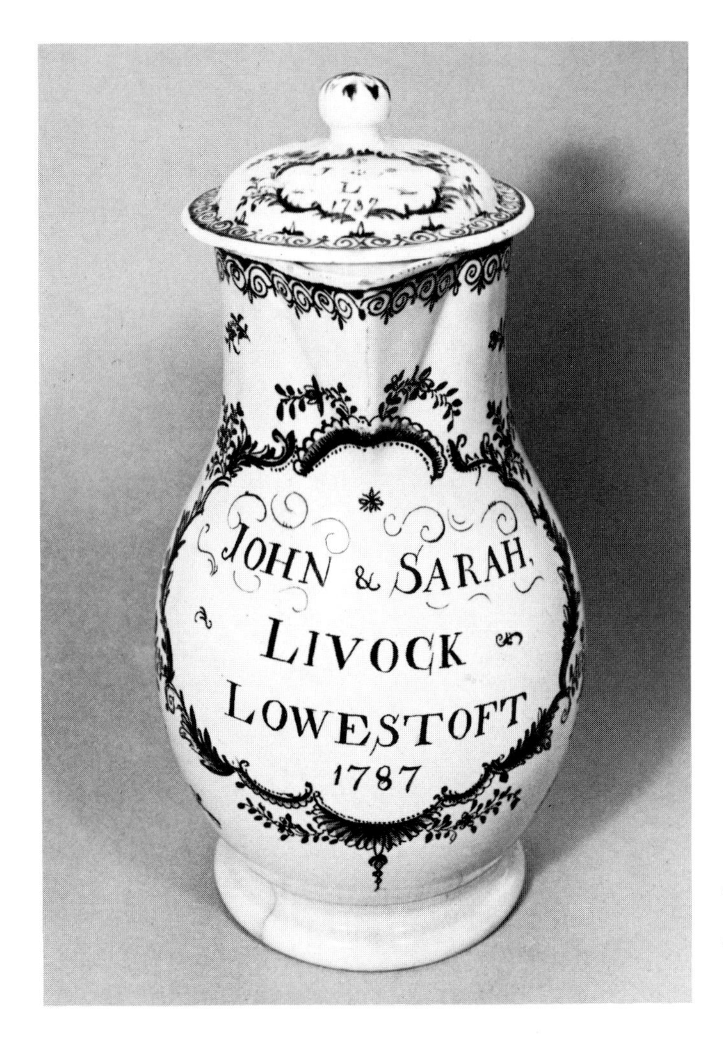

Plate 27. *The Livock marriage jug. John married Sarah Hollands at Lowestoft in October 1787. Sold for £28 in 1948, for £1,850 in 1982. 10ins. high.* Ex Henry Levine Collection.

and some later cup handles. The original sets would have included only one (if any) spoon tray, but Henry could not resist owning two of these rare items. In all his years of collecting Mr. Levine was seemingly unable to locate a covered sugar bowl of this pattern.

Once upon a time (!) complete tea services did exist and were reasonably easy to find. In the mid-1940s, I purchased a near complete Redgrave-type tea service from a leading London firm for £15. Those were the days, and in 1949 the splendid Tulip painter coffee pot shown in Plate 148 was bought at auction for £32.10s.0d. In more recent times the part Redgrave 'two bird' pattern tea and coffee service shown in Plate 26 cost several hundred pounds but still less than half what it might have commanded when split up into separate lots in the Levine sale in November 1982.

Two facts affect this situation. Firstly, pieces from a known collection, as Henry Levine's, will always command a higher price than a similar object from an unknown source especially when, as was here the case, a large number of pieces was offered at a well publicized sale. The quantity of objects brings out all the collectors and dealers, all anxious to add a few pieces from the famous collection to their own selection. Secondly, there is the point that a tea service which is divided up by the auctioneer will usually fetch more in total than would the same set if sold as one lot. This is most regrettable for in a few years there will be no complete services — they are rare enough as it is — and collectors will not know which shapes went with which. Still, a split service does enable perhaps twenty collectors each to own a piece. The enhanced price, of course, arises from the fact that twenty or so people will be bidding for each cup and saucer or for the little jug and at prices they can afford, but only one or two buyers can pay the thousand or so pounds which the whole service could fetch.

Now a few prices from the November 1982 Henry Levine sale:

The inscribed and dated jug shown in Plate 121. Printed in underglaze blue. This is a rare piece but certainly not a thing of beauty. I sat in Sotheby's in April 1948 and was happy to see it then sold for £18. It now commanded bids up to the final one of £640.

The large covered jug shown here in Plate 27, again rare, but not pretty and with reasonably serious damage. At the 1948 Colman sale this was sold for £28. Some thirty-five years later it was purchased for £1,850.

Mr. Levine also had a mug with the same inscription. This too was cracked, but this did not stop it being sold for £1,100. At the Crisp sale in 1935 it fetched just £8, and £16 in the 1955 sale of the Hotblack Collection.

Perhaps even more surprising was the price of £1,400 given for the so-called chestnut basket of the type shown in Plate 130. A rare object, but a straight copy of a Worcester example. A pair of pierced circular baskets of the same Worcester type (as Plate 134) fetched £740 and a salad or junket dish of the type here shown in Plate 127 commanded £310. Apparently there is an awakening of interest in Lowestoft blue printed wares.

Turning to the popular enamelled pieces, we find the coffee pot shown in Plate 192 was sold for a respectable £700. The late but rare and attractive teapot shown in Plate 232 fetched £580. A single saucer of the type shown in Plate 155 was sold for £460.

An initialled flask was sold for £850 and two damaged 'Trifle from Lowestoft' mugs were knocked down for £760 and £580. The attractive and dated 'H. Gillman 1795' mug, here shown in Plate 226, was sold for a reasonably modest £580, a price that reflected the damage.

The highest priced example was a modest blue and white inkpot which sold for £2,200. But it was perfect, and inscribed 'A Trifle from Lowestoft'. It is here shown in Plate 225 with the pounce pot which fetched £1,000.

Yes, I fancy Henry Levine would have been well pleased with the result of this sale, but I am equally sure that he had derived more pleasure in his lifetime from forming the collection, from studying it and showing it to his friends and fellow collectors. It is to be hoped that the many new owners will equally enjoy their ownership of these simple eighteenth century Lowestoft porcelains with their impetuous charm.

CHAPTER I
General History and Marks

This book is concerned solely with the somewhat rare, but charming, products of a small porcelain factory operating from 1757 to c.1799, and situated in the East Anglian fishing port of Lowestoft on the East Coast of England. They are of the variety known as 'soft-paste', an artificial type of porcelain fired at a lower temperature* than the 'hard-paste', or true porcelain as produced by the Oriental potters or by most Continental manufacturers.

This should make it quite clear that we are *not* concerned with that class of hard-paste Chinese porcelain made and decorated for the European (and American) market, and often erroneously described as 'Lowestoft', 'Chinese Lowestoft' or 'Oriental Lowestoft'. These Chinese export market porcelains were produced in vast quantities in the eighteenth and early nineteenth centuries and were shipped from China in every available vessel. This Oriental porcelain comprised every conceivable object (often modelled after European prototypes) and is found decorated in many styles (Plate 28), sometimes exact copies of European prints and sometimes with simpler designs which featured formal floral patterns. A large quantity was decorated with European armorial bearings or initials and much was decorated in underglaze blue only, often with landscape designs of willow pattern type, and these so-called Chinese 'Nankin' blue and white wares were extremely cheap and popular, being at one and the same time the inspiration behind many English porcelain designs and their manufacturers' main competition.

The above explanation is necessary because, in the nineteenth century, the myth was firmly established that this Chinese hard-paste porcelain was made at our little East Coast, Lowestoft manufactory (Plate 1) and the early reference books abound with basic errors that have proved surprisingly difficult to eradicate, although the two types of porcelain are so different that it is hard to see how the early writers were deceived. One would have thought that in over fifty years these nineteenth century errors would have been corrected but this is not so, for the old terms 'Chinese Lowestoft' or 'Oriental Lowestoft' still persist and one book, published as recently as 1967, lists under 'Lowestoft' (in the price section for English porcelains) just six items, all of which are Chinese! It must be admitted that some Lowestoft *designs* are similar to motifs found on Chinese export market porcelains, and that the Lowestoft painters occasionally decorated their porcelain with armorial bearings (Colour Plate 10, Plate 215) but these pieces are of extreme rarity, probably not more than twenty such teasets having been made at Lowestoft, compared with the thousands of armorial decorated Chinese services in existence, and the difference between the two in the porcelain body itself, and in the mode of manufacture, is quite obvious. The following chapters are

---

* Soft-paste porcelain was fired at about 1100°C. Hard-paste at about 1350° to 1450°C.

Colour Plate 3. *The uniquely decorated blue and white Lowestoft porcelain flask showing a shipbuilding scene on the local beach (see Plate 185 for reverse side). 5½ ins. high. c.1780.* Author's Collection.

concerned solely with the soft-paste Lowestoft porcelains. For details of the Chinese porcelains which have in the past been confused with the English Lowestoft porcelains the reader is referred to my book *Oriental Export Market Porcelain.*

The 1750s were momentous years for the English porcelain industry; the new wares, seeking to rival the prized Chinese porcelains, as well as the already famous Meissen or Dresden porcelain, were in great demand. Porcelain factories at Bow and Chelsea in London, as well as at Derby, Worcester and Longton Hall (near Stoke-on-Trent) were established and their wares advertised in the Press. Had the stage not thus have been set, it is doubtful if the chance discovery of a fine clay on the estate of Hewling Luson at Gunton, near Lowestoft, would have attracted more than passing notice. The timing of this discovery was, however, opportune, and from it arose a new industry in Lowestoft, one which was to bring it lasting fame — derived, ironically enough, largely from the mistaken belief that porcelain made by hundreds of Chinese workers, labouring thousands of miles away, came from this English fishing port.

Tradition states, and we have no reason to disbelieve it, that Hewling Luson sent samples of the clay found on his estate to an existing factory in London, probably that at Bow, to test its suitability for the manufacture of porcelain. The reports from London would seem to have been favourable but, unfortunately for Luson, the success

Plate 28. *Part of the famous Owles collection of 'Lowestoft' porcelain, sold by Messrs. Spelman (Auctioneers) at Great Yarmouth, in 1872. With the exception of the mug (top shelf, right), all these objects are of hard-paste Chinese porcelain, made expressly for the European market and formerly attributed to the small East Coast factory shown in the Frontispiece. Similar Chinese wares are still often called 'Chinese Lowestoft' (page 39). All subsequent illustrations are of true Lowestoft, soft-paste porcelains.*

of a porcelain body depends on more than one suitable type of clay; other ingredients, mixed liberally with 'know-how' are essential.

It appears that Luson sought to produce saleable porcelain from his local raw materials in about 1756 but that, for one reason or another, he was unsuccessful. The early writers suggest that the workers, brought in from an existing factory, were bribed to spoil Luson's experimental wares, but we have no evidence to substantiate this story. The fact remains, however, that Luson's trials were unsuccessful, and I do not know of any ware — porcelain or pottery, that can be linked with these first efforts to make a durable ceramic body at, or near, Lowestoft in 1756.

Within a very short time, probably not more than twelve months after the failure of these experiments, a partnership was set up which was to prove so successful that their factory continued to supply local markets with saleable transparent porcelain for a period of some forty-five years, that is, for a longer period than any other English porcelain factory in the eighteenth century, with the notable exception of the Derby and Worcester factories, with their London showrooms and nation-wide markets.

The successful partners included Philip Walker, Robert Browne, Obed Aldred (variously described as a 'brick layer' or 'merchant') and James Richman (or Richmond). Robert Browne was the key figure, being reputedly a chemist, and certainly the manager of the factory, to whom apprentices were indentured. Of the other partners, Philip Walker was the senior, having two of the four shares in the factory, and, judging by a most interesting advertisement contained in the *Norwich Mercury* of June 28th, 1760, he seems to have had previous experience in potting, at least earthenwares:

> TO BE SOLD
> AT CARROW ABBEY STAITHE,
> NEAR CONISFORD GATES,
> NORWICH
> BY MR. WILLIAM HUDSON
>
> Glaz'd and Red Pan-Tiles, Glaz'd and Square ditto, Glaz'd and Red Roofing ditto, from Mr. Philip Walker's Kiln at Gunton, near Lowestoft. Where may be had, all sorts of common white and red ware, and if timely bespoke, white copings, Cornish and Fascia's to any mould or pattern, that nearly resembles Portland Stone. N.B. The Pan-Tiles are (by good judges) thought equal, if not superior, to the Holland Ware and the Square Glazed are esteemed the neatest and most beautiful covering of its kind ever yet invented.

Unfortunately, I have been unable to trace any other reference to Philip Walker's tile-making works at Gunton, near Lowestoft, so that we do not know when this venture started or when it ceased, but it is interesting to note that the site of this kiln was at Gunton, where Hewling Luson is said to have discovered the fine clay which prompted him to have it tested for its suitability for the manufacture of porcelain. Perhaps this clay was really found by Philip Walker, already working a small pottery on Luson's land, using local clay, and that by existing tenancy, or other, agreement Walker had the right to extract it, so ensuring for himself a key position (with two of the four shares) in the subsequent porcelain undertaking. In a Directory published in 1795, Philip Walker is listed as a 'Merchant', and also described as being in partnership with Robert Browne as 'China Manufacturers and Herring curers'. The fact that porcelain was not even the full-time concern of the proprietors should help to convince those who still doubt that the vast quantities of 'Oriental' and 'Chinese' Lowestoft produced could not possibly have originated at this little English factory.

The earliest, indeed the only, recorded announcement regarding the sale of Lowestoft porcelain appeared in the two important local East Anglian newspapers the *Ipswich Journal* and the *Norwich Mercury* early in 1760. This notice is headed 'Lowestoft in Suffolk, Jan, 23rd 1760' and gives the then trading style — Walker & Co.:

> Notice is hereby given to all Dealers in PORCELAIN OR CHINA WARE, that by or before Lady day next will be offered to sale, a great variety of neat Blue and White CHINA or PORCELAIN, at the manufactory in this Town.
>
> 'Tis humbly hoped that most of the Shopkeepers in this County and the County of Norfolk, will give Encouragement to this laudable undertaking, by reserving their Spring Orders for their humble servants, WALKER and Co.

Obviously by January 1760 initial experiments had been completed, most difficulties had been overcome and Walker & Co. were hopeful of having a good selection of 'neat Blue and White China' available for the Trade by March 25th, 1760.

Experienced workmen had almost certainly been brought in from existing porcelain works such as the Bow factory in London (see page 41). It is noteworthy that the same basic type of porcelain body, containing a large percentage of bone ash, or phosphate, was in use at both Bow and Lowestoft, but not at any other contemporary factory. Some painters may have been originally trained at a pottery making Delft-type, tin-glazed earthenware, for much of the early blue painted porcelain displays this influence. By June, 1760, Robert Browne, 'Porcelain Maker', had started to take apprentices and it can be assumed that local persons, including women (an innovation in the trade at that period) were being trained in all aspects of porcelain manufacture and decoration.

The early Lowestoft porcelains are discussed fully in Chapter II, but it should be stated here that the products were painted in underglaze blue only, no overglaze enamels having been used before about 1765, and that the designs and shapes are in the main unique to the Lowestoft factory, showing little or no influence from other factories.

One of the very few recorded contemporary accounts of the factory is given in Edmund Gillingwater's *An Historical Account of the Ancient Town of Lowestoft* (the preface of which is dated 1790) and reads:

> The only manufactory carried on at Lowestoft is that of making porcelain or china ware, where the proprietors have brought this ingenious art to a great degree of perfection, and from the prospect it affords, promises to be attended with much success.

[Here follows an account of Hewling Luson's unsuccessful experiments, with mention of the theory that the workmen were encouraged to spoil the wares.]

> But, notwithstanding this unhandsome treatment, the resolution of establishing a china manufactory at Lowestoft was not relinquished, but was revived again in the succeeding year (1757) by Messrs. Walker, Browne, Aldred and Richman, who, having purchased some houses on the south side of Bell Lane, converted the same to the uses of the manufactory by erecting a kiln and other conveniences necessary for the purpose; but in carrying their

design into execution they also were liable to the same inconveniences as the proprietor of the original undertaking at Gunton [Hewling Luson's experiments] was, for being under the necessity of applying to the manufactories in London for workmen to conduct the business this second attempt experienced the same misfortune as the former one and very nearly totally ruined their designs, but the proprietors happened to discover these practices of the workmen before it was too late, they took such precautions as to render every future attempt to this nature wholly ineffectual, and have now established the factory upon such permanent foundation as promises great success. They have now enlarged their original plan, and by purchasing several adjoining houses and erecting additional buildings have made every necessary alteration requisite for the various purposes of the manufactory. They employ a considerable number of workmen, and supply with ware many of the principal towns in the adjacent counties, and keep a warehouse in London to execute the orders they receive both from the City and the adjoining towns, and have brought the manufactory to such a degree of perfection as promises to be a credit to the Town, useful to the inhabitants and beneficial to themselves.

We now know, thanks to the researches of Mrs. Elizabeth Adams, that the Lowestoft management had access to the London market by at least 1763, at which period Mortimer's *London Directory* lists:

> Mathews, William, Loestoffe (sic) China Warehouse, Addle Street, Aldermanbury.

The *Public Advertiser* of December 1st, 1768 records the transfer of agents in the following brief manner:

> Lowestoft China Warehouse, is removed from Mr. Mathews, Addle St. to Clark Durmford (sic) No. 4, Great St. Thomas the Apostle; where all merchants and shop keepers may be supplied at the usual prices.

A further advertisement of March 1770 reads:

> CLARK DURNFORD,
> LOWESTOFT CHINA WAREHOUSE,
>
> No. 4. Great St. Thomas the Apostle, Queen Street, Cheapside, London. Where merchants and shopkeepers may be supplied with any quantity of the said ware at the usual prices. N.B. Allowance of twenty-per-cent for ready money.

However, this arrangement probably was not of long duration for by at least 1779 Clark Durnford (various spellings occur) was in partnership with the Staffordshire potter Hugh Booth and by this period Durnford had moved to 18 Knightrider Street, Doctors Commons, in London. He was also engaged in a slightly later partnership with Ralph Baddeley of Staffordshire, this was dissolved on June 16th, 1782. It is perhaps noteworthy that the premises were merely described as a 'china warehouse' without any special mention of Lowestoft wares in the 1783 *New Complete Guide. . . to the City of London.*

We therefore have no means of telling for how long this London china seller was connected with the Lowestoft factory, although it is probable that he continued to stock some of this Lowestoft porcelain, along with an assortment of other goods, for several years, up to his bankruptcy, as recorded in the *London Gazette* of May 20th, 1786.

Two of the many visitors to Lowestoft recorded the fact in their diaries, which were most fortunately preserved. Under the date August 26th, 1772, Dr. Silas Neville recorded:

> Went (from Yarmouth) with Mr. and Mrs. Hide in their chaise to Lowestoft, between which and Yarmouth the country is woody with many small commons. Lowestoft stands upon the cliff very near the beach, consists of one pretty long street...Dined at the Crown. After dinner visited the china manufactory carried on here. Most of it is rather ordinary. The Painting branch is done by women...

A further interesting comment is included in the diary of Thomas Wale,* the entry for Monday, May 19th, 1777, reads:

> Drove down...with Mr. Smith and two sons to Lowestoft, where we saw the china ware fabrick, etc. and all of us bought some of it. Saw ye hanging gardens and ye fine prospect of ye sea. Excellent bathing machines, etc....

It would therefore seem clear that day trippers to this fashionable seaside resort were able to look over the porcelain factory and that the wares were sold direct to these visitors, a fact that perhaps explains the several 'Trifles from Lowestoft', the examples with local views and many of the inscribed specimens, made to special order.

A first-hand description of the factory is quoted in William Chaffers' *Marks and Monograms on Pottery and Porcelain* and extracts are given below, but it must be remembered that the writer was aged eighty-four and can have been referring only to the later days of the factory, as he was no more than twenty years old in 1800. There is, however, no reason to question this description.

> I, the undersigned Abel Bly, of Lowestoft...am now in the eighty-fourth year of my age, was born in, and (with the exception of two years) have always lived in Lowestoft; my father's name was Abel Bly, who was employed in various departments in the china factory at Lowestoft. He died when I was eleven years of age [in about 1792]; my two uncles, John and Philip Bly, also worked in the factory.
>
> The factory was situate in Crown Street, where the brew-house and malting premises of Messrs. Morse and Woods now stand, the rear fronting what is now called Factory Lane. Where Messrs. Morse's counting-house stands was the packing-room; the counting-house of the factory being to the east of the packing-room.
>
> At the rear of the packing-room and counting-room were two turning-rooms and farther to the rear adjoining Factory Lane were two kilns. On the ground floor were also the drying rooms.
>
> The painters worked in a chamber approached by a staircase to the eastwards of the counting-room. Over the east turning-room was a chamber for finishing the turner's work.
>
> There was a chamber approached from the east kiln, in which the ware

* Published by Messrs. Chapman and Hall in 1883, under the title *My Grandfather's Pocket Book, 1707-1796, The Diary of Thomas Wale.*

was tested as to its shape. Over this was an attic in which women were employed painting the blue and white ware. . . .

Abel Bly. November 2nd 1865.

To return to the general history of the works, Robert Browne the elder died in 1771 and his son, of the same name, succeeded him as manager of the factory having most probably been employed in the works for some time previously. At about this period several new features appear, the most noteworthy being the increased production of overglaze enamel painting. Many of these new, coloured designs were influenced by the popular imported Chinese porcelains with mandarin-type figure compositions and formal floral designs and, surprisingly, there is some evidence that the Chinese potters had soft-paste English Lowestoft porcelain to copy (page 109).

A popular series of designs in the Oriental style combined the use of underglaze blue with overglaze enamel colours (Colour Plate 7 and Plates 143, 146, 203-5). These designs are associated with the Redgrave family of china painters and are often called 'Redgrave patterns' although individual names such as 'two bird pattern' or 'house pattern' are also employed. Of course, other enamelled designs were entirely English in feeling but these European patterns are rather rare.

A unique class of enamel painting of the 1770s comprises bold, powerfully painted flower sprays, featuring prominently a large tulip, and these pieces by the so-called 'Tulip painter' are probably the most accomplished examples of Lowestoft porcelain. Typical examples are shown in Plates 147-153.

Some very rare figures were made, as were small animals, cats, sheep and rams, swans and at least two different dog models, and this aspect of the factory's production is fully discussed in Chapter III. In the 1790s simple sprig patterns in the then popular French taste were introduced, and were continued until the factory's closure. These late Lowestoft sprig patterns are surprisingly rare, typical examples of which are shown in Plates 217, 220 and 231.

While the use of overglaze enamel patterns was commenced in about 1767 (the earliest recorded dated specimens are of 1774), the use of underglaze blue was by no means neglected, the blue and white designs continuing right through the factory's working period. Apart from the continuation of the standard, child-like, Chinese scenic and floral compositions, the later wares from about 1768, include two innovations. One of these was the introduction of blue printed patterns, some of which are unique to this factory, while others were almost exact copies of popular Worcester and Caughley blue printed designs. This copying of the patterns and shapes of other factories constitutes the second departure from earlier practice and includes the use (or misuse) of standard marks such as the crescent device of Worcester and the rare use of the cross swords mark of the Dresden factory, see Plates 127-8, 131, 141-2.

Just as the exact date of establishment of the Lowestoft factory is open to doubt, so too is the year of closure. Different authorities give this as 1802 or 1803 and several theories are put forward to explain the failure of the factory. Llewellynn Jewitt, in his *Ceramic Art of Great Britain* (1878 and revised edition of 1883), states:

> . . .One great loss was caused by the failure of their London agents; another and more serious one by the destruction of a very large quantity of Lowestoft china in Holland, with which country an extensive trade was carried on, as thus stated — 'When Napoleon crossed the river during a hard frost and captured Holland, amongst the British property destroyed was a quantity of Lowestoft China at Rotterdam, in value several thousand

pounds'. The trade with Rotterdam was very large, and the ware was sent weekly in hogsheads by way of Yarmouth. . . .

It is difficult to know how much, if any, credence to place on the above views, which have been repeated by many subsequent writers. The taking of Rotterdam took place in 1795, but I doubt very much if several thousand pounds' worth of Lowestoft porcelain was in the docks, or that Lowestoft porcelain was exported, in any quantity, for while its shapes and simple designs were well suited to the needs of the local East Anglian population, they can hardly have excited much attention on the Continent but see page 31. There is also the point that the weekly output from the one or two kilns at Lowestoft could not have been very great. It is, of course, possible that the Lowestoft partners were also dealing in wares other than their own and that they were shipping to the Continent the highly popular 'Queen's ware' made by Wedgwood and other Staffordshire pottery manufacturers, and that this was destroyed, to the embarrassment of the Lowestoft partners. It is also possible, although this is only a guess, that the Lowestoft partners were importing from Holland Delft-tiles as a profitable side-line.

I believe that to all intents and purposes the Lowestoft factory had ceased production by 1800, and that it can be considered to have been entirely an eighteenth century factory. Certainly some of the key personnel left in September, 1799, and were employed at Worcester in that year (page 174) and I do not know of any dated examples of *factory decorated* Lowestoft porcelain of a later date. It is my belief that the run down of the factory was gradual from about 1795, and that the Lowestoft porcelains could not compete in popularity and cheapness with the Staffordshire earthenwares, which were so well suited to the middle class markets in which the Lowestoft factory specialised, and that the new porcelain factories, for instance the Spode and Minton works in Staffordshire and the Chamberlain factory at Worcester, were producing porcelain which was finer and more up to date both in form and decoration than the traditional Lowestoft wares. The post-1795 Lowestoft wares are surprisingly rare suggesting a rapid decline from this time. My views are confirmed by a letter written by Robert Browne's son, and quoted by William Chaffers:

> I have heard my father say that they discontinued the works principally because they could not produce the ware so cheaply as the Staffordshire potters, and that they were getting old and wished to retire from the business,* not from want of capital, as they were all wealthy men for the period. . . .

It is a matter of wonderment that the partners could have continued the factory from 1757 to at least 1799 in such an unlikely position, distant from the main markets, London and the other large centres of population, when other porcelain factories were far better situated. The porcelains were, however, made originally for the use and enjoyment of ordinary folk, and now, nearly two hundred years later, the self-same objects give joy to a host of collectors who appreciate their naïve charm and unpretentious friendliness.

Now follows, first, a brief résumé of the marks, and then a more detailed account of

* It is interesting to read that the proprietors were 'getting old and wished to retire', for there is no mention of Philip Walker's death (a reason given by some writers for the closure of the factory) which occurred in 1803 at the age of eight-one, a fact that suggests that, as I believe, the factory closed before this date of 1803.

the objects made and the styles of decoration, and the artists employed. Also lists of the various shapes made and one of the key, dated, specimens which help materially to trace the changing shapes and styles of decoration.

Marks

Although no factory mark as such was employed at the Lowestoft factory, the painters' personal number, or tally marks, and the placing of these on the inside of the footrim form a reliable pointer to their Lowestoft origin.

The painters' number marks were employed from about 1758 to the early 1770s. The numbers '3' and '5' are frequently found, especially on the finer examples and those rare pieces bearing names and dates. Apart from these, letters and signs (such as a circle) were also employed as piece rate tally marks, but these are rarer than the standard number marks. It must be stated that these painters' numbers are found on other porcelains, including the similar Bow products, but it is their being painted on the inside of the footrim (Plates 48, 82 and 89) that is the characteristic but not unique feature of the Lowestoft porcelains after about 1760. Obviously, however, this practice could not be carried out on pieces having a flat base devoid of any footrim. It should be noted that on some very rare *early* pieces the number appears near the centre of the base, not inside the footrim.

The painters' numbers were not consistently applied, for instance only one of a matching pair of sauce boats, or one of a pair of vases, might be marked and many pieces do not bear any painter's number at all.

It is extremely difficult to identify the work of the different blue painters, even the

Plate 29. *Selection of 'wasters' from the Lowestoft factory site, showing fragments of early blue and white wares of the 1757-60 period.* Author's Collection.

Plate 30. *Two plaster of Paris moulds, and two unglazed 'wasters' found on the factory site. These relate to the Hughes-type relief-moulded designs (page 54).* City of Norwich Museums.

Plate 31. *Selection of Lowestoft factory wasters, including part of an inkpot (top left) and a patty pan (top right) with (centre) a ribbed teapot cover missing its flower knob (Plate 142). The small early fragment 'A' is part of a 'waster' submitted for analysis (page 53).* Author's Collection.

relatively common painters numbered '3' and '5', for, except in the cases of individual inscribed presentation pieces, the designs were stock ones copied either from some form of pattern book or from stock pieces kept in the painters' room. This means that, for example, the same blue painted designs appear in the panels of the relief-moulded Hughes-type teawares (Plates 54, 55, 60 and 61, 62, 64 and 65 right, compare also 63 with 75) with little scope for the painter's personal style to be spotted.

One characteristic I have noticed in the early pieces by painter number '3' (page 158) is that the Chinese fisherman, so often introduced in the designs, holds a very long, straight fishing rod with a large spider, or cross-like bait, see Plates 43 and 81.

The standing Chinese figures on pieces bearing the number '5' are often very slim and tall (Plate 57).

Although these painters' numbers are rarely found on the early Redgrave patterns of the 1770s, which combine overglaze enamels with underglaze blue, a small red enamel cross is very occasionally found on these Redgrave-type wares, placed on the inside of the footrim, perhaps as a rebus for one of the Redgraves. Only one wholly enamelled piece has been reported with a painter's tally number, so that it can be stated that for all practical purposes the post-1770 Lowestoft enamelled porcelains are not marked in any way. The post-1775 blue and white porcelains do *not* bear painters' numbers, for these occur only on the early examples. The inscription 'A Trifle from Lowestoft', found on the front of some late pieces (Plates 223-5, 233) should not be regarded as a true mark, as similar examples bear the place names of other villages and towns where such pieces were sold, so that the inscription, 'A Trifle from Bungay', does not mean that the porcelain was made at that place.

Close copies of Worcester blue and white porcelains sometimes bear the Worcester crescent mark, which may be open (that is, not shaded) on hand painted designs, or shaded, with cross lines, on printed patterns, while the Dresden crossed swords mark is also found on some examples bearing versions of standard Continental designs (Plate 142). These marks are normally applied to the base, not the inside of the footrim.

The reader may wonder how it is that the Lowestoft porcelains have been identified, if they bear only workmen's numbers, or copies of the Worcester crescent or the Dresden crossed swords mark, and if the enamelled examples are devoid of all marks. Much of the evidence lay undiscovered on the factory site until 1902 when, during rebuilding operations, a mass of original moulds, together with unfinished or spoilt fragments were found. These important finds received much publicity at the time and examples are illustrated in two reference books (W.W.R. Spelman's *Lowestoft China* of 1905, and F.A. Crisp's *Lowestoft China Factory and the moulds found there in December, 1902,* of 1907). A later work featuring some interesting factory 'wasters' is Christopher Spencer's *Early Lowestoft.* These factory wasters and moulds are now housed in several museums, notably at the Castle Museum, Norwich, but few are on general display. However, these all-important finds are known to several specialist authorities and collectors, and they are still helping to identify fresh types of Lowestoft porcelain, such as the pug dogs shown in Plate 165.

Sixty-five years after the first factory wasters were discovered under a raised floor, major rebuilding operations on the site (on which now stands a multistorey block of flats) uncovered a further selection of mostly small broken fragments. Selections from both the 1902 and the 1967 finds are featured in this book, the later pieces by courtesy of the Lowestoft Archaeological and Local History Society. The author has a selection of factory wasters and a few part moulds in his reference collection at Worthing. These are available for inspection, by appointment.

CHAPTER II
Pre-1770 Blue and White Porcelain

The earliest Lowestoft porcelains which we believe were made between about 1757 and 1760, are extremely scarce, and many collectors are not even aware that they exist as they are rarely illustrated in the standard reference works, are not at present adequately represented in public collections and bear little resemblance to the better-known later products. Present-day students of Lowestoft owe much to the researches of the late D.M. Hunting and in particular to his Paper, read to the *English Ceramic Circle* in 1948, which was published in the *Transactions* of the Society, Volume 3, Part I (1951), under the title 'Early Lowestoft'. In 1981 Christopher Spencer published a detailed study of these rare early blue and white porcelains under the same simple title — *Early Lowestoft*.

In general appearance the very early pieces display a likeness to the tin-glazed Delft wares, their translucency is poor (the body has the appearance of glazed pipe clay) and several of them have a pinkish tone, with the glaze sometimes quite dull, clouded by innumerable minute bubbles, unlike the very glassy, clear glaze found on later pieces. The style of painting, too, on these 1757-60 pieces, is characteristic. The tone of the underglaze blue is light and a rather dry blue-black, as if applied to a very porous surface, and contrasting with the full, liquid, vivid blue found on many post-1760 examples.

The painting technique gives the effect of fine penwork rather than full brushwork, although the pen-like outline of leaves, etc., has been filled by a brush (Colour Plate 5 and Plates 32-6). The subjects in the main are restricted to Chinese-styled flowering trees, with quaint birds or waterfowl added. These patterns and styles of painting are

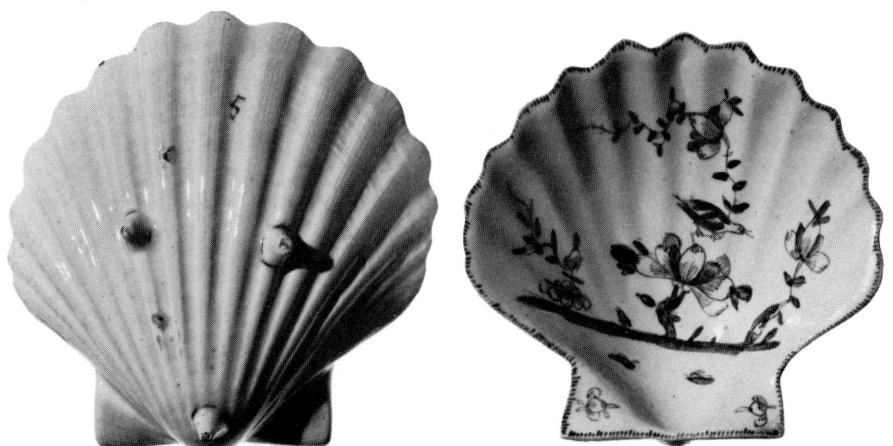

Plate 32. *Two early scallop shell dishes (pages 52 and 212), painted in typical early style, in underglaze blue. One is reversed to show moulding, and also conical feet with blue line at the joint, and painter's number '5'. 4½ and 4¼ ins. high. c.1757-9.* Author's Collection.

Plate 33. *Three early leaf-shaped dishes (page 207), painted in underglaze blue with the same design as that on the shells (Plate 32). Two dishes reversed to show relief-moulded veining and, right, incised veining, three moulded feet, with blue lines at joints and indistinct painter's numbers. 6¹/₁₀ and 5⅔ ins. high. Painter's number '8' or '6'. c.1757-9.* Author's Collection.

Plate 34. *Two rare small mugs painted in underglaze blue, in the early style. 2⅜ ins. high. Painter's number '7' on inside of footrim. c.1758-9.* Dr. B. Watney Collection.

difficult to describe, but once seen they should be unforgettable (Plates 32 and 33). Some rare coffee (or chocolate) pots are painted with a standing Chinese figure in landscape (Plate 35).

These early Lowestoft porcelains are, I repeat, extremely rare, and the recorded forms include the coffee, or chocolate pots with the handle at right angles to the spout (Plate 35); a narrow shaped-edge tray (Colour Plate 5); some shell-shaped scallop dishes, on conical feet (Plate 32); leaf-shaped dishes (Plate 33); baluster-shaped vases (Plate 36); knife and fork handles (Plate 40); beakers with outward flared rims; washhand basins and ewers; bottles; inkwells; porringers; salt cellars; tea canisters; a cane handle (Plate 2); relief-moulded sauce boats; bell-shaped mugs, and circular patty pans. Tea services were obviously made at this period (as is evidenced by factory 'wasters'), but examples are extremely rare; covered sucriers are recorded, and a creamer (Plate 3), straight-sided coffee cans, or small mugs (Plate 34), and coffee cups and saucer-shaped cake plates, see Christopher Spencer's *Early Lowestoft.*

That these rare and unusual porcelains are Lowestoft may be proved by matching spoilt fragments, or 'wasters' found on the factory site, by the continuation of the painter's hand on later pieces, by the reissue of some shapes at later periods, and by the painter's number tally marks on several of them. Unfortunately, no dated specimens of this early type have been discovered, but the whole class is obviously earlier than the earliest known dated example of Lowestoft porcelain bearing the moulded date 1761, and from this period an almost yearly sequence of dated pieces can be traced (see Chapter IV), so that these Delft-like porcelains should belong to the 1757-60 period.

As no analysis has been published revealing the composition of this early Lowestoft body, I requested that the Ceramic Testing Laboratory of the North Staffordshire College of Technology at Stoke-on-Trent, should test a typical example found on the factory site. This factory 'waster', a fragment of a slop bowl (Plate 31), gave the following result:

	Per cent
Silica	51.24
Lime	21.65
Phosphate	17.15
Alumina	6.76
Soda	.80
Potash	.67
Magnesia	.63
Ferric Oxide	.58
Titanic Oxide	.50
Loss (Calcined at 950°C.)	.47
	100.45

Plate 35. *A fine and early chocolate pot and cover (page 199) painted in underglaze blue in typical style, with early type of open flower knob as shown in Plate 29. 9¼ ins. high. Painter's number '1'. c.1758-9. See sale record 232 (page 250).* Sotheby's (ex Hunting Collection).

Plate 36. *A fine early vase and cover (page 217), painted in underglaze blue, in the early style (compare with later examples, Plate 48). 6½ ins. high. Painter's number '2'. c.1758-9.* Sotheby's (ex Hunting Collection).

This fragment contains over 40 per cent of bone ash, and is similar to some Bow porcelains of a like period. A published analysis of a Redgrave pattern Lowestoft fragment of a post-1770 period gives a rather different result, with 41 per cent Silica, 25 per cent Lime, 19 per cent Phosphate and 10 per cent Alumina, to give the main constituents in round figures.

From about 1760, several changes took place in the general appearance of the Lowestoft porcelains. Firstly, the tone of the underglaze blue became darker, and seems to have been more generously applied by a fully charged brush. Secondly, the glaze has a very shiny surface, like glass (contrasting with the rather dull, cloudy earlier glaze) and is clear, although where it has been thickly applied or has run into pools, for instance under the base, it is very prone to bubbling, with dark specks on the surface (Plate 82); it can also be slightly blue in tone. The post-1760 porcelain body is very compact, and feels heavy, and in general the potting is thicker than that associated with the rare pre-1760 examples.

An interesting early class of ribbed moulded wares occurs in about the 1760 period. To some degree these may have emulated similar Worcester teawares. The Lowestoft essays of this type are shown in Plates 49-52.

One of the most charming and characteristic features of the post-1760 Lowestoft porcelains was the moulded ware, mainly teasets, typical examples of which are displayed in Plates 53-79, showing relief-moulded floral motifs and borders surrounding small panels, which were painted in the normal way with underglaze blue. The teawares in this style are associated with James Hughes, and the tradition is strongly held that a teaset was made to commemorate the birth of James Hughes (to Susannah and James Hughes) in February, 1761. This belief rests on the fact that some examples of these wares bear the initials 'I.H.' moulded into the relief ornamentation, with the date 1761, 1762, 1764 and very rarely 1765, but these initials are so

Plate 37. *An early moulded sauce boat (page 211), sparsely painted in underglaze blue, shown with a factory 'waster' from a similar sauce boat. 5½ ins. long. Painter's number '2' in the centre of the underside of the base (not inside footrim). c.1758-9.* Victoria and Albert Museum (Crown Copyright).

Plate 38. *A moulded sauce boat from a similar mould to that shown above, but with a simplified handle, and with the relief-moulded panel borders painted in underglaze blue. 6¾ ins. long. Painter's number '3' (indistinct) on inside of footrim. c.1758-60.* Author's Collection.

inconspicuously placed that they need to be searched for, quite unlike the bold inscriptions found prominently placed on other commemorative Lowestoft porcelains. There are also the points, first, that several teasets bear these moulded initials, although articles from these sets are attributed to *the* James Hughes teaset as if only one was made, and, second, that the same initials are found on porcelains other than teawares, for instance, the sauce boat shown in Plate 59, an unlikely object to commemorate a child's birth!

I am sure, although I can offer no supporting evidence, that these initials are those of the master modeller who first conceived and made the designs. These were then mass-produced by means of plaster of Paris moulds, taken from the original master mould. The designer, rightly proud of his work, incorporated his initials in the design, and it is possible that this modeller and designer was James Hughes, the father of the child for whom, according to tradition, a teaset was made. A second son William, was employed at the factory as a modeller, in the 1780s and 1790s (page 157).

Plate 39. *An early, crisply potted jug, painted in underglaze blue. Note the early handle form. 6 ⅜ ins. high. c.1760.* City of Norwich Museums.

The reader's attention is, however, drawn to Mr. John Howell's researches as contained in his 'Early Lowestoft' Paper (E.C.C. *Transactions,* Vol. 11, part 2, 1982) where he states that James Hughes' occupation as stated on his October 1760 marriage licence was 'China Painter' not a modeller or designer. Mr. Howell then stated "I feel this rather dashed all ideas of the initials 'IH' being those of James Hughes". I do not wholly agree with this view, for the date of the marriage — October 1760 — with the description 'China Painter' was prior to the introduction of the initial marked moulded wares which, when dated, commence in 1761. The Lowestoft management in 1760 would not have had any need for a full-time modeller or indeed for a full-time mould maker, for most of the early pieces were thrown on the wheel. My case is, however, weakened by the fact that when acting as a marriage witness in July 1769 Hughes' occupation is again recorded as 'painter'. This may well have been because a painter was a full-time occupation whereas china modelling was part-time at Lowestoft. Or perhaps simply because 'painter' had a better sounding ring!

Mr. Howell was unable to suggest another contender for a modeller with a J forename (it was, of course, normal practice in the eighteenth century to render J as an I) and an H surname. Right or wrong I am sure that most Lowestoft collectors will continue to describe these so collectable relief-moulded wares as Hughes type.

These early moulded Lowestoft porcelains were made in great variety and for

Colour Plate 4. *A typical Lowestoft globular shape teapot, painted in overglaze enamel colours with a formal floral pattern in the style of the Chinese export market porcelains. 6ins. high. c.1785-90.* Geoffrey Godden, Chinaman

N.B. This and all subsequent pieces are of soft-paste English porcelain, not hard-paste so-called 'Oriental Lowestoft' Chinese imports.

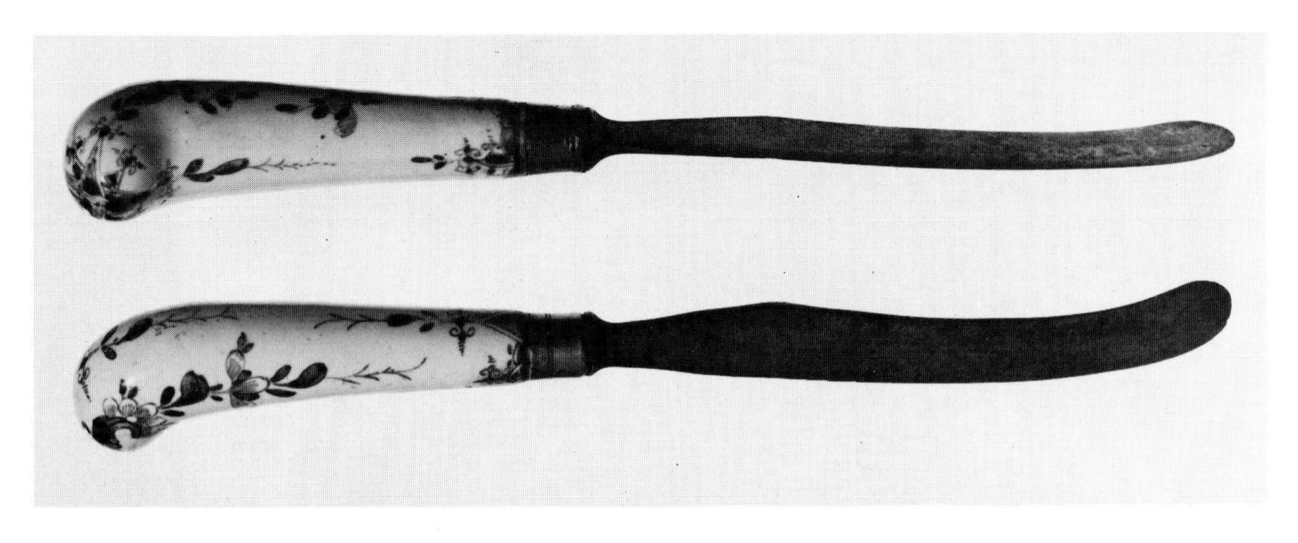

Plate 40. *Two rare, early knife handles (page 206) of unusually large size, painted in underglaze blue in early style. Several unglazed fragments of similar handles were found on the site. Porcelain handles 4 ¾ ins. long. c.1760.* Author's Collection.

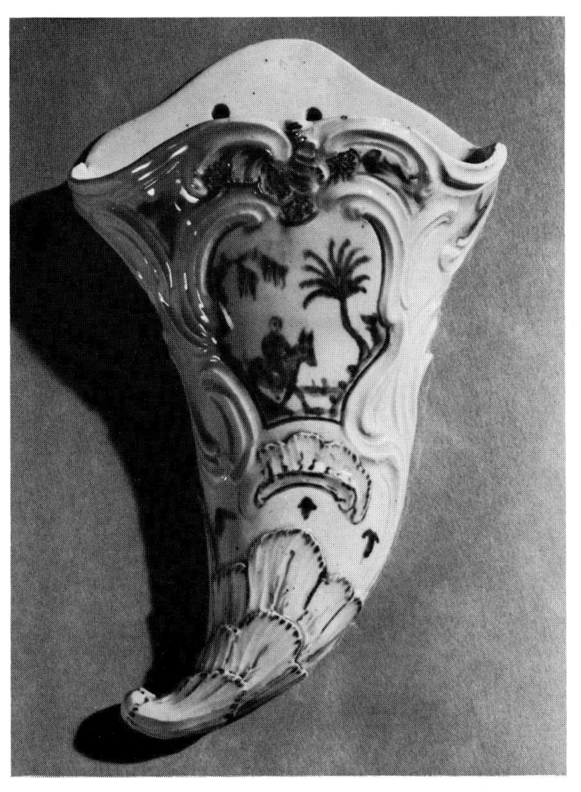

Plate 41. *A beaker, or vase (page 196), of a form made from the earliest days of the factory, with typical blue motifs. 3⁹⁄₁₀ ins. high. Painter's number '3'. c.1765 (or earlier).* Author's Collection.

Plate 42. *Wall pocket showing unusual relief moulding. This early example is glazed with the rare clear, warm, wet looking glaze found on some pieces of about 1760 (Plates 43 and 44) and it shows the crisp moulding to good effect (pages 20 and 217). 8⁹⁄₁₀ ins. high. c.1760.* Author's Collection.

Plate 43. *Early hand-pierced basket (page 196) with particularly clear, wet looking glaze seen also in Plates 42 and 44. These small baskets were made in several sizes. Diameter 5½ ins. Indistinct painter's number '3' (?) on inside of footrim. c.1760.* Author's Collection.

anyone seeking to form a small, select collection this class is ideal. Examples are now rare, teawares, especially cups and saucers, outnumbering other articles, but these are found with several different relief-moulded designs or variations in the painted underglaze blue borders. The earliest design, which probably dates from 1760 or possibly earlier, is noteworthy for the absence of the chrysanthemum, or sunflower-like flowers prominently placed on later wares (Plate 54, right) and a *single* line of raised beads surrounds the circular panels on early wares.

The rather more common 1761 designs often with the initials 'I.H.' and the date worked into the design, normally have chrysanthemum-like flowers growing upwards from the base of the trellis-like division between the circular panels (Plates 54, left, 55, etc.,) and a border of scrollwork (with or without leaves) is added just above the foot of cups, bowls, etc.

A later set of moulds was used with the date '1764', instead of the earlier '1761' (or very rarely '1762') year marks. The characteristic feature of these later moulded teawares is the painted underglaze blue border, reproduced below, which is found on the outside of bowls, cups and other objects, and takes the form of square clock face

Plate 44. *An attractive blue and white jug, with the clear, wet looking glaze seen also on objects depicted in Plates 42 and 43. 7ins. high. c.1760.* Formerly at South Quay Museum, Great Yarmouth.

Plate 45. *A fine large jug of the heavy compact body, turned to show the reverse side. Note the characteristic berry border at the top edge (page 71). 9¾ ins. high. c.1760.* Author's Collection.

Plate 46. *A large jug of rare form, without the normal turned foot (see Plate 45). The basic underglaze blue design is the same but obviously by a different hand. 8ins. high. c.1760.* S. Spero Collection.

Plate 47. *A rare, early, covered sugar bowl (page 214) painted in underglaze blue. 5⅜ ins. high. c.1760.* Victoria and Albert Museum (Crown Copyright).

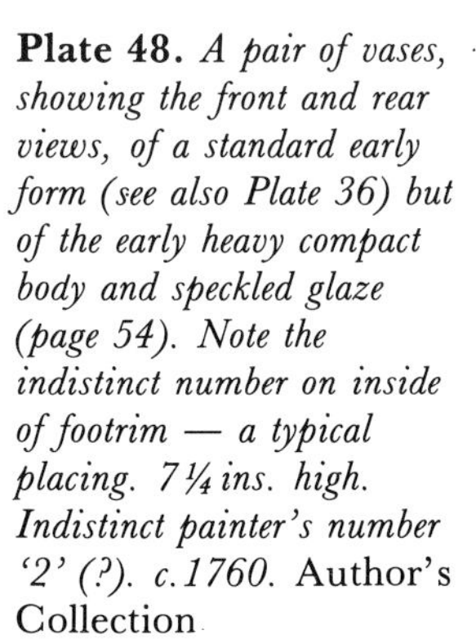

Plate 48. *A pair of vases, showing the front and rear views, of a standard early form (see also Plate 36) but of the early heavy compact body and speckled glaze (page 54). Note the indistinct number on inside of footrim — a typical placing. 7¼ ins. high. Indistinct painter's number '2' (?). c.1760.* Author's Collection

Plate 49. *A rare, early, ribbed teapot, painted in underglaze blue. Note the blue dashes at the juncture of the handle with the body. 5¾ ins. high. Painter's number '8'.* Formerly at South Quay Museum, Great Yarmouth.

motifs with key-like cyphers between. This design appears to be restricted to the Lowestoft wares, so that its presence is a useful guide.

At least one teaset was made to be sold in the white, without the addition of the blue painted panels or border (a teabowl, with the moulded date 1764, is shown in Plate 76), for it is glazed, and the blue painting, if this had been intended, would have been painted on the once-fired body, *before* glazing.

Originally the cups and saucers discussed above formed part of complete teasets, which would also have included a teapot and cover (Plate 75), a slop-bowl (Plate 55), a jug (Plate 72, right), a tea canister and cover, a covered sugar bowl (Plate 74), two bread or cake plates, although I only know of one surviving specimen of plate with relief moulding, and the sugar bowls are also extremely rare. The guides to dating given when discussing the cups apply equally to the other objects which do not always bear the moulded date. It must be remembered that, when one speaks of 1761 or 1764 dated pieces, this is only the earliest possible year of manufacture; a '1761' dated mould could equally well have been used in 1762 or even in 1763 and it would appear that the 1764 moulds were used for several years. As a general rule it can be stated that the rare, undated, non-chrysanthemum examples (Plate 54, right) were made before 1761, and that the designs showing circular panels surrounded by one circle of raised beads were not made after 1762. Examples which are thinly potted, of a compact body, often showing bubbling of the glaze, are also of the pre-1764 period. The 1764 and later pieces are normally of a new, lighter body, which I describe as 'floury' as it appears open rather than compact, but the reliefs are now not so sharply defined as those made from the earlier compact body, often being quite blunt. The covering glaze is now almost perfect and clear, not blued, and the earlier tendency to bubbling has been

Plate 50. *A rare, early, fluted teabowl and saucer, the underglaze blue decoration similar to the ribbed teapot shown in Plate 49. Saucer, diameter 4 7/8 ins. Painter's number '8'. c. 1760.* City of Norwich Museums.

Plate 51. *An oval stand painted in underglaze blue. 7¼ x 5¾ ins. Painter's number '5' on the inside of the footrim. c.1760-5.* Author's Collection.

Plate 52. *A rare, oval, butter tureen and stand. These may be found with different painted borders (Plate 51). A similar butter tureen, at Norwich, has the ribbing on the cover running lengthwise along the cover. Stand 7ins. long. Painter's number '5' on stand. c.1760-5.* Victoria and Albert Museum (Crown Copyright).

Plate 53. *An early Hughes-type (page 55) relief-moulded sugar bowl (or tea blending bowl, page 214). 4½ ins. high. Indistinct number '5' or '6' on inside of footrim. c.1760-2.* Dr. B. Watney Collection.

Plate 54. *Two Hughes-type (page 55) relief-moulded coffee cups. That on the right is the early type, of c.1760, without the later, standard, sunflower-like motifs (arrowed 'A'). Note also the vertical line of trellis between the circular panels. The 1761 and later versions are tapered downwards, whereas the rare earlier pieces show this feature with nearly parallel lines ('B'). The left-hand cup, of c.1761, has the initials 'I.H.' in a small panel. Painter's number '2'. c.1760 and c.1761.* Author's Collection.

Plate 55. *Two rare relief-moulded, Hughes-type (page 55) bowls of slightly different moulded design. The top specimen has the key border of c.1764 (page 62), the very rare, large bowl an earlier border of c.1761-2 and bears in the moulding an indistinct date, 17??. A very rare moulded bowl in the Castle Museum, Norwich, has oblong, rather than the normal circular, panels. Diameter 5 and 7 1/10 ins. Painter's number '2' or '3' on larger bowl. c.1761-4.* Author's Collection.

Plate 56. *A very rare and early moulded jug, (from a three-part mould, (see page 205), with underglaze blue painting, including typical 'berry' inner border (page 71). 10ins. high. Painter's number '3'. c.1761.* Author's Collection.

Plate 57. *A typical Lowestoft relief-moulded jug (from a two-piece mould) with underglaze blue panel and border. Several different moulded jugs of this general type are recorded and these were popular for about twenty years from c.1761 (page 205). 10¼ ins. high. Painter's number '5'. c.1761-5.* Author's Collection.

corrected. This new body and glaze would seem to have been first introduced in about 1764 and was universally employed from about 1768.

Other Lowestoft moulded teawares are shown in Plates 64, 65 and 72, and these can be found with several variations, of relief moulding, of handle shape or of border or other decoration in underglaze blue. Other moulded teawares are decorated with close parallel ribbing and in these wares the underglaze blue ornamentation is sometimes restricted to the borders (Plate 12). The simple and attractive creamer and teabowl and saucer illustrated in Plate 73 have the cell border associated with the 1764 Hughes moulded teasets (Plates 74 and 75).

Apart from relief-moulded teawares discussed above, several other articles are found with this attractive form of ornamentation, the most numerous being sauce boats, originally made in large quantities and in a variety of designs. They were produced and sold in matching pairs, though perfect pairs are rarely found today. Several different sizes were made of each basic shape or design and some are very small, between four and five inches in length; these small boats were perhaps butter boats, not sauce or gravy boats, which normally have a length of between six and eight inches.

Some moulded sauce boats incorporate the initials 'I.H.' as found on the relief-moulded teawares associated with the name of James Hughes (page 55), such as that shown in Plate 59. Although most moulded sauce boats fall within the 1760-70 period, some designs were popular over a long period, one, showing large sunflower-like flowers each side of the main panel, having been continued into the 1770s and 1780s, and often found decorated with underglaze blue printed patterns (Plate 104). The early pre-1765 boats are of the heavy compact body with its resulting crisp relief motifs, while the later examples are of the softer 'floury' body covered with a thicker glaze which produced rather blurred relief work. The painter's number marks on these articles are normally found inside the footrim, and blue line dashes are often placed each side of the handle where it joins the body (Plate 59). The relief designs found on most Lowestoft sauce boats are unique to this factory, except for those shown in Plates 69 and 70.

Some very fine and large moulded jugs were made at the Lowestoft factory, such as the particularly early and rare model shown in Plate 56. Two other typical designs are shown in Plates 57 and 79, one with a mask head spout is in the general Worcester tradition, although the Lowestoft version is vastly different in detail and this example has some of the main features of the mask spout picked out in underglaze blue. As with other Lowestoft porcelains, the earlier jugs are of a heavy compact body with sharp relief modelling, whereas the later ones are of a softer body and the modelling becomes less and less crisp (compare Plate 57 with Plate 79).

One of the most attractive and rare of Lowestoft porcelains is the cornucopia issued in pairs, with sometimes each member of the pair slightly different from the other (Plate 42) and these represent one of the very few types of article found in both Lowestoft and Bow porcelain. Another attractive moulded object is the so-called cider mug, as illustrated in Plate 66. These, like other objects, are found with different handle-forms and with a variety of added underglaze blue borders and designs.

Other early Lowestoft relief-moulded articles are oval butter dishes with matching stands and covers. Although these often appear identical, several different relief-

Plate 58. *A most attractive moulded sauce boat, shown with a matching fragment from the factory site. This 'waster' appears to be of the 1758-60 period, but the complete specimen is c.1761-2. The other side of this sauce boat is shown as Plate 74 C. of Dr. B. Watney's* English Blue and White Porcelain of the 18th Century *(1963). 8ins. long. Painter's number '3'. c.1761-2.* Author's Collection.

Plate 59. *A relief-moulded Hughes-type sauce boat, with the initials 'I.H.' under the main panel (page 55). The clarity of the relief moulding on these early specimens made from the heavy compact body is here clearly seen. 7¾ ins. high. Painter's number '3'. c.1761-2.* Author's Collection.

Plate 60. *A small Hughes-type relief-moulded butter dish formed from a reversed half of the mould, resulting in downward growing plants on one side (page 68). 4½ ins. long. Painter's number '5'. c.1762.* Author's Collection.

Plate 61. *A larger Hughes-type relief-moulded butter dish and stand, like Plate 60, also with downward growing flowers, due to an inverted mould. 5ins. long. Painter's number '4'. c.1762.* Messrs. T.C.S. Brooke (Wroxham).

moulded patterns are to be found (Plates 60 to 62) and in some instances the two halves of the plaster of Paris moulds were placed together incorrectly, so that one half is upside down, resulting in the sunflower-type plants growing downwards on one side. Such an example is shown in Plate 60 and one wonders if the workers failed to notice the error, for it has been subsequently decorated and glazed, and there can be very few factories that would place such blatantly faulty objects on the market. Lowestoft collectors are pleased to view such neglect as an amusing error typical of this unpretentious factory, and in fact such faults add to the interest and value of the piece rather than, as one might expect, detract from it. Another form of oval butter dish bears close moulded ribbing and these sometimes have the knob to the cover in the form of a bird; see Plate 52.

One of the rarest classes of the Lowestoft moulded porcelains is that of the tea canisters. A fine pair of these, large and eight sided, is illustrated in Plate 67. An inscription on the ends indicates the type of tea each should contain; for example, my pair are inscribed 'G' TEA (Green or Gunpowder tea) and 'H' TEA (Hyson tea) but others are known marked 'B' TEA and 'Super' Fine. It is possible that these pairs of octagonal containers originally fitted each end of a wooden tea caddy, having a matching sugar bowl, or mixing bowl (for blending the two different types of tea) in the middle. Such an arrangement is well known in wooden tea caddies of the 1760-80 period, but in most cases the tea containers are of silver, tinned metal, lead or wood, rather than of porcelain. If this supposition is correct, then it is likely that the moulded Lowestoft porcelain bowl illustrated in Plate 53 accompanied a pair of porcelain tea containers in a wooden tea caddy. As with other standard shapes, these tea containers are found with different underglaze blue borders and panel subjects, and were made over several years, from about 1760 to about 1768. They normally have flat, glazed over bases on which is added the painter's number, often a '5' (Plate 67). I have been informed that on a similar caddy in an American collection impressions of British silver hallmarks are worked into the design, a fact which tends to emphasise that these were designed to fit into a wooden tea caddy in the same fashion as some rare examples with silver caddies.

Plate 62. *Two relief-moulded stands to butter dishes, as shown in Plates 60 and 61. As with other, seemingly similar, objects, differences in the relief decoration are readily apparent on examination. Left stand, 7⅛ x 6¼ ins. Right stand, 7½ x 5¼ ins. Indistinct painter's number '2' (?). c.1762.* Author's Collection.

Plate 63. *A rare Hughes-type relief-moulded teapot and cover. Initials and date 'I.H.', '1761' incorporated in the design (page 55). Note the line dashes at the juncture of the handle and the body. 4 ¾ ins. high. Painter's number '5'. c.1761-2.* City of Norwich Museums.

On the other hand, small, rather squat canisters with eight equal sides (Plates 64 and 65) were intended to be used with the Hughes-type moulded teasets.

Other articles decorated with moulded relief motifs included eye baths, butter or cream boats, leaf dishes and chamber candlesticks. It must not be thought, however, that all English porcelains decorated with relief-moulded designs are of Lowestoft origin, for most factories made similar wares, especially in sauce boats, but the forms illustrated in Plates 37, 52-68, 72-9 can be regarded as of Lowestoft origin, and the sunflower, or chrysanthemum, motif, seen moulded in slight relief on so much of this East Anglian porcelain, does not appear to have been employed at any other factory.

The relief-moulded Lowestoft porcelains, attractive as they are, represent less than half of the output of this small factory, for most of its products were of simple, plain shape, adorned only by the painting applied in blue on to the unglazed body. For instance, all the mugs or tankards are devoid of any raised decoration, as are most of the vases, bowls, teawares, coffee pots and a host of other articles made there, and listed in Chapter V.

We have read earlier in this chapter that the first Lowestoft porcelains of the 1757-1760 period show little translucency, and that they are painted in a rather dry looking greyish tone of underglaze blue, but soon after 1760 the body became very heavy and compact, and the underglaze blue of a darker tint, normally applied generously with a fully charged brush. On some examples, probably made about 1760, the glaze is extremely fine, giving a thin, clear, liquid-like covering to the porcelain. The porcelains illustrated in Plates 42-4 have this fine, silky glaze but then for a short period, of five or six years, the glaze tended to be very generously applied so that where it was thickest, for instance under the base, a mass of minute bubbles was formed. Some of these bubbles have turned into dark spots, making it appear as if pepper or

Plate 64. *An octagonal relief-moulded Hughes-type tea canister (without cover), with flat, glazed over base. 3½ ins. high. Painter's number '5'. c.1762.* Author's Collection.

Plate 65. *Two octagonal tea canisters (page 214) and covers of a type issued with 'full' teasets of the 1760s. This basic from also occurs with ribbing. 3¾ ins. high. c.1762-5.* City of Norwich Museums.

Plate 66. *Two relief-moulded cider mugs (page 199). Note the slightly different handle forms. The birds in branches is a favourite motif of the 1760s. 3¾ ins. high. Painter's number '3'. c.1763-5. Other later variations are known, see Plate 250.* Author's Collection.

some like substance has been sprinkled over the glaze. It is noticeable that, whilst on some occasions the glaze is slightly blued, it is more often of a greenish tone, but this feature is apparent only where the glaze has gathered into tears, or where it is especially thick.

From the early 1760s a distinctive, but simple, underglaze blue border motif was favoured, and when it occurs it can be taken for an almost sure indication of a Lowestoft origin. This border, which is drawn below and may be seen on articles illustrated in Plates 45, 56, 87, 88, 92, 96, 103 and 109, is difficult to describe, but reminds me of a blackcurrant and I refer to it as the 'berry border' (it has also been called the 'husk' border) and I find myself attracted to any piece bearing it. This border normally indicates a date between 1762 and about 1770.

The feature of the painter's personal sign, normally a number, being placed on the inside of the footrim (as shown in Plates 48, 82 and 89) has already been remarked upon and may be repeated, as it is quite a reliable guide to pre-1775 Lowestoft porcelains. The latest dated piece known to me bearing a painter's number is the Jacob and Mary Bray mug of 1775.

There is, however, one class of pre-1770 Lowestoft porcelain which does not bear painters' numbers, and comprises the pieces decorated with a dark, rather uneven, inky powder blue ground with small panels reserved into the ground (Plates 94-5). The ground is called 'powder blue' because powdered blue pigment was blown or dusted on to the body, not painted with a brush. This system obviated unsightly brush marks but resulted in a rather granular appearance. The outlines of the reserve panels were

Plate 67. *A fine pair of large tea canisters, of a type which may have fitted into a lockable wooden container (page 68). One is turned to show the narrow end and the flat, glazed base with painter's number. $4\frac{9}{10}$ ins. high. Painter's number '5'. c.1763-5. Other earlier variations are known.* Author's Collection.

Plate 68. *A large and a small relief-moulded sauce boat, similar to models known in salt-glazed stoneware. 8 and 6ins. long. Painter's number '5'. c.1763-5.* Author's Collection.

Plate 69. *A rare relief-moulded sauce boat, shown with part of the original plaster mould. A similar model was made at some other factories. This example has a flat glazed over base. 6ins. long. Painter's number '3'. c.1763-5.* Mould, Christchurch Mansion Museum, Ipswich. Sauce boat, Author's Collection.

Plate 70. *A moulded sauce boat. A similar model was also made at the Worcester factory. This is a large example, 7ins. long, but this popular form was made in several different sizes. c.1763-5.* Author's Collection.

Plate 71. *A selection of small, relief-moulded butter boats (page 198). The top example and that shown bottom right occur also as full-size sauce boats. Top butter boat 4 ¼ ins. long. Middle row left has the painter's number '6', and middle right the number '5'. c.1763-70.* Author's Collection.

Plate 72. *Two relief-moulded milk jugs from tea services of the 1760s. Part of the mould for the example on the left was found on the factory site. Several slight variations of the right-hand jug are known, with different handle forms (see also Plate 7). 3¼ and 3¾ ins high. c.1763-5.* Author's Collection.

Plate 73. *A teabowl and saucer, with a jug, from an attractive ribbed tea service, showing the 1764 + key border (page 62). Creamer 3⅖ ins. high. Indistinct painter's number '17' (?). c.1764-5.* Author's Collection.

Plate 74. *A very rare relief-moulded sugar bowl from a Hughes-type tea service (page 214). Note 1764 + key border. 4⅕ ins. high. Painter's number '5'. c.1764-5.* Author's Collection.

Plate 75. *A rare relief-moulded teapot from a Hughes-type tea service (page 215). Teapots of this type are also known with an open flower knob, such as occurs on the sugar bowl in Plate 74, or with a ball-type knob. Note the late, simple loop handle and straight spout, and compare with Plate 63. 5½ ins. high. c.1764-5.* Sotheby's (ex Hollond Collection).

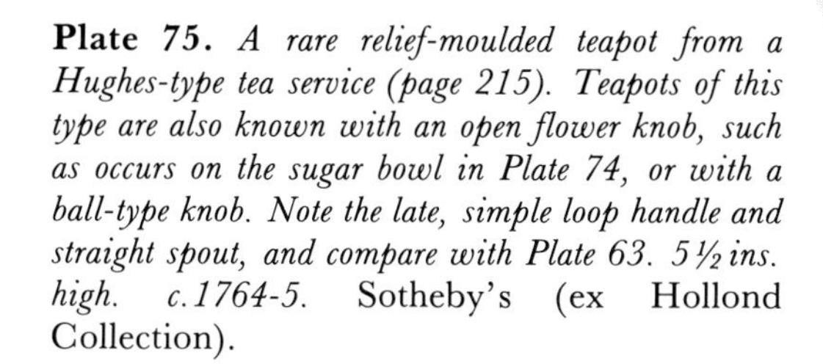

Plate 76. *A decorated teabowl and saucer from a Hughes-type tea service, shown with a very rare undecorated teabowl (page 62). Diameter of saucer 4⁷⁄₁₀ ins. c.1764-6. Some very rare, large size teabowls and saucers were made.* Author's Collection.

Colour Plate 5: *An extremely rare, early Lowestoft spoon tray (page 17), painted in typical early style. Note the dull, thinly applied underglaze blue, finely painted as if with a mapping pen, then filled in with a brush. Note also the typical birds, or waterfowl, and compare with Plates 32 and 33. $7\frac{1}{5}$ ins. long. c.1758-9.* Author's Collection.

Colour Plate 6. *Interior view of a superb bowl, showing the inscription and fine quality painting in underglaze blue. Diameter $5\frac{1}{2}$ ins. c.1770-5.* Victoria and Albert Museum (Crown Copyright).

Plate 77. *A barrel-shaped teapot from a tea service relief-moulded with carnations. In this case the moulding has been painted over (perhaps but not certainly, some years after it was originally made) with enamel colours, but in many cases this design has only the underglaze blue borders. 6ins. high. Painter's number '5'. c.1764.* Victoria and Albert Museum (Crown Copyright).

Plate 78. *A rare relief-moulded eye bath, painted in underglaze blue. 2¹⁄₁₀ ins. high. c.1765.* Author's Collection.

Plate 79. *A relief-moulded jug of the late 'floury' body. Compare the sharpness of the moulding with that seen in Plates 56 and 57. Note the typical Lowestoft mask spout (page 206). 8¾ ins. high. c.1765-70.* Formerly Author's Collection.

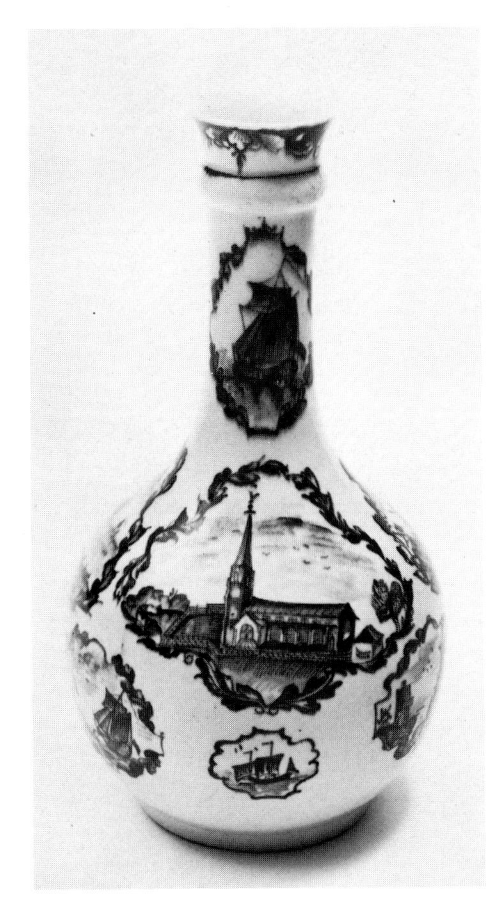

Plate 80. *A superb ewer and basin (not a pair) painted in underglaze blue with local views, the centre panels depicting St. Margaret's Church, Lowestoft, and, on the basin, the High Light. Ewer 9½ ins. high. Inscribed under the base 'E.A. Lowestoft. 1764'. Painter's number '3'. Diameter of basin 9⅜ ins. Painter's number '5'.* Ewer, City of Norwich Museums. Basin, Sotheby's (ex Colman Collection).

painted in by hand (and often the added powder blue ground does not exactly match the pre-painted outline). The reserve panels were hand painted with small Chinese-style landscapes, and in the smaller panels with floral sprays. The basic style was copied from Chinese porcelains and similar powder blue wares were made at the Bow, Caughley and Worcester factories.

Often in the past Bow powder blue porcelains have been attributed to Lowestoft, but really there is little excuse for this error, as the Bow examples are of a typical soft bone ash body, whereas most Lowestoft pieces are of the early compact body with a glossy glaze, quite different from that used at the Bow factory. Further, the Bow (and Worcester) examples are nearly always marked with a series of mock Chinese characters, whereas the Lowestoft pieces are, with one exception, unmarked. A further very important difference between Lowestoft and most other essays in powder blue decoration lies in the different shapes of the larger reserve panels, those of Lowestoft having a multi-curved outline like some Chinese examples, the other factories favouring fan shape. The typical Lowestoft form can be clearly seen in Plates 94-5. All powder blue examples are now rare. One, a perhaps unique plate in the British Museum, has in the centre panel a view of St. Margaret's Church, Lowestoft, with other local views in the smaller panels. A very rare coffee pot has panels painted with flowers in overglaze enamel, which indicates a post-1768 date for this particular piece, but most examples are rather earlier and a mammoth tea, or punch, pot in the Castle Museum, Norwich has the incised date 1763. Another teapot is dated 1768. Nearly all Lowestoft powder blue porcelains are teawares, a possible exception being a small tray in the City Museum, Birmingham, which could, however, be a spoon tray from a tea service. Dessert wares, such as shaped dishes, do not appear to have been made at Lowestoft, although they were certainly made at the Bow, Caughley and Worcester factories with a powder blue ground.

The early pre-1775 Lowestoft mugs or tankards were often of a graceful bell shape with a good scroll handle, having an outward kick at the bottom and a thumb grip near the top of the handle. Plate 4 shows a particularly fine bell shape mug with a typically early handle form. Other more usual bell shape mugs are shown in Plates 81, 82 and 98 and other dated examples are listed in Appendix I. The cylindrical mug shown in Plate 5 is a rare early example of a slightly flared form with a rare thin strap-like handle. The later mugs were nearly always of a plain cylindrical shape (Plates 147, 160 and 186).

A useful guide to attribution is the extent of the glazing, for in general the Lowestoft workmen endeavoured to cover completely the porcelain body with glaze. For instance, when a base was flat, that is without a footrim, it would be glazed, whereas one from the Liverpool factories would not, and while the flat bases of Lowestoft teapot

Plate 81. *A typical early shaped mug, painted in underglaze blue and inscribed in the front: 'Ann Hammond. Woodbridge, Aprill (sic) 9th, 1764'. Painter's number '3', signed, or inscribed, under the return at the bottom of the handle 'Richard Phillips' (page 158).* Castle Museum, Norwich.

Plate 82. *Two, of a set of three, typical bell-shaped mugs, painted in underglaze blue, and inscribed under the base: 'Ab^{rm}. Moore. August 29th 1765'. Painter's number '3' on the larger example. This pattern and inscription were copied in Continental hard-paste porcelain (page 253 and Plate 241). 6 and 4 ¾ ins. high.* Sotheby's.

Plate 83. *A rare early cylindrical mug, 'pencilled' in black and inscribed: I.*[s] *Hughes. Sept 4th 1766. Lowestoft' (page 154). 4⅜ ins. high. Painter's number '3'.* Christchurch Mansion Museum, Ipswich.

Plate 84. *A rare and early octagonal inkpot painted in underglaze blue, and inscribed on the base: 'S.A. Curties, July 4th 1766'. Diameter 3¼ ins., 2½ ins. high. Painter's number '3'.* Victoria and Albert Museum (Crown Copyright).

Plate 85. *A unique plate, painted in underglaze blue, the base inscribed as shown. Similar doodling is seen on an inkpot (also dated 1766) now in the British Museum, with an indistinct painter's number, perhaps '3'. See* The Connoisseur *magazine, June 1927. Diameter 9ins.* Sotheby's.

stands and spoon trays were glazed, similar objects from the Worcester or Caughley factory would be wiped clean of glaze. This preoccupation with glazing is particularly helpful in identifying a Lowestoft teapot, for the inside flange of the cover is always glazed (except, sometimes, for the bottom edge) whereas flanges of similar Worcester or Caughley teapot covers after about 1770 are wiped, or left free of glaze.

Another distinguishing potting detail is the triangular shaped foot of Lowestoft teapots, contrasting with the square or rectangular foot found on Caughley pots, or the undercut footrim often, but not always found with Liverpool examples.

By about 1765 the earlier compact body was replaced by a lighter one of more open texture which I have termed 'floury' (indeed, the two bodies could be compared with a bad and a good sponge or cake, one doughy, the other open and light). This new, post-1765 body was not so well suited to the production of the moulded designs discussed on pages 54-69 because, as I have explained, the relief work appears rather blunted. On the other hand, the post-1765 glaze is always pure, devoid of the speckling and excess bubbling sometimes (but by no means always) found with the earlier body, and I have never seen a specimen of Lowestoft porcelain with a crazed glaze, that is, with that network of fine lines which breaks up the glaze on so much porcelain, recent as well as eighteenth century.

With the introduction of the open 'floury' body the objects were, as a general rule, rather thicker than their equivalents of the earlier compact body, a difference which is especially noticeable in saucers, for the early ones were often turned or trimmed to a very thin gauge. The Lowestoft saucers display to a marked degree the method of support in the glost kiln (that is, after they have been glazed) for the post-1765 saucers show three blemishes, spaced equally, round the top edge of the saucer where the 'stilts' or spacers, were placed to stop each saucer from sticking to its neighbour in the

Plate 86. *A teabowl and saucer painted in underglaze blue with a typical fanciful Chinese landscape within the berry border (page 71). Diameter of saucer 2⁴⁄₅ ins. Painter's marks, a cross and a circle on the inside of the rim. c.1764-6.* Author's Collection.

Plate 87. *Part child's tea service painted in underglaze blue with one of the popular 'toy patterns'. Note painter's number on foot of tilted waste bowl. Teapot 3¹⁄₁₀ ins. high. c.1765.* Author's Collection.

pile. The blemishes, often an extra gathering of glaze or a discoloured mark, are frequently quite obvious, and help materially to identify a Lowestoft saucer for, while some other factories (not Caughley or Worcester) employed this method, the tell-tale signs are not nearly so obvious as those to be seen on the top edge of nearly every Lowestoft saucer, from about 1765 to the closure of the factory some thirty-five years later. It is noticeable, too, that the post-1765 Lowestoft saucers with these 'stilts' or spacer marks are fired upside down, so that if any of the underglaze blue has run it is towards the outside edge rather than to the centre. This rule, however, applies only to post-1765 (or perhaps post-1768) saucers, for the earlier examples do not normally show stilt marks on the outside edge, and appear to have been fired with footrims downwards, not in the later, reversed position.

The early, pre-1770 Lowestoft porcelains are illustrated in Plates 32 to 108, and the various articles made during both periods are listed alphabetically in Chapter V, while notes on the painters are given in Chapter IV.

Plate 88. *Two simple, but charming, early milk jugs painted in underglaze blue. Note the dashes at the juncture of handle and body, also the berry border on the left-hand specimen. 3¹⁄₁₀ ins. and 3¼ ins. high. Painter's numbers '5' (right) and '6' (left) on inside of footrim. c.1764-6.* Author's Collection.

Plate 89. *Two very rare sauce boats, without the normal relief-moulded decoration, painted in underglaze blue with typical birds and foliage. One boat is turned to show the painter's number '5' in normal position on inside of foot. 7¼ ins. long. c.1764-6.* Author's Collection.

Plate 90. *A rare oil (or vinegar) bottle (page 209). Note the pierced holes in the handle. 6ins. high. c.1765.* H.C. Wolton Collection.

Plate 91. *A very rare* hors d'œuvre *dish made in one piece (page 205). c.1765.* Messrs. T.C.S. Brooke (Wroxham).

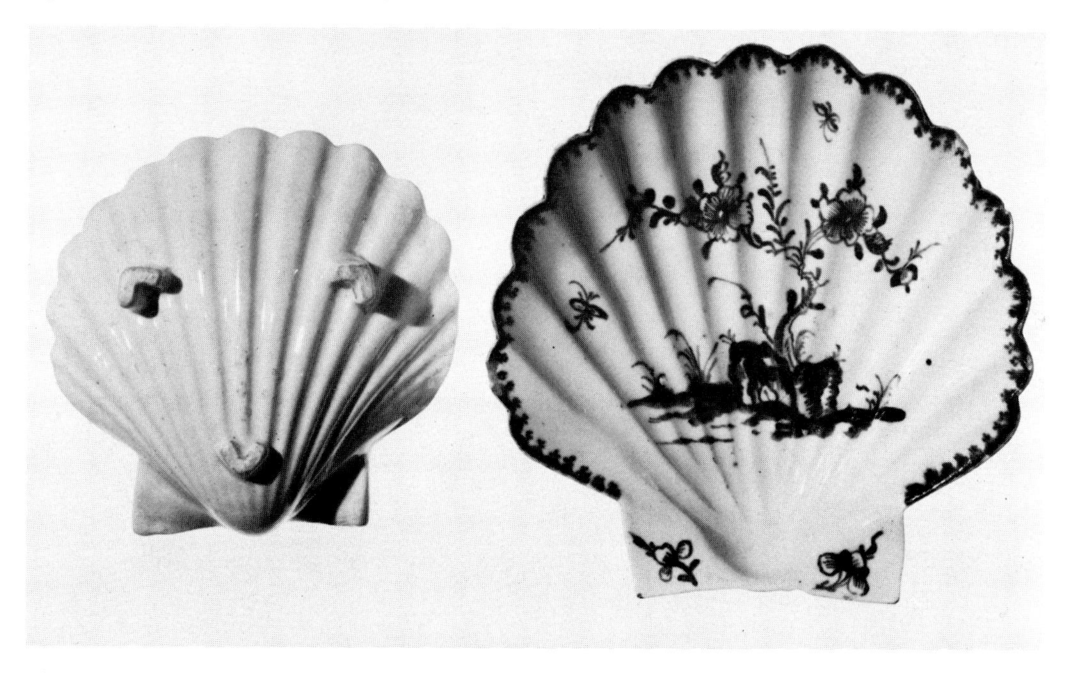

Plate 92. *A pair of moulded scallop shell dishes. Note the triangular feet, the 'berry' border and dark tone of blue, and compare with earlier examples shown in Plate 32 and a later example, Plate 105 (page 212). 5½ ins. high. Painter's number '3' inside one foot. c.1765.* Author's Collection.

Plate 93. *Large bowl, painted in underglaze blue. Birds and foliage on the exterior. Diameter 8¾ ins. c.1765.* Author's Collection.

Plate 94. *A very rare, small teapot with powder blue ground (page 71) and a rare coffee cup and saucer. Teapot 5ins. high. c.1765-8.* Formerly Godden Collection.

Plate 95. *A rare coffee pot with particularly dark, powder blue ground and a bread plate from a similar tea service. Coffee pot 9ins. high. c.1765-8.* Author's Collection.

Plate 96. *A rare tray, perhaps a spoon tray, from a tea service (page 213). Other rare square trays of this type have a more scalloped edge. 4½ ins. square. c.1765-8.* Author's Collection.

Plate 97. *A large dish, from a dinner service (page 203). A fine tureen with this design is recorded. Note the bubbled glaze. 12¾ x 10ins. c.1768.* S. Spero Collection.

Plate 98. *A fine and typical bell-shaped mug, with formal floral sprays each side of the central panel. 5¾ ins. Painter's number '3' on inside of footrim. 1768.* Author's Collection.

Plate 99. *A rare pair of blue-painted small vases (page 217) with middle period bubbled glaze. 6ins. high. Painter's number '5'. c.1768.* Author's Collection.

Plate 100. *A superb blue painted shallow bowl, inscribed under the base, 'Elizath (sic) Buckle. 1768'. Diameter 11ins. Painter's number '5' (page 145).* Castle Museum, Norwich.

Plate 101. *A rare fluted salad bowl (page 211). Formal floral motifs in a style found on several objects of the period c.1765-70. Diameter 8½ins., 2¼ins. high. c.1768.* Author's Collection.

Plate 102. *A rare circular coaster-like object, all the blue and white decoration being on the exterior, (see page 200). Diameter 4¾ ins., 2⅞ ins. high. c.1760-5.* Author's Collection.

Plate 103. *Three leaf dishes, the top example of a popular form made at several factories, but note the 'berry' border (page 71). The right-hand form appears unique to Lowestoft and is 6¼ ins. long. c.1768-70.* Victoria and Albert Museum (Crown Copyright).

Plate 104. *A 'pap warmer', made in three separate pieces (page 209). The mask head varies, as does the blue decoration. The aperture is to insert the oil burner, of the type shown below, with an unglazed cover, from the factory site. Note the pierced knob for the wick. 10½ ins. high. Painter's number '5'. c.1768-70.* City of Norwich Museums.

Plate 105. *A scallop-shaped shell dish, a late version of a form illustrated in Plates 32 and 92, but now with a continuous footrim (page 212). 4½ x 4¼ ins. c.1768-70.* Author's Collection.

Plate 106. *A typical Lowestoft bottle-shape vase of small size, here turned to show the amusing and so typical Lowestoft prancing bird on the reverse. Painter's number '3'. 6¼ ins. high. c.1765-8.* Author's Collection.

Plate 107. *A rare small beaker mug, painted in an amusing manner. 2½ ins. high. c.1768-70.* Photograph, N. Baker, Esq.

Plate 108. *A rare small mug, with typical handle form. 3½ ins. high. c.1768 (or earlier).* Messrs. T.C.S. Brooke (Wroxham).

Colour Plate 7. *A fine, post-1775, tall coffee-pot attractively decorated with the 'Two-bird' pattern in the Redgrave style (page 103 and Plate 26), showing typical combination of underglaze blue with overglaze enamel colours and slight gilding. 9¾ ins. high. c.1775-80.* Godden Collection.

CHAPTER III

Post-1770 Porcelains

As we have seen, the post-1770 Lowestoft porcelain body, which I have described as 'floury', was rather soft and open in texture, in contrast to the compact body of the 1760-4 period (page 81), and the covering glaze is normally free of imperfections such as bubbling, spotting or crazing.

The top edge of the saucer rims display the three 'stilt' marks mentioned in the previous Chapter (page 81) and on occasions these blemishes have been so pronounced that a dealer has reduced the price owing to what he thought were 'chips' but which were in reality a firing characteristic, and a most useful guide to identification. A further pointer is a roughish patch under the article where the glaze is very thin, as if the glazer's thumb had gripped the piece just inside the footrim when he dipped the piece in the glaze, or when he shook off the surplus glaze. However, this feature is not always present.

All the pre-1765 Lowestoft porcelains discussed in the previous chapter were decorated by hand in underglaze blue, and this standard method of decoration was continued right through to the closure of the factory, although its use had declined greatly by the 1790s, and from about 1785 the blue is much lighter in tone than the earlier, rather inky colour. Some late blue and white designs have a dark green or brown line near the rim, perhaps in an effort to imitate a gilt edge, or the coloured rim found on some Chinese export porcelains.

There were two important innovations in the mid-1760s. The first is the belated introduction of overglaze enamel colours (pages 25-9). The second is the introduction of the blue printed designs, some of which designs are surprisingly scarce.

To discuss first the printed designs in underglaze blue, which fall into two categories; those which are clearly copies of popular Worcester blue prints, and those designs are unique to the Lowestoft factory. The copies of standard Worcester patterns nearly always bear also a copy of the Worcester crescent mark, and these prints are applied to forms which were favoured at the Worcester (and Caughley) factory. These Worcester-type prints are:

(A) The so-called pine cone design (Plates 127, 128, 133 and 136) which is found amongst other objects on Worcester-styled openwork baskets and stands (Plate 133), on pierced cress dishes (Plate 136), on rare shaped-edged Worcester-styled salad dishes (Plate 127), and on plates.
(B) The Worcester fence pattern, found mostly on teawares (Plates 131 and 132).
(C) The Worcester rose pattern (Plates 123 and 126) which is found on Worcester-type covered butter dishes (Plate 126), on rare Worcester-styled moulded cabbage leaf jugs, and on other articles.
(D) The Worcester three flower design (Plates 129 and 131), was also copied mostly on teawares.

(E) Several near copies of Worcester Chinese-styled landscape designs, of general 'Willow pattern' style, were also made, and one of these is called the 'Argument' pattern because two figures are shown, at a window, in belligerent attitudes.

(F) The printed design shown inside the sauce boat (illustrated in Plate 124) is also found in Worcester porcelains.

Full details of all the known Lowestoft blue printed designs are listed and illustrated in John Howell's E.C.C. Paper 'Transfer-printed Lowestoft Porcelain' published in the *Transactions of the English Ceramic Circle,* Vol. 7, Part 3 (1970).

It should be stressed that these Lowestoft printed designs are copies of Worcester prints, *not* of the post-1775 Caughley versions of the same Worcester designs, and for the differences between the wares of these two factories the reader is referred to the author's *Caughley and Worcester Porcelains, 1775-1800.* The first dated example of Lowestoft blue printing is of 1771, before, in fact, the Caughley porcelain factory was established. It is also worth mentioning here that in the 1770s and early 1780s the Lowestoft factory issued copies of some hand painted Worcester designs, for instance, the floral pattern seen on the teapot in Plate 127, or the mustard pot shown in Plate 114.

The reader may well ask how is he to tell the Lowestoft copies of Worcester blue printed designs from the original Worcester, or from other copies of the Worcester designs. This is, indeed, relatively simple for anyone familiar with Lowestoft porcelain, but judging by the many errors of attribution which can be seen today, accurate knowledge on the subject is not as widespread as one would wish.

(A) Taking first the porcelain body, the Lowestoft porcelain is a relatively soft, bone ash 'floury' porcelain, often thickly potted. This contrasts with the harder, crisp soapstone body employed at Worcester and at Caughley.

(B) In regard to shapes, the typical Lowestoft copy of the Worcester flower knob found on teapots, covered sugar bowls, tea caddies, etc. is supported on a

Plate 109. *Three rare egg cups, the left-hand example with 'berry' border c.1765, the centre example printed in underglaze blue c.1775 and is 3ins. high. The low egg cup is in a late, bright blue, c.1785-90.* Dr. B. Watney Collection.

Plate 110. *A rare inscribed plate, dated on reverse, 1770. Diameter 9ins. 1770.* Christchurch Mansion Museum, Ipswich.

characteristic high solid hump (Plates 127, 129, 141 and 142). The applied leaves on teapot covers, Worcester-styled baskets, butter dishes and similar objects are thick, and quite different from the same features on Worcester and Caughley porcelains (Plate 126). The Lowestoft saucers show the three stilt marks on the upper edge (page 81) not found on the Worcester and Caughley examples.

(C) The prints themselves have rather a spidery, uncertain appearance, and where shading was required this portion has often been rather carelessly washed over by hand with underglaze blue pigment (Plates 129, 132 and 245).

These pointers should enable the reader to differentiate between Worcester blue printed porcelains and the copies made at the Lowestoft factory and in some cases the prints will be found on purely Lowestoft shapes, forms not made at Worcester or Caughley, cases in point including the coffee pot shown in Plate 132, and the milk jug on the left side of Plate 131. Both these specimens have applied leaves under the handle.

The printed designs previously discussed were copies of popular Worcester patterns. However, many Lowestoft prints are unique to this factory. Some fine prints incorporating a sportsman are traditionally associated with a Bungay printer named

Plate 111. *A rare jug, with the appearance of being a typical bell-shaped mug (Plate 82) with spout added. Inscribed 'Willm. Callow, Ludham, 1773'. 5ins. high. Painter's number '5'.* Sotheby's.

Plate 112. *A typical Lowestoft inscribed and dated teapot, from the Rev^{d}. C.J. Sharp Collection.* Photograph, Ceylon Tea Centre, London.

Plate 113. *A possibly unique miniature feeding cup, painted in black with a man shooting fowl, perhaps on a local lake or 'broad'. 2ins. high. c.1765-70 (or earlier).* E.D. Levine Collection.

Plate 114. *Two rare Lowestoft mustard pots, that on the left being the earlier, c.1765, and having the painter's number '5'. The right-hand example is painted with a copy of a Worcester pattern (often employed at Lowestoft) and has a late handle form. This is 3¼ ins. high. c.1765 and 1785.* Victoria and Albert Museum (Crown Copyright).

Plate 115. *A charming and typical blue and white covered jug. Note the handle form, and also the typical dashes on the knob. 7ins. high. c.1770-80.* Victoria and Albert Museum (Crown Copyright).

Plate 116. *Three leaf dishes; that shown on the right appears to be unique to Lowestoft, the other two being versions of Worcester, Derby and Caughley dishes, but note the blue lines at handle joints. Left-hand dish 3⅗ x 3ins. c.1770-80.* Author's Collection.

Plate 117. *A rare relief-moulded, leaf-shaped chamber, or hand, candlestick, as seen from above. An unglazed fragment of such an example was found on the factory site. 6ins. long. c.1770.* Formerly at South Quay Museum, Great Yarmouth.

Plate 118. *A rare, small, barrel-shaped creamer, painted in underglaze blue. $2\frac{9}{10}$ ins. high. c.1770-5.* Author's Collection.

Plate 119. *A very rare Lowestoft salt, one of a pair from the Wallace Elliot and Colman Collections. $1\frac{4}{5}$ ins. high. c.1770-5.* Author's Collection.

Plate 120. *A rare form of shell-shaped creamer, of a basic type made at several other English factories, most of which employed a dolphin-like handle, instead of this rather skimpy Lowestoft one. $2\frac{4}{5}$ ins. high. c.1770-5.* Author's Collection.

Gamble, but I do not know of any evidence to substantiate this, and it is interesting to digress for one moment to see how, in this case, the opinion of one person became in time established as fact. Llewellynn Jewitt, writing in the *Art Journal* magazine of July, 1863, referred to a blue printed jug 'handed down from father to son in the family of the most active proprietor, (that) is preserved, with a memorandum that the copper plate from which it was printed was given to Mr. Browne by a Mr. Gamble of Bungay, who, with his family, was in the habit of visiting Lowestoft. Probably the plate was given that the family might be supplied with ware printed from it. The design is a sportsman with dog and gun, and on the spout of the jug are the letters 'S.A.', the initials of Samuel Aldred.' Handed down family traditions are notoriously suspect, yet in a recent standard reference book we find this early opinion passed on as an unqualified statement of fact: 'the print...was made by Gamble, of Bungay'. Mr. Howell has been unable to trace an engraver of this name.

Other Lowestoft blue printed designs are simple and include: two pheasant-like birds in foliage (Plate 128), a framed castle-like building (believed to represent the local 'Good Cross Chapel', and often referred to by this name (Plate 125), an amusing print depicting a seated Eastern lady with a squirrel on a fence (Plate 125), and a rare one showing two dromedaries on a raft (Plate 128). Another rare Lowestoft print depicts a Chinese tea party (Plate 13). Several other prints can be seen in Room 140 at the Victoria and Albert Museum in London, of which some show representations of Chinese-styled temples in landscapes, often referred to as 'Willow pattern', although they bear little resemblance in the main details to the famous Willow pattern as we

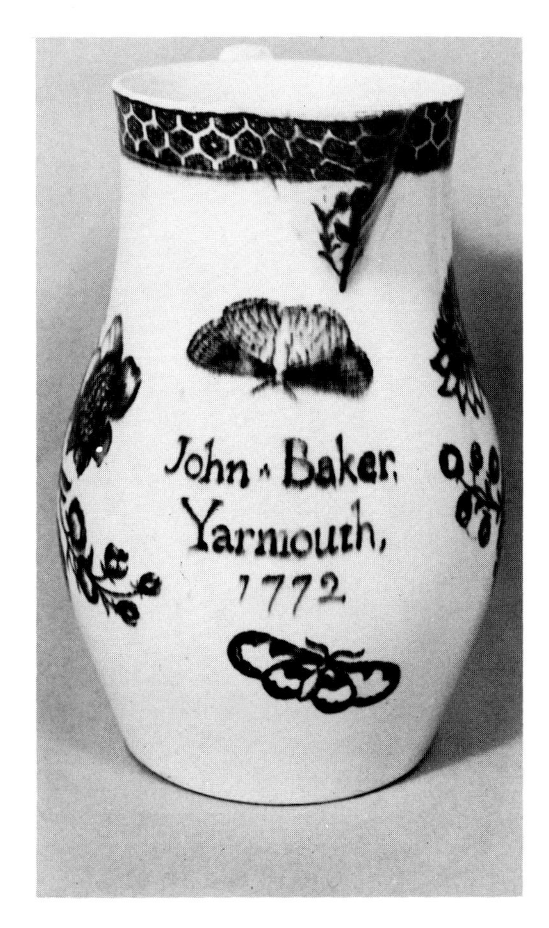

Plate 121. *An early example of underglaze blue printed motifs in the Worcester style, but applied to a typically Lowestoft form. 6½ ins. high. 1772.* Ex Henry Levine Collection. See sale record 248.

Plate 122. *Two forms of Lowestoft feeding cup, bearing Worcester-type underglaze blue printed motifs. The shaped-sided example is the rarer type, but several variations of size and shape occur. 3⁵⁄₁₆ ins. high. c.1772-5.* Left. W.W. Warner (Antiques) Ltd. Right. Dr. B. Watney Collection.

know it today, a design which, in spite of many statements to the contrary, would seem to date from the nineteenth century, not the eighteenth.

The borders of Lowestoft printed designs can vary, and in fact were sometimes painted by hand, while conversely, a printed border can occur on a piece which is otherwise hand painted. The pieces which bear prints unique to the Lowestoft factory, those which are not copies of standard Worcester designs, do not bear any factory mark.

Before leaving the subject of printed patterns one disclaimer must, regretfully, be recorded. A charming design of two Chinese figures climbing rococo scrolls*, very much in the manner of the painter Jean Pillement, has been illustrated on several occasions as Lowestoft but all examples that I have handled appear to be of Derby, or perhaps of Bow, manufacture.

It is not known for certain when the Lowestoft management first started to use overglaze enamel colours, instead of the underglaze blue of the earlier period. I originally wrote that such overglaze coloured designs dated from about 1770 but this belief has been superseded by the researches of John Howell as given in his E.C.C. Paper 'Some notes on the introduction of Polychrome Decoration at Lowestoft', published in the *Transactions of the English Ceramic Circle,* Vol. 9, part 3 (1975). In brief Mr. Howell, a noted collector of Lowestoft porcelain with his wife, suggests that the overglaze patterns were introduced in about 1766. I now agree with these thoughts and have shown in Plates 18-19 on page 27, two early type teapots but it must be stated that overglaze designs produced before about 1775 are decidely rare.

Turning for a moment from the pieces decorated only with overglaze colours we have a quite large selection of porcelains which combine underglaze blue with overglaze enamels and often slight gilt enrichments. These Imari-style pieces show a strong eastern influence, showing Chinese-type landscapes or formal 'Famille Rose' floral designs (Colour Plate 7, Plates 143-6 and 203-5) and some of which are in fact

* See Dr. B. Watney's *English Blue and White Porcelain of the 18th Century*, Plate 84B.

Plate 123. *A rare Lowestoft copy of a Worcester moulded cabbage leaf jug, bearing printed underglaze blue designs. Note the large, typically Lowestoft, mask head spout (see also Plate 79). These jugs, with or without the mask spout, were made in different sizes and at several factories. 9ins. high. c.1772-8.* Author's Collection.

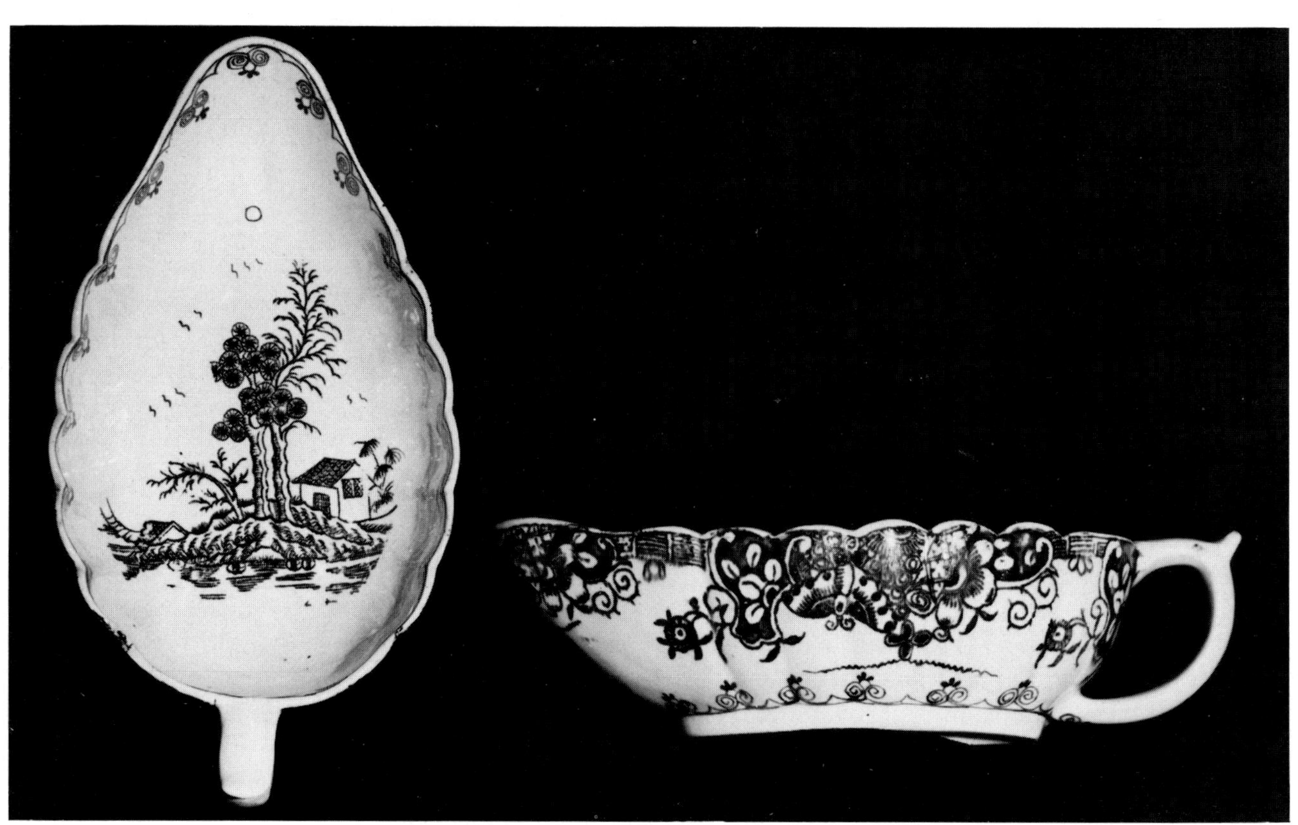

Plate 124. *A rare pair of transfer-printed Lowestoft sauce boats in imitation of a Worcester model, also made at the Caughley and Derby factories. 8½ ins. long. c.1772-8.* Formerly Author's Collection.

also found on Chinese porcelains of the 1770-90 period. The new overglaze enamel colours on these designs are mainly a bright red, a pale green and a pinky-red enamel, with rather thin, brassy gilding on some specimens.

This family of related blue and enamelled designs, simple but charming, are found only on tablewares and very rarely on bowls (Plate 143). They are called 'Redgrave patterns' but, although they are associated with painters of this name, I think it probable, as I explain on page 163, that these freely painted designs were the responsibility of the female painters, perhaps of a team of young painters working under Mary Redgrave. They are normally unmarked but some very rare specimens have a small red enamel cross painted inside the footrim, a perfect rebus for the name Redgrave.

In contrast to these rather naïvely executed Redgrave patterns we have a very fine range of enamelled porcelains delicately painted by an accomplished flower painter. His compositions very often include a prominent full-blown tulip and the artist is generally known as the 'Tulip painter', although this flower is not always present. Plates 147-53 illustrate typical specimens of the work of this artist who was painting at Lowestoft by at least 1774, as pieces bearing this date are preserved, see Plates 147 and 151.

The selection of pieces from the Castle Museum, Norwich, shown here in Plate 147, illustrates well this painter's style and his dislike of over-ornamentation. His compositions stand out clearly from the white porcelain backcloth and the eye is not distracted by clumsy borders, many of the pieces lacking even a single line border. Apart from the famous tulip, this painter favoured a pair of lily-like flowers with very long trumpets, characteristic motifs sometimes found on the cover or back of a piece, and the close-up of a teapot cover shown in Plate 149 illustrates this flower clearly.

Apart from floral compositions in full enamel colour, the 'Tulip painter' also worked

Plate 125. *A blue printed Lowestoft saucer with the Good Cross Chapel design, and a teabowl and saucer with the popular printed squirrel pattern, which is to be found with different hand painted borders. Saucers, diameter 4¾ ins. c.1772-8.* The late Mr. and Mrs. E. Hutchinson Collection.

Plate 126. *A Lowestoft oval butter tureen, cover and stand, a close copy of a Worcester model and also copied at the Caughley factory (page 198). Printed in underglaze blue. Note the typically thick, applied leaves and six-petalled flowers (also found on figures, see Colour Plate 8 and Plate 179). Stand 7½ ins. long. c.1772-80.* Author's Collection.

Plate 127. *A rare blue printed Lowestoft salad bowl (page 211), a circular butter tureen (page 199), and a hand painted teapot. All three pieces are modelled, and decorated, after Worcester originals. Salad bowl, diameter 10ins. A blue painted open crescent mark on the teapot. c.1772-85.* Godden of Worthing Ltd.

in monochrome, an example being the teabowl and saucer from a service, said to have been the wedding service made for Robert Browne, the factory manager, illustrated in Plate 154, and painted in pink monochrome with a gilt border, with the characteristic lily-like flowers at the top of the saucer.

Although the 'Tulip painter' is associated with flower painting, I believe that on occasions he painted figures. At least one fine service is painted with pink figure compositions and has a gilt border very similar to that found on the Browne wedding service (compare Plate 154 with 155) and the treatment is identical, the enamel being very thinly applied with the underlying white porcelain used to serve for the highlights. Porcelains painted by the 'Tulip painter' occasionally also bear armorial bearings (see page 182 and Plate 152) and sometimes initials and/or, names and dates. All examples of this artist's work are now rare and very desirable and he seems to have been employed at the Lowestoft factory for only a few years, almost certainly for less than ten. With great courage, or foolhardiness, I have attempted, on page 186, to identify this 'Tulip painter'.

While the 'Tulip painter's' work displays an English, or at least a European feeling, most of the Lowestoft enamel painting imitates the Chinese porcelain that was brought into this country in large quantities, and which proved so popular. Many teasets were painted with Chinese figure compositions and the teapot shown in Plate 187 is a good, typical example. Some fine, straight-sided tankards were also made (Plates 191 and 194) but these are very much rarer than the Chinese hard-paste porcelain examples which they sought to imitate. Vases were also decorated with panels of Chinese figures and, while even pairs are rarely seen today, these vases were originally issued in sets of five (Plates 198-9 and 201).

A further class of decoration made in imitation of the Chinese export market

Plate 128. *A rare, shaped-edged Lowestoft plate, printed in underglaze blue after a Worcester original. Two Lowestoft blue printed teabowls and saucers bearing patterns unique to this factory. Plate, diameter 9¼ ins. Blue printed, shaded crescent mark. c.1772-1785.* Godden of Worthing Ltd.

Plate 129. *A blue printed Lowestoft tea canister and cover (page 215), the print taken from a Worcester original, although the shape is typically Lowestoft. 5ins. high. c.1775-85.* Victoria and Albert Museum (Crown Copyright).

Plate 130. *A rare Lowestoft covered basket of a form produced also at Worcester and at Caughley. A mould for the matching stand was found on the Lowestoft factory site. 8½ ins. long. c.1775-85.* Private Collection.

porcelains comprised formal floral designs such as cornucopias of flowers, ornate Oriental baskets of flowers (Plates 198 and 199) or straightforward floral compositions often within wide ornate Oriental cell or diaper borders, typical specimens of which are to be seen in Plates 200, 207, 210, 213 and 214. These styles are associated, on traditional grounds, with a painter named Curtis (page 152).

Some Chinese export market porcelains were painted in black enamel, sometimes heightened with gilding, work which can be very fine, and is often called 'pencilling' and has been associated with the Jesuit missionaries. The Lowestoft factory in England also copied this style on their soft-paste porcelain, and the garniture, or set of vases, shown in Plate 201 serves as a good example of this rare style. The flare topped vases are rather top heavy but are based on the standard shape favoured by the Chinese potters. Several different black and gold 'pencilled' patterns were painted on Lowestoft teawares and these have a decided Oriental air. The teapot illustrated in Plate 188 is probably the finest example of this style known, although some very delicate black pencilling depicts European scenes (Plate 113).

We are still by no means certain if the Lowestoft painters were in fact copying the Chinese, or if the Chinese potters were sent samples of Lowestoft porcelain which they copied and sent back to Europe. This latter, rather improbable situation mainly arises from a document found at The Hague, relating to patterns sent to China by the Dutch East India Company, where the instruction* — '...the director especially requested that dragons and other chimerical animals should not be sent to Europe ... but instead the small flowers in the taste of Lowestoft ware' — would appear to indicate that the English wares were well known to the Dutch merchants and perhaps even to the Chinese potters. It must be remembered that the Chinese potters had little, or no, knowledge of Western art or their customers' requirements, so that samples, in the form of prints, or drawings, or even silver articles, or European pottery and porcelain, were taken out to China by the trading vessels and the Chinese potters and painter simply copied what they were given. This occasionally gave rise to amusing situations when the china was brought back to Europe and a distinguished family found the centre painted with the inscription 'my arms here', or 'these are my arms', the instructions on the original sketch!

I do not wish to confuse the reader or resurrect the old myth that Chinese porcelain was painted at the Lowestoft factory, but Plate 195 is interesting. The saucer on the left is Chinese hard-paste porcelain, copied from a European design, or at least depicting a European vessel, while the bowl is English soft-paste porcelain, made and painted at Lowestoft, yet the decorations are so similar and unusual that one must be a copy of the other — but which was the original?

One of the best known types of Chinese porcelain decorated especially for the European market is that which was painted with the family armorial bearings, crest or initials (Plate 28). The Lowestoft factory (in keeping with most other English porcelain factories of the period) did occasional essays in this style, but the soft-paste English examples are very much rarer than the Chinese (which are often called 'Lowestoft' in error, see page 39).

Perhaps the most famous of the true Lowestoft armorial services is that made for the Rev. Robert Potter, Vicar of Lowestoft and Prebendary of Norwich (Plate 215) but only the cups and saucers to this set would appear to have survived. Another set was

---

* Quoted from John Goldsmith Phillip's *China-Trade Porcelain* (but previously published by J.P. Van Goldsenhoven in *La Céramique Chinoise sous les Ts'ing* (1936).

Plate 131. *Two blue printed Lowestoft milk jugs, the patterns taken from Worcester originals, shown with a pair of relief-moulded sauce boats of a design found in the 1770s and 1780s. Sauce boats 7¾ ins. long. Blue printed crescent marks. c.1775-85.* Formerly Godden Collection.

painted with the stag crest of Townshend of Honingham, Member of Parliament for Yarmouth, but the most complete Lowestoft crested teaset is that known as the Ludlow service, which bears a gilt lion crest above the initials 'E.L'. This set is attractively decorated in black enamel and gilding, with festoons of flowers and slight floral sprays, and is very similar in decoration to some Chinese hard-paste services made for the English market.

This Ludlow service is illustrated in Colour Plate 9 and Plate 202, and, apart from the cups (both handleless teabowls and handled coffee cups) and saucers, the set comprises:

Coffee pot and cover, of tall, post-1775 shape, with floral knob.
Teapot and cover, of standard globular shape.
Teapot stand, of typical octagonal shape.
Spoon tray, of typical octagonal form.
Sugar bowl and cover.
Milk jug and cover.
Waste bowl.
2 bread and butter plates.

It is probable that the set originally included also a tea canister and cover.

Other crested or armorial decorated examples are shown in Colour Plate 10, Plates 147, 152, 215 and 216. A rather amusing story concerns the rather late, but superb, perfect mug shown in Plate 216, which was purchased at an Antique Fair for the

Plate 132. *A rare form of Lowestoft coffee pot with an unusual handle shape (page 201). Decorated with a version of the popular Worcester and Caughley 'Fence' pattern. 8¾ ins. high. c.1775-85.* Formerly Godden Collection.

Colour Plate 8. *A superb pair of Lowestoft musicians (page 136), as Plate 181, but with floral 'bocage' above the base. The female figure (which should be holding a lute-like instrument) is turned to show the supports to the 'bocage', and the typical way in which the supporting tree stump is painted. The front view is shown in Plate 180. Flat, glazed-over bases (Plate 174). 6¾ and 7ins. high. c.1780.* Author's Collection.

Plate 133. *A blue printed Lowestoft oval basket and stand (several fragments of similar examples were found on the factory site). A close copy of a popular Worcester and Caughley design. The stand is particularly rare. Stand 12½ ins. long. c.1775-85.* H.C. Wolton Collection

Plate 134. *A rare pair of small openwork baskets, one reversed to show the base and exterior. The potting is thicker than that on similar Worcester baskets, and the applied flowers are deeper. Note also the hesitant printing washed in by hand. Diameter 4⁹⁄₁₀ ins. c.1775-85.* Author's Collection.

Plate 135. *A noble covered jug (not a coffee pot, see page 206), printed in underglaze blue, the printed design washed in by hand as is often (but not always) found on Lowestoft specimens (Plate 245). Prints of this type are often called Willow pattern in error, but this design as we know it today was not introduced until the nineteenth century. 9ins. high. c.1775-85.* Author's Collection.

Plate 136. *A rare Lowestoft version of a Worcester blue printed, pierced cress dish and stand (page 202). Decorated with the so-called pine cone design, seen also in Plates 127, 128 and 133, and on much Worcester and Caughley porcelain. Diameter 9ins. c.1775-85.* H.C. Wolton Collection.

extremely low price of eleven pounds. I learnt later that the dealer from whom I purchased this piece had shown it to an internationally respected expert who, on account of its mint state and unusual style of decoration, had pronounced it a fake. Having accepted this advice, the dealer was presumably relatively happy to sell it for eleven pounds. The buyer was, however, far happier and this story is related to encourage the collector, or dealer, to trust his own judgment,

As I have already stated, the true Lowestoft armorial decorated porcelains are much rarer than the hard-paste Chinese porcelains painted in similar styles. Most readers can probably differentiate between the two basic types of porcelain body, but, for the benefit of those who have not learnt this all important first step in china collection, I have included two illustrations which should prove helpful in correctly identifying a Lowestoft or a Chinese armorial teaset, and, of course, the comparisons also hold good for wares bearing any other form of decoration. These direct comparisons are illustrated in Plates 242 and 243.

Almost without exception the Chinese teapot covers will be found to have the glaze wiped away (or trimmed off by turning on a lathe-like instrument) from the flange under the cover while the Lowestoft flange is generally covered with glaze, as can be seen in Plate 242.

A Chinese saucer is normally turned to a much thinner gauge than a soft-paste Lowestoft one and the edge of the footrim on a Chinese hard-paste saucer has been trimmed to a sharp point, causing a coloured line to appear where the body has been exposed. The true Lowestoft saucer has a thicker footrim with a glazed rim which very seldom ends at a point (Plate 142). Apart from these differences in potting technique there is, of course, the basic difference in the porcelain body, and many Chinese shapes were not employed at Lowestoft and several Lowestoft forms are not found in Chinese porcelains. The standard globular teapot was made in both places but the post-1770 shapes bearing Chinese-style designs, shown in Plates 189, 190, 192, 193, 196, 197, 200, 203, 206, 211 and 213, occur only in English porcelains.

The vast majority of the known Chinese armorial decorated porcelains made for the English market are illustrated, described and dated by David Sanctuary Howard in his standard book *Chinese Armorial Porcelain* (Faber and Faber, London, 1974).

The superb set of three mugs shown in Plate 160 represents a very rare class of porcelain that can be linked both with German, Dresden (or Meissen), porcelain, and with Chinese export market wares, for riverside or harbour scenes of this type are found on both and are very similar in treatment to these three mugs and a bowl in the Victoria and Albert Museum in London. They may have been painted by a Lowestoft trained watercolour artist named Richard Powles, who went to Denmark and later worked in London, and was probably working at the Lowestoft factory during the 1776-84 period (page 159).

Several fine specimens of Lowestoft enamel painting are associated with Richard Powles' name, including a most attractive teapot in the Fitzwilliam Museum at

Plate 137. *A rather rare form of Lowestoft patty pan, the standard form of which is reproduced on page 209. Painted in underglaze blue in a typical manner. 2ins. high. c.1775.* J. Howell Collection.

Plate 138. *A very rare form of moulded Lowestoft cream boat, with animal panels each side (page 201). 4ins. long. c.1775.* E.D. Levine Collection.

Plate 139. *Two Lowestoft spoon trays of typical form, unique to this factory. The undersides are flat and glazed over. The blue design with the wavy, scale motif design is known as the Robert Browne pattern, after a teaset of this pattern which was said to have been made for the proprietor of the works. 6¼ ins. x 3¼ ins. c.1775-80.* The late Mr. and Mrs. E. Hutchinson Collection.

Plate 140. *A hand painted Lowestoft covered jug (not a coffee pot, see page 206) of simple form without turned foot. Note the typical handle and knob. The slight discoloration around the old crack by the spout is quite normal owing to the soft body. 8½ ins. high. c.1775-80.* Author's Collection.

Cambridge. The teapot shown in Plate 159 is also considered by some to be by his hand, as are several pieces, including pictures of shipping, painted in underglaze blue, such as the flask shown in Plate 185, though pieces of this nature are of extreme rarity, and it must not be thought that Powles was the only Lowestoft artist to have painted shipping.

Other rare enamelled designs include ruins and local views, several of which were painted to special order and also bear names, inscriptions or dates. The majority of enamel patterns of the 1770s and 1780s, however, are standard designs, mainly comprising floral motifs or Chinese figures of the types shown in Plates 187-201, 207 and 210. In the 1790s very simple sprig motifs of cornflower type came into general favour, not only at Lowestoft but at several other factories and the fashion seems to have originated in France. Apart from the style of decoration, the shapes of the 1790s bear little relation to those of the 1780s. Nearly all Lowestoft enamelled porcelain comprises teawares (the exceptions being vases, mugs and the rare figures), for enamelled dessert and dinner services do not appear to have been made.

Plate 141. *A fine ribbed Lowestoft coffee pot, painted in underglaze blue with a continental formal floral design. Note the thick leaf on the cover and the solid hump supporting the flower knob. 11 ¼ ins high. Dresden, crossed swords mark in underglaze blue. c.1775-80.* Victoria and Albert Museum (Crown Copyright).

Plate 142. *Representative pieces from a moulded and ribbed teaset, such as would have accompanied the coffee pot (Plate 141). Note the thick leaves on the covers and the solid humps supporting the flower knobs. Note also the large size of the milk jug which contrasts with the earlier, small cream jugs. Milk jug 5 ¼ ins. high. Some pieces with the crossed swords mark, others with the open crescent mark (see upturned teabowls). c.1775-80.* Godden of Worthing Ltd.

Plate 143. *A rare large bowl decorated with an ornate and scarce 'Redgrave' pattern (pages 105 and 163), incorporating underglaze blue, with overglaze enamels — mainly red and a light green. Diameter 7¾ ins. c.1775.* Author's Collection.

Plate 144. *A typical Lowestoft teapot and jug decorated with the Redgrave 'Two-bird' design in underglaze blue and overglaze enamel colours (Colour Plate 7). Teapot 6½ ins. high. c.1775-80.* Sotheby's.

Plate 145. *A rare form of Lowestoft cream or milk jug and a teacup and saucer decorated with an Imari-type design in the Redgrave manner (page 105). Note the typical blue line dashes by handles. Creamer 3ins. high. c.1780-85.* Author's Collection.

Plate 146. *Representative and typical parts of a Redgrave pattern (page 105) tea service, including an octagonal teapot stand and two spoon trays, a teapot and a fluted slop bowl, a sparrow beak creamer and a tea caddy (missing its cover). Teapot 6½ ins. high. c.1780-5. See sale records 256-62, and page 35.* Ex Henry Levine Collection.

Plate 147. *A selection of Lowestoft porcelains painted by the Tulip painter (page 105). The upper teapot has armorial bearings painted on the reverse side. The inscribed mug, in the foreground, is one of a set of three, see Sale record 119, and D.75A, pages 243 and 226. Large teapot 8ins. high. c.1770-6.* City of Norwich Museums.

Plate 148. *A superb, and typical, Lowestoft coffee pot of the early shape (page 200) with rare open flower knob. Painted by the Tulip painter and including, near the foot at the left, the characteristic lilies (Plate 149). 8¼ ins. high. c.1770.* Formerly Godden Collection. Christchurch Mansion Museum, Ipswich.

Plate 149. *Detail of a teapot cover showing two lily-like flowers with very long stamens. These characteristic flowers are found on many pieces painted by the Tulip painter (Plates 147, 148, 151, 152 and 154 and page 180).*

Plate 150. *A Lowestoft 'Chelsea ewer' creamer (page 202) painted in slight manner by the Tulip painter. 2¼ ins. high. c.1775.* Author's Collection.

Plate 151. *The front and side view of a rare inscribed and dated Lowestoft mug, painted in colours by the Tulip painter. 4½ ins. high.* Sotheby's.

Plate 152. *A sugar bowl (an inverted saucer-like cover should go with this article, see Plate 187), decorated by the Tulip painter. The reverse side is painted with ornate armorial bearings and crest. 2¾ ins. high. c.1770-5.* Author's Collection.

Plate 153. *A very rare porringer-like handled bowl (page 210) decorated by the Tulip painter. 3½ ins. high. c.1775.* City of Norwich Museums.

Plate 154. *A teabowl and saucer, decorated in pink monochrome by the Tulip painter. Note the lily-like flowers at the top of the saucer (Plate 149 and page 180). A service of this design is traditionally believed to have been made as a wedding service for Robert Browne, the proprietor of the factory. Diameter of saucer 5ins.* County Museum, Truro.

Plate 155. *A rare Lowestoft teabowl and saucer painted in pink monochrome in a style similar to that seen on the flower compositions by the Tulip painter (page 182). Diameter of saucer 4¾ins. c.1775.* T.C.S. Brooke (Wroxham).

Plate 156. *A rare Lowestoft bowl painted in the same style as that employed by the Tulip painter (see Plates 154, 155 and 157 and page 182). 2⅖ ins. high. c.1775.* Formerly Dyson Perrins Museum, Worcester.

Plate 157. *A very rare, sparrow beak creamer, with handle form found only on early enamelled pieces of the 1770s. This piece matches the teabowl and saucer shown in Plate 155. 3ins. high. c.1775.* A.W. Denney Collection.

Plate 158. *A unique covered jug (not a coffee pot, see page 206) amusingly painted with local scenes and inscribed and dated. The lettering and date appear to be by the same hand as the inscribed pieces by the Tulip painter (page 180). 9¾ ins. high. 1775.* Mrs. D. Westrop Collection.

Plate 159. *A Lowestoft teapot of typical form but rare (or unique) decoration painted in a style similar to the Gooch jug (Plate 158), attributed by some collectors to Richard Powles (page 159) but perhaps by the Tulip painter. 6¾ ins. high. c.1775-80.* Formerly Godden Collection. Christchurch Mansion Museum, Ipswich.

Plate 160. *A superb set of three Lowestoft mugs, painted in the style of some Meissen porcelain, of a type copied on Chinese porcelains made for the European market. Perhaps painted by Richard Powles (page 159). 5¾, 5 and 3½ ins. high. c.1775-80. Sale record 158, (page 246).* Photograph, Messrs. Sotheby's. Formerly Hotblack and Godden Collections.

Colour Plate 9. *Representative pieces from the 'Ludlow' crested and initialled tea and coffee service (see also Plate 202). Such special services are extremely rare, and this is the only one recorded still intact with its main pieces, although a few other services are known, through some surviving cups and saucers (page 109). Teapot 6¾ ins. high. c.1785.* Author's Collection.

Trifles

One of the best known classes of Lowestoft porcelain comprises those pieces with the inscription:

'A Trifle from Lowestoft.'

Typical examples are shown in Plates 223-5 and 233, and in the main they belong to the 1790s, and are decorated in overglaze enamels, although earlier examples are known and pieces painted in underglaze blue were certainly made. The majority of these are mugs of the standard straight-sided form, or of the rare, late barrel shape (Plates 223 and 224) but teapots, pounce pots and inkpots (Plate 225) are also inscribed in like manner.

Apart from these, examples are also recorded with the following place-names — Bungay, Hingham, Holt, Lynn and Wangford. A study of a collection of these rare 'Trifles' shows that the inscription was painted by the same hand (see page 146). The charm and individuality of these 'Trifles' explain the high regard in which collectors of Lowestoft have always held them.

The new collector is, however, warned that fakes have been produced, and that many of these are antique in their own right!

Animals

It is clear that small china models of animals were made at the Lowestoft factory as, apart from the similarity of paste and finish, moulds and fragments were found on the factory site.

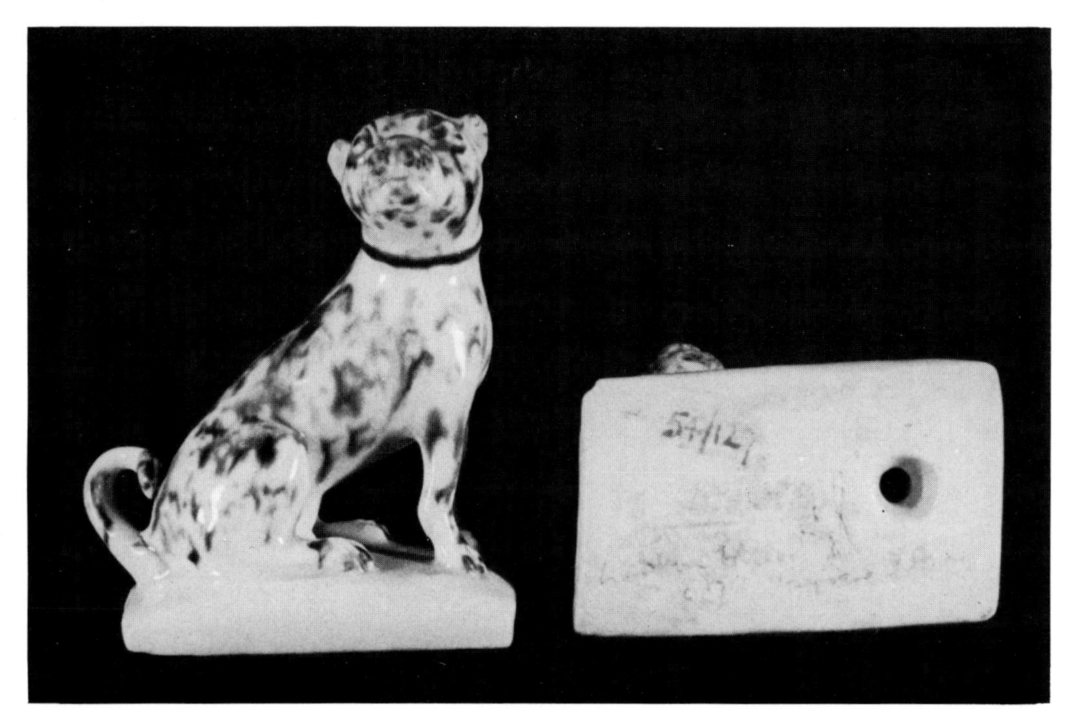

Plate 161. *A pair of porcelain pug dogs, one turned up to show the flat base and vent hole. This model, with manganese colouring and with underglaze blue collar and eyes, has formerly been attributed to Longton Hall, but recent research suggests that these may have been made at the Lowestoft factory (page 131). 3 ⅝ ins. high.* Worthing Museum and Art Gallery.

Plate 162. *A rare model of a pug dog, on a puce cushion. A further model that has recently been attributed to the Lowestoft factory. Base 2¼ x 1¼ ins.* E.D. Levine (Cromer).

The two best known of these rare animal models are the simple swans which are found both white and coloured, and the cats (Plate 166A and B). These are normally solid and therefore heavy for their size, have a base which is flat (except for a vent hole) and which has been glazed over. An original plaster of Paris mould for the cat was found on the factory site and a rough cast taken from this is shown in Plate 166A.

Less well known are the small images of a sheep and a ram. The basic model is similar to the relatively common Derby sheep, and to the rarer Bow models, but some of the rare Lowestoft examples can be distinguished by their greater weight and the flat glazed base. Others are smaller and have a hollowed out base (Plate 167).

Since 1967, a class of seated pug dog on an oblong base (Plate 161) has been attributed to the Lowestoft factory on account of the presence of bone ash in the body. These dogs are illustrated in nearly every ceramic reference book on Longton Hall (see *Longton Hall Porcelain* by Dr. B. Watney, 1957, Plate 35A) and they normally feature patches of brownish manganese colour. While I cannot present any evidence to disprove the recent reattribution of these dogs to the Lowestoft factory, the question of their provenance must, for the moment, remain open. However, if the new attribution is proved correct, it is possible that the very rare cow milk jugs, also with manganese markings, are also of Lowestoft make, a good example of which is illustrated by Dr. Watney in Plate 35B, and another, here, in Plate 163. In this case the glazed-over base appears to be Lowestoft and is similar to fragments of bases found on the factory site. The author has not handled the model shown in Plate 162 which is believed to be Lowestoft.

The Lowestoft factory did manufacture another animal model, probably a dog, for unglazed factory 'wasters' have included a flat shaped edge base, with the remains of broken off feet (Plate 164). The dog shown in Plate 165 would appear to match, in shape, the key fragments from the factory site, although these fragments are smaller than the base of this example. This very rare model is known in its plain white state as well as coloured. The reader's attention is drawn to an article by Miss Sheenah Smith — 'Unrecorded Lowestoft Pug Dogs', published in *The Connoisseur* of November, 1968. A pair of hind and stag figures may also have been made, for the moulds on the factory site in 1902 and 1903 included part moulds for these animals.

Plate 163. *A very rare porcelain cow creamer, with manganese markings (page 131). After a silver original, but more often found in earthenware. Note the unusual flat base, glazed on the underside, and compare with rather similar 'wasters' from the factory site (Plate 164). The tail handle is damaged and the lid missing. 3¾ ins. high.* Sotheby's.

Plate 164. *Two flat, shaped-edged, bases (one underglazed) with remains of animal feet affixed, found on the Lowestoft factory site (page 131) and of the same class as is found on the rare standing dog models (Plate 165) and similar to the base of the cow creamer (Plate 163). A trace of manganese is apparent on the glazed base. Complete, unglazed bases 2ins. long.* City of Norwich Museums.

Plate 165. *A very rare dog model, standing on flat base, similar to 'wasters' found on the factory site (Plate 164). This example is decorated with enamel colours but the model is also known in an undecorated state. 2⅛ ins. high.* T.C.S. Brooke (Wroxham).

Plate 166A. *A plaster of Paris mould found on the factory site, with a cast taken from this original mould.* Miss Paul Collection.

Plate 166B. *A Lowestoft porcelain cat of the form produced from the mould shown in Plate 166A. 2 ⅛ ins. high. c.1770-80.* Formerly E.D. Levine Collection.

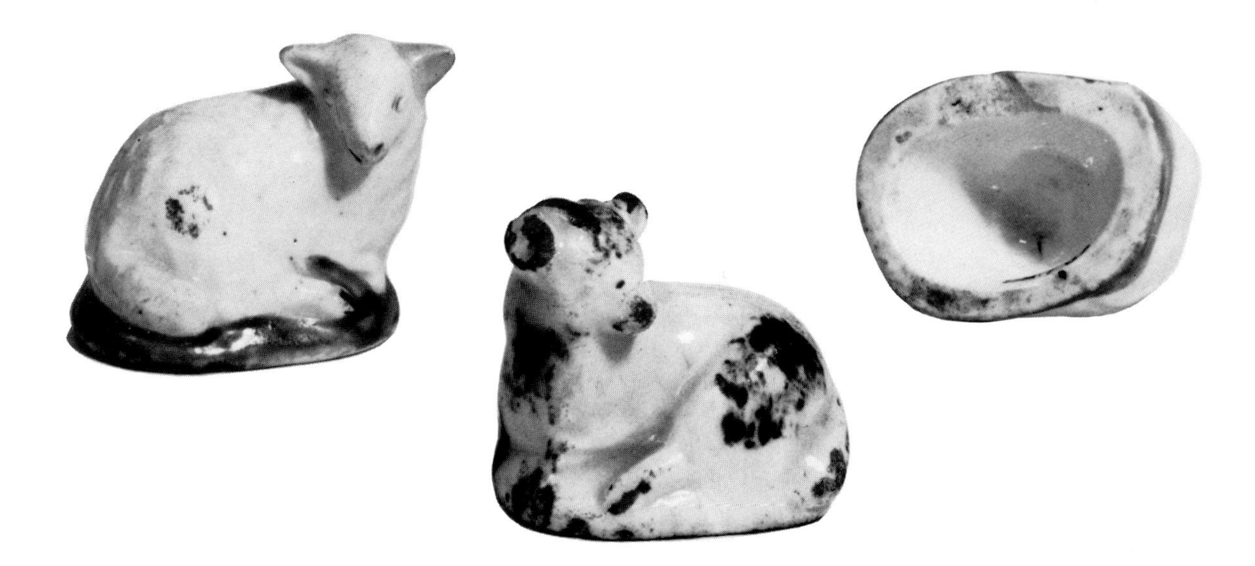

Plate 167. *Three rare, small size sheep and ram models, attributed to the Lowestoft factory, but with recessed bases, instead of the flat base found on most other animal and figure models. 1 ⅜ ins. high.* E.D. Levine and City of Norwich Museums' Collection.

Figures

There are many collectors who still do not believe that this factory produced figures, although the evidence for their existence is strong, and comprises part moulds and unglazed fragments found during rebuilding operations on the factory site.

Unfortunately, soon after these factory wasters were discovered, the late W. Spelman, in 1905, sought to attribute to Lowestoft a class of apparently Staffordshire figures of a body quite unlike that employed at Lowestoft. For some fifty-two years after this, the question of Lowestoft figures was largely allowed to stagnate until the publication of my article on the subject in *The Connoisseur Year Book* for 1957.

Before discussing the figures that are undoubtedly of Lowestoft origin, mention must be made of a class of small figures of putti holding baskets of fruit or flowers, as shown in Plate 169. These are often called Lowestoft and sometimes the description 'Bow-Low', coined by Mr. Kiddell, is used, but they are, in fact, more Bow than Low. In other words, they seem to be of Bow manufacture.

Plate 168. *A rare (or unique) enamelled porcelain cane handle in portrait form. The high hairdressing suggests a 1775-80 dating. This object is hollow, similar pottery examples were used as boxes as they have a screw cover. 3½ ins. high.* Victoria and Albert Museum (Crown Copyright).

The evidence that has helped to identify correctly the true Lowestoft figures comprises the original mould for part of the female figure, one for the supporting tree stump and one for an arm, together with two unglazed arms, part of a base, and fragments of the characteristic leafy bocage found at the back of some figures (Plates 172, 182 and 183). Supporting evidence is found in the similarity of the thickly moulded leaves found on typical Lowestoft porcelains of the 1780s and on the bases and bocages of these figures (Colour Plate 8). A rare cover has a head knob* which matches that of the Lowestoft putti.

The Lowestoft putti as shown in Plate 173 are of two different models forming a pair, the hands raised and holding a small flower, one putto swinging to the left, the other to the right. The bases are irregularly shaped and are solid with a flat, glazed-over underside and a small vent hole (Plate 174). The supporting stump at the back is

---

* See article by Mr. A.J.B. Kiddell in *The Connoisseur* of October, 1937.

Plate 169. *Three porcelain putti of a type sometimes attributed to the Lowestoft factory but which show none of the typical characteristics of this factory (page 135). 3½ and 3ins. high.*

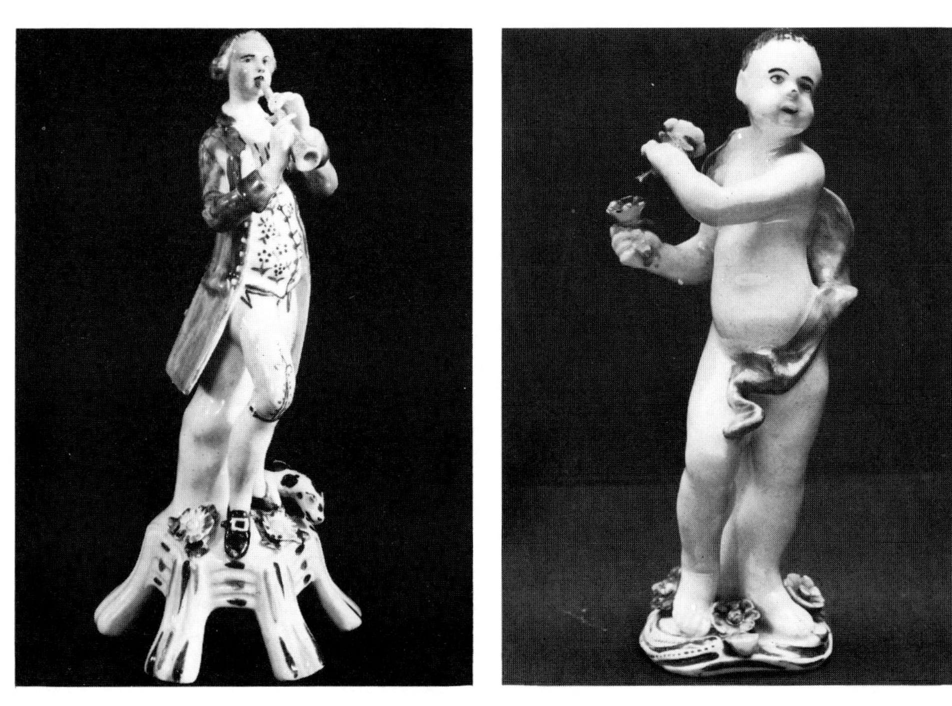

Plate 170. *A rare standing musician of a type which links with some Lowestoft-type models (Plate 176) but with several differences of body, glaze and decoration (page 139). 6½ ins. high.* Formerly Godden Collection. Christchurch Mansion Museum, Ipswich.

Plate 171. *A rare standing putto, of a model known in obviously Lowestoft porcelain (Plate 173), but with slight differences, for instance, the applied flowers and leaves on the base (see page 130 for my recent thoughts). 5⅛ ins. high. c.1770.* City of Norwich Museums.

painted over to represent a tree trunk and the base is ornamented with typically Lowestoft applied leaves and flowers, and with puce brushwork picking out the moulding.

The other pair of figures so far discovered (other models may well turn up subsequently) is a pair of musicians, a man in a tricorn hat playing a triangle, and a hatless female playing a lute-like instrument, but these figures are nearly always damaged and often lack the fragile and accident-prone instruments (Plates 180 and 181).

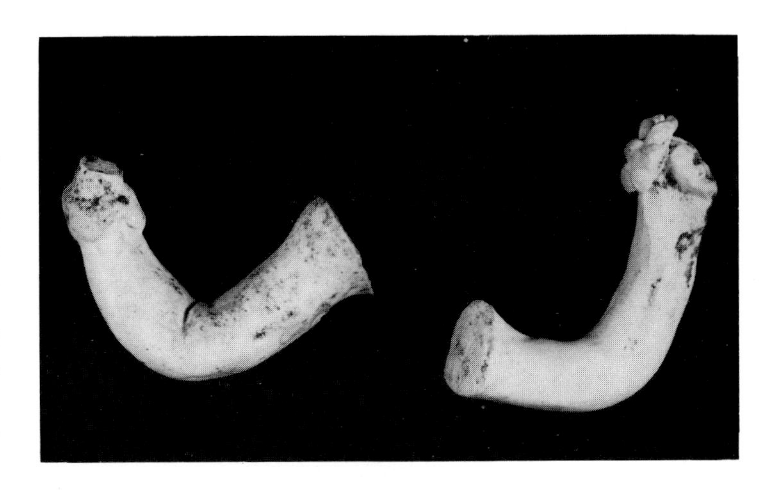

Plate 172. *Two unglazed arms found on the Lowestoft factory site. The right-hand arm matches that found on the putti (Plate 173) but with different, and probably later, flowers. The left-hand unglazed arm matches that on the female lute player (Plates 180, 181 and 183).* City of Norwich Museums.

Plate 173. *A rare pair of Lowestoft putti (page 135) of typical body, with flat, glazed-over bases (Plate 174) with applied leaves and flowers as found on Lowestoft baskets, butter tureens, etc. (Plates 126, 133 and 179). The flesh of these putti is slightly coloured. 5 ¼ ins. high. c.1780-5.* Author's Collection.

The original plaster of Paris mould for the upper part of the body of the female lute player was found on the factory site, and an impression from it is shown in Plate 182. An unglazed hand, also from the factory site, is shown in Plate 183, and this arm matches that of the female figure. Like the putti just discussed, the bases are solid, the underside flat (with a vent hole) and glazed over. The tree stump support at the back is enamelled in a characteristic manner (Colour Plate 8) and the applied leaves and flowers on the base (and the bocage background) are of the same type as those on the putti and on other Lowestoft late porcelains. The woman's skirt and the man's coat and trousers are enamelled with simple, small, single flowers (Colour Plate 8 and Plates 180, 181 and 184).

A unique example of the female musician is mounted on a high stepped circular base (Plate 184), the puce painting on which is reminiscent of the 'Trifle from Lowestoft' pieces. This example came from the Aldred family (Obed Aldred was one of the original partners in the factory) and may be the one referred to by William Chaffers in the nineteenth century — 'Mr. Aldred possessed a figure cleverly modelled by his father's hands in the factory; it is a well-dressed, modest housekeeper-looking woman in the costume of the time in which it was made (1790).' This figure is now much damaged and lacks both arms as a result of its use as a plaything by successive generations of Aldred children who can have had no idea that it was a unique porcelain figure worth hundreds of pounds in an undamaged state.

The term unique must be used with caution, for while at the time of writing only one example may be recorded, there is always the likelihood that others may be discovered. The pipe stopper illustrated in Plate 182 appeared to be unique until I found a second example! This rare figure-type object is shown together with an impression from the original mould from the factory site.

It would be most convenient to close this section on Lowestoft figures at this point,

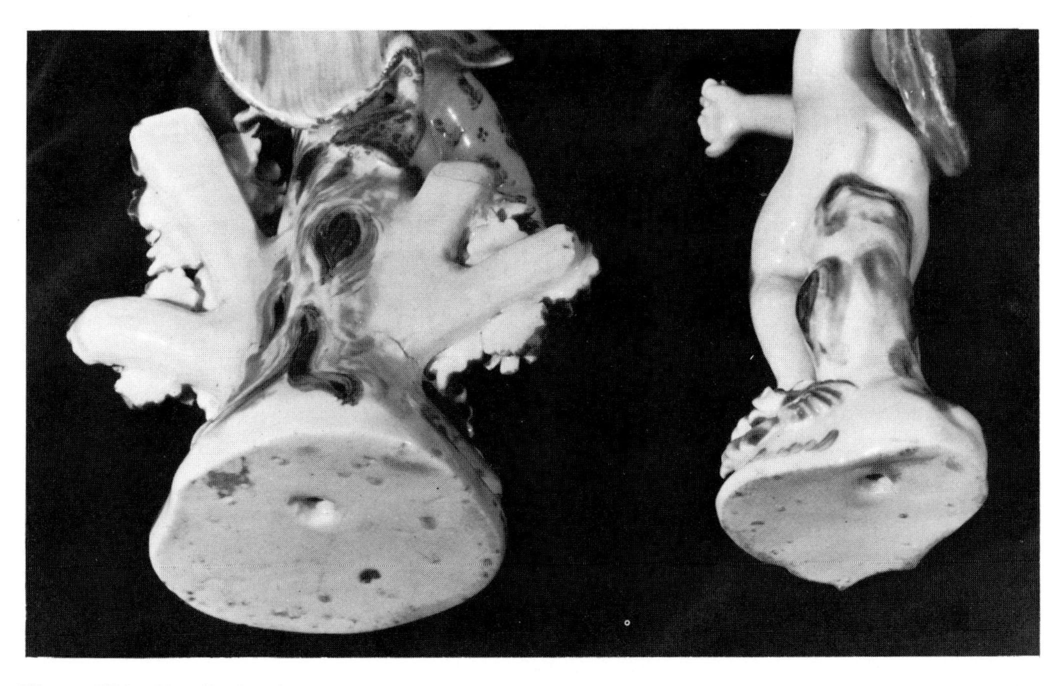

Plate 174. *Detail showing flat, glazed-over bases found on Lowestoft figures and also the enamelled decoration found on the back of the supporting tree stump (page 135).* Author's Collection.

Plate 175. *A rare, undecorated figure of the same basic design as the Lowestoft lute player (Plates 180 and 181) but with untypical base and applied flowers (page 139). The lute is missing on this example, see Plate 176 for complete example. 7¼ ins. high.* Sotheby's.

Plate 176. *A rare pair of enamelled musicians, complete with musical instruments. Apart from the bases and applied flowers the enamelling also differs from that on undoubted Lowestoft specimens (Colour Plate 8 and Plates 180 and 181), see page 139.* City of Norwich Museums.

Plate 177. *An enamelled lute player (as Plate 178) but with lute missing. This figure has previously been attributed to the Longton Hall factory 'about 1755'. The model is, however, similar to the Lowestoft one (Plates 180 and 181) and to the related 'problem' pieces (see below). 6¼ ins. high.* County Museum, Truro (Photograph ex Dr. B. Watney).

Plate 178. *One of a pair of white, undecorated Lowestoft figures similar to the basic models shown in Plates 175-7, 180-1, 183-4. 6¾ ins. high. c.1780.* Phillips.

having described examples that are clearly of Lowestoft origin, (Plates 180-4), but the position is complicated by a series of figures of similar form to those discussed above and illustrated in Plates 170, 171, 175-7. All are now generally accepted as Lowestoft, but I have slight reservations in my own mind, and I shall list the basic differences between the two types in order that the reader can form his own opinion, or a future student be encouraged to continue the quest for a definite resolution to the puzzle.

(1) The glaze appears thinner and harder than the thickly applied soft-glaze found on the true Lowestoft figures, as shown in Plates 173-4, 178, 180-4.

(2) The body gives the appearance of being slightly harder and more compact than the late 'floury' type of body used for the other Lowestoft figures. Therefore the modelling is sharper on the problem pieces which sometimes have applied ribbon bows on the shoes, etc., not found on the late Lowestoft figures with the more blurred modelling.

(3) The applied leaves and flowers on the bases of these figures are quite different from those found on the late Lowestoft figures and from the leaves on Lowestoft butter tureens, etc.

(4) The bases are quite different, the problem pieces are usually mounted on four-

footed pedestal bases, whereas the late Lowestoft figures are on low solid bases.

(5) The applied enamel decoration is different:

(a) The characteristic single flower sprigs found on late Lowestoft figures do not appear on the problem pieces.

(b) The tree stump at the back of these figures is not coloured on the problem pieces as it is on the true Lowestoft pieces (Colour Plate 8).

(c) The painting of the faces is quite different, for on the late figures the lips are not detailed and normally are represented by a line only, whereas the problem pieces have shaped lips, thick at the centre with thin, upward 'grin lines' each side (compare Plates 180-1 with Plate 176). On the problem figures the two nostrils are represented by two enamelled spots, but on the late Lowestoft figures the nostrils are not painted. The treatment of the eyes is also different, on late Lowestoft figures the pupils of the eyes being represented by an enamelled spot touching the upper line of the eye, and the lower outline of the eye represented by a thin line, not present on the problem figures.

These differences listed under number five may show only that the two classes of figures were painted by different enamellers, but those set out under numbers one to four represent differences in basic make-up. It is, of course, possible that both classes of

Plate 179. *A blue printed Lowestoft butter tureen cover (similar to that shown in Plate 126) showing the typical thick leaves and six-petalled flowers found on the standing figures (Plate 180 and Colour Plate 8).* Reproduced by permission of the Syndics of the Fitzwilliam Museum, Cambridge.

Plate 180. *A Lowestoft lute player (missing the instrument, which is shown in Plates 176 and 178), with extremely rare floral 'bocage', the reverse side of which is seen in Colour Plate 8. 6¾ ins. high. c.1780.* Author's Collection.

Plate 181. *A rare pair of Lowestoft musicians (the female has been incorrectly repaired, and she should be holding a lute, as Plates 176 and 178). Note the similar style of decoration to the figures shown in Colour Plate 8, Plates 180 and 184. 6¾ ins. high. c.1780.* Messrs. Winifred Williams.

Plate 182. *Left, a cast for a pipe stopper taken from a mould found on the factory site. Centre, a cast from an original mould, matching the top half of the female lute player (Plates 180, 181 and 183), and right, a complete and decorated pipe stopper (page 137).* British Museum (Crown Copyright).

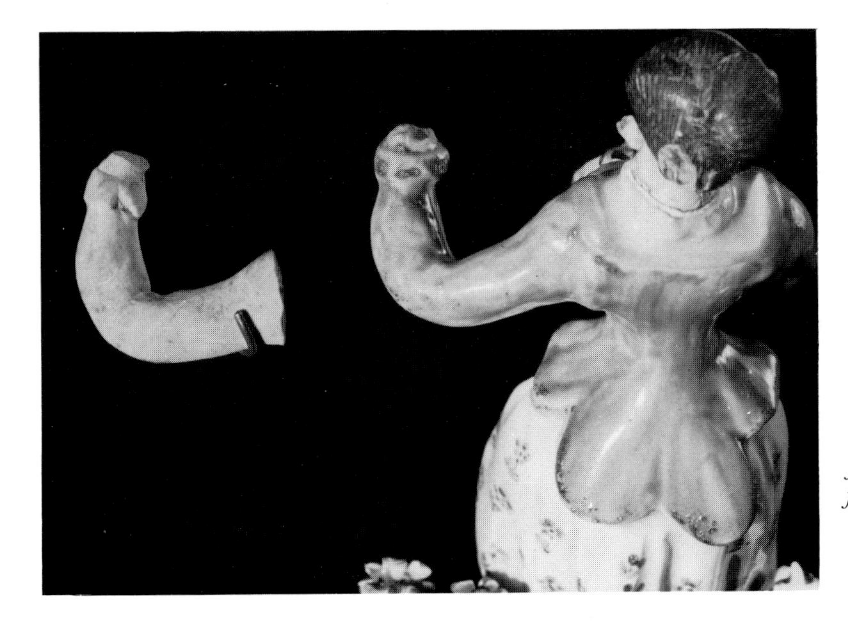

Plate 183. *Detail of the back of the female lute player, as shown in Plate 180, with an unglazed fragment arm found on the Lowestoft factory site.* Unglazed arm is in the Lowestoft Borough Library Collection.

figures were made at the same factory but at different periods, the true Lowestoft figures being obviously rather late and probably of the 1780s and early 1790s, so that the other figures would be earlier, rather than later. If we take it that enamelled colours are not found on Lowestoft porcelains before about 1768 these enamelled figures could be of the same period providing, of course, that the reader accepts them as of Lowestoft manufacture.

The problem examples of the musicians so far discussed are mounted on strange four-footed bases as shown in Plates 175 and 176, but there exists a damaged female figure in the Museum of the Royal Institution of Cornwall at Truro which would appear to be of the same model as the problem class lute player, and this example is on a low, irregularly shaped base (Plate 177). It is in general appearance unlike the late, true Lowestoft product and has, in fact, been illustrated in a recent book as Longton Hall, 'about 1755'.

It is, of course, noteworthy that the late Lowestoft models — the pair of putti and the

Plate 184. *Detail, showing the, perhaps unique, high circular base on which stands a much damaged lute player (as Plates 180-1), from the Aldred family (pages 42 and 137). 8¾ ins. high.* Formerly Godden Collection. Christchurch Mansion Museum, Ipswich.

musicians — are the same as those in the problem group, but one further figure is known in the problem class (Plate 170) and as yet a duplicate has not been discovered in the late Lowestoft body and style of finish.

I am unable to suggest the resolution to this problem of the two types of Lowestoft figure, but at least the reader is now aware of their existence, and perhaps time, and the researches of an enquiring collector, will supply the answer. In my view the problem figures do not readily link with any other identified class of English porcelain figure and on balance I now regard them as the first essays in figure manufacture by the Lowestoft management, in perhaps the late 1760s. This view has recently been strengthened by the discovery of a putto of the early type which when compared with the undoubtedly Lowestoft later specimen (Plate 23) leaves little or no doubt of the common origin. In this case the pieces are from the same moulds, the flat-glazed base and vent hole are identical as are the features of the faces. The other differences of colouring and of the added flowers and leaves, are I believe, due to the difference in period — not of place of manufacture (see page 30).

CHAPTER IV
The Artists and Work People

Little is known of the workmen and workwomen employed at the Lowestoft factory, but this Chapter gives some information and endeavours to link some styles with known artists.

The dates of birth and marriage quoted here have been extracted from *The Parish Registers of Lowestoft, Suffolk,* published by Frederick Arthur Crisp, in 1904.

We have seen that most pre-1770 Lowestoft porcelains bear a painted number in underglaze blue and that these painters' personal tally marks are normally placed on the inside of the footrim, and although several collectors have endeavoured to link these numbers with individual painters, there are many difficulties involved. One of these is that we know the names of so very few early Lowestoft painters of the period when these numbers were employed, that is, up to about 1775. Another difficulty is that the numbers are often indistinct, being very small in size and, as they were placed on the upright inside part of the footrim, an accidental dot or spot of pigment could run downwards and be mistaken for a '1', making for instance the number '2' into '12' or '21'.

The numbers reached at least seventeen (and some writers cite very much higher numbers) but the number '10' has not been reported and '15' is open to question. In addition to these numbers, some letters and signs are known. Of the painters' numbers, three and five are those most often met with and these two are (with one exception) the only ones recorded on the several inscribed and dated pieces, so that we may assume that painters numbered three and five were the most talented ones, entrusted with the decoration of special orders. They were also employed from the earliest days as these numbers are found on pre-1760 articles as well as on later products. See notes on Robert Allen and on Richard Phillips.

Chaffers and the early writers, such as Jewitt, had a source of information on some of the Lowestoft painters and work people, for they list:

The Artists and Work People

James Balls	painter
Abel Bly	
John Bly	painter, died at Worcester
Joseph Bly	
George Butcher	kiln man
Mrs. Cooper	blue painter
Thomas Curtis	artist
William Hughes	modeller, went to Worcester
James Mollershead	painter
Margaret Redgrave	painter
James Redgrave	flower painter

John Redgrave	painter
Mrs. Simpson	blue painter
John Sparham	artist
John Stevenson	modeller, went to Worcester
Mrs. Stevenson and daughter	blue painters
William Stevenson	finisher, went to Worcester.

These persons, with some additions, are discussed in alphabetical order on the following pages. Remember, however, that this list of named persons totals only eighteen out of the ninety to a hundred reported in 1784 (see page 31).

Robert Allen

The painter's number '5' is that most commonly found, appearing on approximately a quarter of all the Lowestoft pieces which bear a painter's mark. The reason why this artist was so prolific and other artists' work and numbers are almost non-existent is not known, but the number '5' also differs from other numbers in that, while most numbers are very small, the numeral '5' is often quite large, and on occasions the tail has spread from the footrim on to the bottom of the article.

The number '5' is traditionally associated with the painter Robert Allen. The early writers, who had the benefit (?) of gathering information from descendants of the Lowestoft painters, reported that Robert Allen commenced at the factory in 1757 when he was but twelve years old. He was therefore about twenty-three when he painted a service for his aunt, Elizabeth Buckle, in 1768. These pieces, which are inscribed 'Elizabeth Buckle', are quite charmingly decorated with pastoral figures and represent the high watermark of Lowestoft underglaze blue porcelains. A superb shallow bowl now at the Castle Museum, Norwich, is painted with Eastern figures (Plate 100), and other pieces bearing the painter's number '5' are shown in Plates 32, 41, 51, 52, 57, 60, 62, 63, 64, 67, 68, 74, 77, 80, 88, 89, 99, 104 and 111.

Robert Allen married Ann Landifield on January 12th, 1783, but his wife soon died and he married for a second time on September 15th, 1785, when his bride was Tryphoena Richmond. In December 1786, a daughter, Elizabeth, was born to this couple; another daughter, Mary, arrived in April 1788, and in April 1790, twin daughters, Lucy and Sarah were born, but Sarah died in 1794. Yet one more daughter, Maria Sarah, was born in January 1796. It is strange that no birth tablets are recorded commemorating the birth of these children to the wife of a leading Lowestoft decorator, although several are known relating to the Redgrave family.

Chaffers and other writers state that Allen became foreman of the works and eventually the manager, but the former also states that Allen was employed up to the time of the factory's closure and that, 'after the close of the works Allen opened a shop at Lowestoft as stationer and china dealer, and having erected a small kiln in his garden, he decorated the Wedgwood, Turner and other Staffordshire wares. . . .' Chaffers' account, gleaned from family sources, was incorrect in at least one instance, for Robert Allen is included in a Directory of 1795 as a trader with a 'China-shop', a fact that suggests that Allen may have been decorating on his own account at least by 1795 and that he certainly had an interest outside the factory at this period.

The difficulty is to tell if Robert Allen was still employed at the factory when he had his own china-shop in the 1790s. Certainly he later had a small kiln for firing enamel decoration on to wares he purchased from various sources and these articles were normally of the standard cream coloured earthenwares as manufactured in

Staffordshire and at most potteries of the period. One Chinese porcelain teapot was the cause of much confusion to nineteenth century writers as it bears Robert Allen's name, but there is no direct connection between this solitary Chinese example and the Lowestoft factory. The key question is: when did Allen start to paint and fire wares on his own account? Was it only after the factory closed, or from the 1795 period, and did he then employ some of the factory painters to assist him after the factory closed in about 1799? The lettering on some supposedly Allen decorated creamwares is very similar to that found on factory decorated 'Trifle' pieces, see page 130 and compare Plates 223-5 with 239. The creamware jug dated November 10th, 1799, is a fine and interesting piece in the Allen style and indicates that he was ordering earthenwares to decorate at this period; was this because the local porcelain factory had already closed?

The range of Lowestoft *porcelain* 'Trifles' all seems to have been inscribed by the same hand (in a manner similar to, but not as fine as, the Redgrave examples, Plates 227-9. These inscriptions are seen in Colour Plate 11 and Plates 223-5, 233, 235 and especially in the detail shown in Plate 244. A few of these 'Trifles' are painted in underglaze blue (Plates 225 and 233), a fact that suggests strongly that these pieces were decorated by a factory hand as a commercial line not by an outside decorator. The style and form of lettering found on these Trifles is, however, continued on to the pottery pieces bearing dates after the factory's closure and, as we know that Robert Allen was both a factory painter and that he had a kiln where he decorated and fired

Plate 185. *The front and reverse sides of a superb Lowestoft porcelain flask, painted in underglaze blue, by an artist noteworthy for his swirled clouds and dotted ground. This painter was perhaps Richard Powles (page 159) and the shipbuilding scene is one of the finest examples of Lowestoft underglaze blue painting. 5½ ins. high, diameter 4⅘ ins. c.1780. (See also Colour Plate 3).* Author's Collection.

Staffordshire earthenwares after the factory closed, it is reasonable to assume that Allen inscribed all these related 'Trifle' pieces which in the main were made in the 1790s.

The Allen style of lettering and date numerals can also be found in the porcelains shown in Plate 226, probably in Plate 221 and also in several pieces which are not illustrated in this book.

Robert Allen died in 1835, aged ninety-one.

Miss Sheenah Smith in her catalogue of *Lowestoft Porcelain in Norwich Castle Museum* lists many blue and white pieces which can be attributed to Robert Allen.

James Balls

Chaffers listed James Balls as a painter and he could have been employed during the early pre-1770 period, for a James Balls was married to Mary Jones in February 1769. Children were born to this couple in October 1769, September 1770, May 1771 (a son also named James but this son died in 1773), January 1774, July 1776, and September 1779, but the situation is complicated by the fact that a further set of parents with the same name were at Lowestoft at the same period and we have a christening entry relating to them before the above-mentioned marriage, 'October 11th, 1767. Mary of James and Mary Balls': and as a further complication a son named James was born of these parents in February, 1769. We therefore have two James Balls of marriageable, and working age at Lowestoft in the late 1760s, and a son of the same name born in 1769, and therefore of working age in the late 1780s.

Abel Bly

Abel Bly's son may have been the source of Chaffers' information on the Lowestoft work people, and if this supposition is correct it would indicate that all persons listed by Chaffers were employed towards the end of the factory's working period. We have read on page 45 that Abel Bly, aged eighty-four in 1865, gave Chaffers a statement relating to the factory premises as he remembered them in his youth. This statement included the information — 'my father's name was Abel Bly, who was employed in various departments in the china factory at Lowestoft. He died when I was eleven years of age. . . . .' (that is in 1793).

Abel Bly, the Lowestoft workman, was born of John and Laetitia Bly in about 1756. On October 30th, 1780, he married Sarah Shuckfer and in 1782 Chaffers' informant, Abel Bly, was born. Abel Bly, senior, died in January, 1793, at the age of thirty-seven. It is unlikely that Abel Bly was a painter, or his son would have said so, instead of using the phrase 'employed in various departments', which suggests a potter or handyman rather than a decorator.

It is unlikely that Abel Bly, junior, was employed at the factory. He was born in 1782 and so would have been only about seventeen when the factory closed in about 1799, and in his statement to Chaffers he recorded only the fact that 'from my father working at the factory I was in the habit of going daily to the premises. . . . .' On February 24th, 1807 Abel Bly, junior, married Deborah Barker and a son, also named Abel, was born to them in December 1807.

John Bly

Chaffers refers to John Bly as a painter at the factory who 'died at Worcester'. Abel Bly, junior, referred to John (and Philip) Bly as his uncle, so that Abel Bly, senior,

Colour Plate 10. *A fine cylindrical mug, enamelled with a view of the Lowestoft High Light, together with the Low Light and shipping in the Roadstead. Above the main panel are the arms and motto of Trinity House. 4½ ins. high. c.1785-90. A similar mug, from the Colman Collection, is in the Castle Museum, Norwich.* Victoria and Albert Museum (Crown Copyright).

John and Philip Bly were brothers, all employed at the Lowestoft factory.

The situation is, however, complicated by the fact that we have records of two John Blys, father and son. John Bly, senior, born in about 1753 of John and Laetitia Bly, married Mary Cooper (who died in January 1789) on November 27th, 1775. A son, also named John, was christened on September 2nd, 1779, and John Bly, senior, died at Lowestoft in January 1792, at the early age of thirty-nine. It is probable that John Bly, senior, was not the Lowestoft painter referred to by Chaffers, for Chaffers added, 'died at Worcester', and it was John Bly, junior, who moved to Worcester in 1799, after his father's death at Lowestoft. However, we can assume that John Bly, senior, was certainly employed at the Lowestoft factory in some capacity, for Abel remarks 'my two uncles John and Philip also worked in the factory', and if he was referring to John Bly, junior, he should have used the term cousin.

John Bly, junior, was born in February 1779, and consequently he could not have been usefully employed at the factory until the mid-1790s. Chaffers related that a Mrs. Johnson (the daughter of Robert Allen, the Lowestoft artist) had a china mug, 'painted by a Lowestoft apprentice named Bly, who, on the suspension of the works, had been transferred to the Worcester China Manufactory, and sent this specimen of his progress to his old master; it formed part of a service made expressly for the Duke of Cumberland, whose arms it bears. Mr. Chaffers had a sketch by Bly of a coat of arms, painted just before his death, for a Worcester service made for Lord Amherst.' One Chamberlain service was made with the Duke of Cumberland's arms in 1806, and a Flight, Barr and Barr service was made for Lord Amherst in 1823.

The use of the term 'apprentice' is interesting and underlines the youth of John Bly, junior, during his period of employment at the Lowestoft works. It is interesting to discover from the wage records of the Chamberlain factory at Worcester that John Bly was employed there from the week ending September 28th, 1799, at a period when other former Lowestoft work people were taken on at this Worcester factory (page 174).

It would appear that John Bly later changed his allegiance to the other Worcester factory worked by Messrs. Barr, Flight and Barr (c. 1804-13) and subsequently by Messrs. Flight, Barr and Barr (c.1813-40) and a fellow Worcester artist related, 'John Bly, who came from Lowestoft excelled in shading the gold in Arms, and was unequalled in giving a natural expression to the Lion in the Royal Arms or wherever it occurred, and took that part in the grand service made for His Majesty William IV'* (c.1831).

John Bly had married Ann Poultney on October 5th, 1813, at Worcester, and a son, also named John, who was subsequently employed as a landscape painter on Worcester porcelain, was born almost exactly a year later. John Bly, the Lowestoft trained armorial painter and gold shader, died in Worcester in September 28th, 1833.

---

* R.W. Binns in his *Century of Potting in the City of Worcester* (1877) illustrated an engraving of a plate from the William IV service of c.1831 and he states that the Worcester firm, then Messrs. Flight, Barr and Barr, 'was rich in crest painters, and it is on this account, we believe, that the design made for His Majesty was of a purely heraldic character. . . . The centre of the plate is decorated with the Royal Arms of England, excellently painted. The gilding of this plate is very elegant. . . Altogether this is the handsomest work of Messrs. Flight (Barr) and Barr's which we have seen.' We have already observed above that John Bly worked on this service which was so different in its style from the simple Lowestoft wares (made for local markets) on which he had been trained.

Joseph or Philip Bly

Chaffers, in his list of Lowestoft workmen, gives the name Joseph Bly but I cannot trace records of any person of this name, and Abel Bly mentions that his 'uncles John and Philip Bly also worked at the factory'. I have, therefore, assumed that Chaffers wrote 'Joseph Bly' in error for 'Philip Bly', a brother to Abel Bly, senior, and John Bly, senior, both of whom were employed at the Lowestoft factory.

I have been unable to trace any references to Philip Bly's birth, marriage or death in the available local Church Registers, but we do have records of children born between 1777 and 1787 to Philip and Ann Bly. These records suggest that Philip could have been employed at the factory from at least 1770, as he was married and had fathered a child by 1777. Chaffers does finish his list of Lowestoft workmen with 'Philip Bly, carter', and he may have been correct in this description.

Mrs. Bull

There is a tradition set out in the catalogue of the Seago Collection (1873) that figures were painted by Mrs. Bull, one of the painters of the factory, but I have been unable to substantiate this, and the early writings on the subject of figure production at the Lowestoft factory are notoriously unreliable! The Registers list Sophia Bull, wife of James Bull, in the 1750s and 1760s; Lydia Bull who married James Bull in 1794; Margaret Bull (who died in February 1791, aged seventy-nine), wife of William, and Rebecca Taylor, who married John Bull in December 1785.

Plate 186. *A very typical Lowestoft cylindrical mug, painted in underglaze blue and inscribed in the front — 'Ann Cotton, 1780'. 4½ ins. high.* Author's Collection.

Plate 187. A. *A finely enamelled teapot of typical shape and Chinese styled figure pattern.* **B.** *A Chinese shaped covered sugar bowl, enamelled with the same design. Teapot 5ins. high, bowl 3¾ins. high. c.1780-5.* Victoria and Albert Museum (Crown Copyright).

George Butcher

Chaffers listed George Butcher as a kiln man at the Lowestoft factory but I have been unable to trace any information about workmen, apart from records in the Church registers, where eight children are recorded as being born to George and Mary Butcher between June 1770, and March 1787.

Family tradition believes that this artist worked at the Lowestoft factory. He was born in 1750, indicating an employment date after at least 1765.

Mrs. Cooper

Chaffers listed 'Mrs. Cooper — blue painter' but I have been unable to discover any information about her, except that in November 1775, John Bly married a Mary Cooper and it is possible that Chaffers' Mrs. Cooper may have been John Bly's mother-in-law. The Mrs. Coopers listed after 1770 are: Rebecca, wife of Francis; Susanna (died in childbirth in August, 1787) wife of William; Mary, wife of John; Elizabeth, wife of William Cooper, and Mary, wife of James Cooper. Mary died in July 1779, aged 35.

We have already read that in 1772 'the painting branch is done by women' (page 45) and at this period it would seem that underglaze blue painting was being referred to, for no dated enamelled piece is known before 1774. What we do not know is how long female painters had been employed. Was it from the earliest days of the factory (if so, they would have been a novel innovation in the ceramic industry) or were they introduced in about 1770, perhaps to produce the new printed designs? Abel Bly related that, about the time when the factory closed, the women blue and white painters worked in an attic over the testing room, whereas the other painters worked over the counting room (page 46).

Other female painters on Lowestoft porcelains were Mrs. Simpson, Mrs. Stevenson and her daughter, but several more must have been employed, and their names have not been recorded. Jewitt, writing in 1878, lists several workmen, and adds, 'besides these, several women were employed in painting and gilding'.

Thomas Curtis

Thomas Curtis, listed by Chaffers as an 'artist' rather than an 'painter', is an interesting person, and would appear to have been employed for a long period and was of an old Lowestoft family. Thomas Curtis was born of James and Mary Curtis in December 1759. A blue and white bell-shaped mug bears the inscription:

JAMES AND MARY
CURTIS
LOWESTOFT
1771

and tradition has it that Thomas Curtis painted it for his parents, but, if the Thomas born of these parents in 1759 was the Lowestoft artist of this name, then Thomas would have been only about twelve years old, and the traditional Curtis attribution would appear to be incorrect. The local Church Registers show that Thomas Curtis married twice and remained at Lowestoft until at least 1799, his name being associated, I believe correctly, with overglaze enamelled floral designs normally found with ornate Chinese-styled cell borders (Plates 208-10). Dated specimens of this type are of the late

1780s and of 1790, the enamel colours are noticeably full and wet-looking, as if painted with a fully charged brush.

If the lettering on inscribed examples was painted by the artist responsible for the rest of the decoration, then it would appear that two different artists painted in the traditional Curtis style, for the lettering on examples shown in Plates 208-10 is different from that seen in Plates 211-2 (page 189).

Thomas Curtis' style of formal floral decoration, sometimes incorporating a cornucopia-like device, is also found on late eighteenth century Chinese porcelain made for the European market, and it is not clear if the Lowestoft potters were emulating the Chinese or if the Chinese potters were copying Lowestoft wares or patterns sent out with the tea clippers (page 109). Thomas Curtis' second marriage was in 1797, and Chaffers states that his occupation as given in his will was 'china painter', an occupation he would seem to have enjoyed from about 1775 to the closing of the factory.

James Hughes

As has been explained on page 54, James Hughes' name is traditionally associated with the charming, early relief-moulded designs of the type illustrated in Plates 53-79. Many of these do, in fact, incorporate the initials 'I.H.' in the raised design, and a 'J' of that period was nearly always written as 'I', so that there is some reason for the traditional attribution. The dates 1761 and 1764 (and very rarely 1762) are also found worked into the raised pattern teawares bearing the initials 'I.H.'.

We have few facts regarding James Hughes: he had sons born to him in 1761 and in

Plate 188. *A Lowestoft teapot of typical form, very finely painted in the Chinese style with black enamel and gilding. Several similar patterns in black 'pencilling' were made, but not of this quality. 6ins. high. c.1780-5.* Godden of Worthing Ltd.

Plate 189. *A rare jug (the cover missing, of similar form to Plate 158), enamelled with brick red ground and gold trellis design, the panel painted with Chinese figures in a typically simple and amusing style. 8¼ ins. high. c.1780.* Sotheby's (Sale record 200, page 249).

1768, so that he was presumably of working age in 1757 when the factory was established, although the typical raised patterns associated with his name were probably not introduced until 1760. There is a fine mug in the Christchurch Mansions Museum and Art Gallery at Ipswich which bears the inscription, 'Is Hughes. 1766. Lowestoft' (Plate 83), and this may have been made by, or for, this Lowestoft workman. As I have explained on page 20, Mr. John Howell has discovered that James Hughes described himself in 1760 and in 1769 as a 'painter' not a modeller or mould maker, as we have previously believed. My comments on this point are previously recorded, (see page 56).

In January 1768, James and Susan Hughes had a son, William. He was to continue the family association with the factory after his father's supposed death, for Chaffers records the fact that he was a modeller late in the eighteenth century, earning on an average three pounds per week, a high wage at that period (see next entry).

Plate 190. *A fine, rather squat coffee pot, enamelled with Chinese figure design, one of many such Oriental patterns. 7ins. high. c.1775.* T.C.S. Brooke (Wroxham).

Plate 191. *Three superb Lowestoft mugs enamelled in the Oriental style. The right-hand example is particularly fine and can perhaps be linked with the painter of the mugs shown in Plate 160. 5⅜ and 5½ ins. high. c.1780-5.* Sotheby's (Colman Collection, see Sale records 148 and 149, page 245).

Plate 192. *A fine, large coffee pot of the later, tall shape (compare with Plate 190), finely enamelled in the Oriental style. 12ins. high. c.1785.* Ex Henry Levine Collection (see Sale record 266).

Plate 193. *A rare and attractive tea caddy and cover (not a vase, page 215) bearing a rare teaware pattern. 4½ins. high. c.1785.* Mr. and Mrs. Peter Bennett Collection (Photograph, John Howell).

Plate 194. *A rare enamelled mug, with characteristic scroll handle decorated in the Oriental style with typical border, perhaps by the same hand as Plate 191, right. Note the foreground and the strange leaves on the trees. 4¾ins. high. c.1785.* T.C.S. Brooke (Wroxham).

William Hughes

Chaffers' list of Lowestoft workmen includes two modellers, William Hughes and John Stevenson, although one would not have thought that this small factory would have supported two modellers in the accepted sense of the term, especially in its closing years, when few new shapes were being introduced. Perhaps by 'modeller', Chaffers, or his informant, did not mean one who designed new shapes and figures, but rather a workman who formed, either on the wheel or by plaster of Paris moulds, the basic, repetitive shapes which were turned out hour after hour.

Local registers record the christening of William Hughes on January 24th, 1768, the parents being James and Susan Hughes (for an account of James Hughes see previous entry). At a date before November 1791, William Hughes had married Ann Williams, and a son, Edward, was born to them in November 1791.

The period of William Hughes' useful life at the factory would have been c.1785 to c.1799. Chaffers appears to state that William Hughes (as well as John Stevenson) went to Worcester, but I have been unable to trace Hughes' name in the available records of the Chamberlain factory. John Stevenson certainly moved to Worcester with his family and his name appears in the Chamberlain wages book from September 22nd, 1799 (page 170).

James Mollershead or Mottershead

James Mollershead is listed by Chaffers as a Lowestoft painter, but the spelling is probably an error for Mottershead, and Jewitt in 1878 gives Mottershed. A James Mottershead was at Bow in London in the 1760-7 period according to the researches of A.J. Toppin, and Mrs. Elizabeth Adams, and this artist may be one of the Bow artists who reputedly came to Lowestoft. He had left Lowestoft before October 1793, for Chaffers recorded a letter from a James Mottershead of Hanley dated November 5th, 1793:

> Sir, I received yours dated October 28th on Saturday and answer as soon as possible and have done the best in my power to give you an account of all my methods in the preparation (the process for preparing the gold) as exact as I can which if you follow you cannot mistake. I have your drauft (sic) it was thirty days before date.
>
> From your humble sarvan (sic) and wellwisher.

I have been unable to trace further information on this painter, but see commments on page 186.

Richard Phillips

The painter's number '3' is associated with Richard Phillips because one mug (Plate 81) with this mark has also the name 'Richa[d] Phillips' painted under the handle. This

Plate 195. *A rare, perhaps unique, Chinese-style sugar bowl (missing the cover), enamelled in the style of Chinese porcelains made for the European market. In fact the saucer plate shown with this bowl is of Chinese hard-paste porcelain (page 109). Diameter of bowl 4½ ins. c.1790.* Bowl, formerly Godden Collection. Chinese Plate, Messrs. Earl D. Vandekar of Knightsbridge Ltd.

article was not made for Phillips, for the owner's name is clearly painted on the front:

'Ann Hammond. Woodbridge. April 9, 1764.'

A further example has the initials 'R.P.' under the handle and this is inscribed:

'John Cooper. 1768.'

Good illustrations of these important inscribed and dated mugs are given by both Sheenah Smith and Christopher Spencer in their recent books.

An entry in the local Church Register of christenings under the date March 6th, 1744, probably relates to this artist:

'Richard, son of James and Elizabeth Philipps.'

The spelling of Phillips is incorrect, but spelling errors of this type abound in eighteenth century records.

Apart from inscribed pieces, the painter's number '3' is found on the examples illustrated in Plates 38, 43, 56, 58, 59, 66, 69, 80, 81, 82, 83, 84, 92, 98 and 106, but little has been recorded about this early Lowestoft painter.

Miss Sheenah Smith carried out interesting research on the calligraphy found on the various inscribed specimens. In this way she has suggested many pre-1770 pieces which could well have been painted by Richard Phillips. The reader is referred to Chapter 8 of *Lowestoft Porcelain in Norwich Castle Museum.*

Richard Powles

The obituary of this artist was published in the *Monthly Magazine* of February 1808, and stated that Richard Powles was taken on at the Lowestoft china factory as a boy, and that he remained there until he was grown up. He then joined his uncle in Denmark and later returned to England. A good draughtsman, and celebrated local painter, several of his watercolour drawings are known, including one depicting Lowestoft High Street, and he also furnished views for Gillingswater's *History of Lowestoft* of 1790.

To fix some dates, the local Church Register states that Richard Powles was christened on October 15th, 1764, the son of Richard and Elizabeth Powles, so it follows that he can hardly have painted Lowestoft china before 1775, and 1780 would be a more realistic date.

Richard Powles apparently went to Denmark in about 1784, but in February 1787, he was married at Lowestoft to Deliana Williams. The family then apparently returned to Denmark for their first son, John Diston Powles was born at Elsinore on December 16th, 1787. Richard Powles also wrote to the *Gentleman's Magazine* from Elsinore in 1790. Another son Richard was, however, born at Lowestoft in January 1791. Richard Powles then spent several years in London, but returned towards the end of 1807, one report saying that he returned ten weeks before his death.

His death is recorded in the Lowestoft registers on December 30th, 1807:

'Richard Powles, husb. of Deliana, aged 44, died.'

Richard Powles' name is associated with several well-known examples of Lowestoft porcelain, some of which show a similarity to his watercolour drawings. One circular tablet painted with figures adapted from Fontaine's Fables 'The Princess betrothed to the King of Garba', has the initials 'R.P.' painted on the reverse, and the style of painting is like that seen on other specimens which would seem to fall within the period of Richard Powles' supposed stay at Lowestoft in the early 1780s. While he is mainly associated with overglaze enamel painting, it is quite possible (but by no means certain) that he also painted some of the most charming underglaze blue designs, such as those shown in Colour Plates 3 and 6 and Plate 185.

James Redgrave

The following four entries relate to the Redgrave family of Lowestoft decorators. The name is well known to collectors and is associated with a class of Oriental styled landscape designs incorporating areas of underglaze blue in conjunction with overglaze enamel colours (Colour Plate 7 and Plates 143-6 and 203-5).

It is difficult to trace the various members of the families. For example, Chaffers refers to James Redgrave as a flower painter but, as the only person of this name whom I have been able to trace was not born until 1778, he could not have been usefully employed at the factory until the 1790s.

On January 23rd, 1803, James Redgrave married Mary Bly, and children were born to this couple at Lowestoft in 1803, 1805, 1807, 1808, 1809, 1811 and 1812. A James Redgrave of the correct age group was still alive at Lowestoft in 1841, then described as a shipwright, and his father was John Redgrave, (see next entry).

John Redgrave, Senior

John Redgrave, senior, was born in about 1721, so that he could well have been employed at the Lowestoft factory from its commencement in 1757 to quite late in its history, for he did not die until December 1801, when he was eighty, and had probably retired from painting in the 1780s or early 1790, although this is only conjecture. It is quite possible, indeed probable, that the Redgrave family came from London and that some were employed at the Bow factory.

At a date prior to 1770 (or perhaps 1762) John had married Mary, and they had children christened as listed below:

March 30th, 1770	Edmund
September 18th, 1772	Susanna
July 3rd, 1775	John, see next entry
August 17th, 1778	James, see previous entry

Plate 196. *A typical Lowestoft sparrow beak milk jug form with very rare pink enamel decoration. 3¼ ins. high. c.1775.* H.C. Wolton Collection.

Plate 197. *Two typical Lowestoft sparrow beak milk jugs, showing simple scroll handles, without the earlier thumb rest seen in Plate 196. Also a milk jug with ribbed handle. 5 and 3¼ ins. high. c.1785-90.* Author's Collection.

An elder daughter, Mary, was born in November 1761, for a porcelain birth tablet is inscribed, 'Mary Redgrave, born Nov. 19th, 1761', and this appears to relate to John and Mary's first child (it is generally considered that this tablet was made and decorated some years after the date it bears, see page 220. Mary's birth, late in 1761, is reflected in a register entry for her death on May 4th, 1795:

'Mary Liffin, daughter of John and Mary Redgrave, died aged 33.'

A unique 'birth tablet' served both to record the arrival of a daughter, Martha Liffin, in August 1794, and, on the reverse, the death of the mother, Mary Liffin, who was born in 1761.

To return to John Redgrave, senior, he died in December 1801, at the age of eighty, his wife Mary having died in March of the same year, aged sixty-two. If we can assume that John Redgrave was employed at the factory from its early days, as is possible from his date of birth in the 1720s, then he could have been only one of the early blue painters, perhaps with the tally number '1' or '2'. That is, if we are correct in associating the other early numbers '3' and '5' to Richard Phillips and Robert Allen (pages 145 and 158).

John's son, Edmund, who married Elizabeth Welton at a date before 1796, and was still living in 1841, remained in Lowestoft and may, or may not, have been employed at the china factory. A Lowestoft porcelain birth tablet was made and inscribed 'Ann Redgrave, born Novbr 4 1795' to commemorate the birth of their daughter, Ann.

John Redgrave, Junior

I believe that the John Redgrave listed by Chaffers was really the son of the person of the same name listed above, for the other workmen listed appear to relate to the closing

Plate 198. *A superb garniture of five small vases painted in the manner of Chinese porcelains made for the European market. This type of decoration is associated with Thomas Curtis (page 152). Covered vases 9ins. high. c.1785-90.* T.C.S. Brooke (Wroxham).

years of the factory, when John Redgrave, senior, was approaching eighty and must have retired.

John Redgrave, junior, was christened on July 3rd, 1775, and married Ann Stevenson on July 15th, 1792, and the couple bore the following children who were christened on the dates given below:

January 4th, 1794	Ann (Birth tablet gives date of birth as January 2nd)
June 23rd, 1795	Jane (died August 30th, 1795)
July 9th, 1797	Jane (died July 23rd, 1798)
July 14th, 1799	Jane

On the evidence of age, John Redgrave could have been employed at the factory from about 1790, but he had left with other workers by November 1799, although he was presumably still at Lowestoft in July of that year, when his daughter Jane was christened.

The evidence that John left in November 1799, is contained in the Chamberlain wage records, which show John Redgrave's name as a painter (or gilder) from November 16th, 1799. His wife, Ann, was taken on as a burnisher of gold from April 12th, 1800, and both were employed at Worcester for many years. The fact that Ann was employed at Worcester as a burnisher may indicate that she was so employed while at Lowestoft.

Margaret Redgrave

Chaffers lists Margaret Redgrave as a Lowestoft painter, but I have been unable to trace the name in the available records. However, a Martha Redgrave is recorded in a marriage entry: 'November 25th, 1792, John Gall and Martha Redgrave' and a birth tablet inscribed 'Martha Redgrave born Augt ye 12th 1765' confirms the name.

There were other female members of the Redgrave families:

Plate 199. *A selection of Lowestoft enamelled vases, in the manner of the Chinese export market wares. Large vase 9ins. high. c.1785-90.* A.W. Denney Collection.

Ann Redgrave, née Stevenson, married John Redgrave, junior, July, 1792 (moved to Worcester by April, 1800, see page 162).

Mary Redgrave (senior) wife of John Redgrave, senior (born c.1739, died March 1801).

Mary Redgrave (junior) married John Liffin, December, 1785 (died May, 1795, aged 33).

Susanna Redgrave, daughter of John Redgrave, senior (born September 1772).

I believe that the so-called Redgrave patterns (as illustrated in Colour Plate 7 and Plates 143-6 and 203-5) were painted by the female Redgraves or the children, for without intending to be disrespectful, the designs are quite simple, repetitive ones, requiring no special training or particular talent. The probable period of these designs is c.1775-90.

Now, if we have been successful in tracing all members of the Redgrave family, we can proceed to eliminate some from the list on account of age, in an endeavour to discover the persons responsible for the Redgrave patterns.

Ann Redgrave	not a Redgrave until she married John Redgrave, junior, in 1792, too late for these typical 'Redgrave' designs.
Edmund Redgrave	not born until 1770
James Redgrave	listed by Chaffers as a flower painter, and not born until 1778.
John Redgrave, Senior	born c.1721 and perhaps working at the factory from its commencement. He would appear to have been too talented, or too old a hand, to have introduced or worked on the simple, so-called 'Redgrave' designs in the 1775-90 period, although this is only conjecture.

John Redgrave, Junior	not born until 1775.
Martha Redgrave	born August 1765; could possibly have assisted in the decoration of Redgrave-type designs. She married John Gaul (or Gall) in November, 1792. Lowestoft birth tablets were made for their children.
Mary Redgrave	wife of John Redgrave, senior (born c.1739); probably employed at the factory before 1775 as a blue painter and she may well have introduced, or supervised, the painting of the new 'Redgrave' patterns with their underglaze blue and overglaze enamel colours. Probably a small team of women, apprentices or children were employed on this range of patterns.
Mary Redgrave Junior	born c.1762, the daughter of Mary Redgrave, senior (see above). This paintress may well have assisted in the decoration of the 'Redgrave' patterns.
Susanna Redgrave	born 1772, too late to have been associated with these designs.

Thomas Rose, Senior

Llewellynn Jewitt, who visited Lowestoft early in 1863 for the purpose of seeking information regarding the Lowestoft China Factory, for an article, which was published in the *Art Journal* of July 1863, subsequently noted, 'at that time literally nothing was known, and after a vast deal of research. . . . I succeeded in obtaining the information which is embodied in this Chapter' (of his *Ceramic Art of Great Britain,* published in 1878). Jewitt then printed quite a full account of Thomas Rose, some of which is here quoted, but it must be stated that Jewitt picked up much local gossip

Plate 200. *A very rare covered preserve pot (?), painted with formal floral designs in the Curtis style (page 152). 3⅝ ins. high. c.1785-90.* Christchurch Mansion Museum, Ipswich.

Plate 201. *A very rare garniture of miniature vases in the Oriental taste, enamelled in black enamel with slight gilding. c.1785-90.* Sotheby's.

which has not stood the test of time, and he illustrates as Lowestoft several pieces of clearly Chinese origin. In the sixty odd years between the closure of the factory and Jewitt's visit, several myths seem to have been planted and nurtured by the local population to be harvested and repeated as fact by the nineteenth century ceramic historians. Having given this warning, we can quote Jewitt's account of Thomas Rose, for it is the only one available to present day collectors. Jewitt wrote in 1863.

> . . . A French refugee of the name of Rose, one of the cleverest of the French porcelain painters, found his way to Lowestoft, and was engaged by the company. He became the principal, and by far the best, of the artists employed, and probably introduced the rose more generally, in allusion to his name, than would otherwise have been done. To him may probably be ascribed the finest and most minutely finished specimens of painting which the works produced, and it was his taste which gave that French character to the general style of ornamentation which is so discoverable on many of the services. [It would appear that at this point Jewitt was referring, in error, to Chinese porcelains made for the European market and which were then often referred to as Lowestoft; Jewitt illustrated several such examples in his book] . . . He was an aged man when he came to Lowestoft, and he remained at the works till his eyesight failed him and he became very poor. A subscription was entered into, and a couple of donkeys to help him carry water in the town purchased, and thus he passed his last few years.'

If we can believe Jewitt's account of the standing of this artist, 'one of the cleverest of the French porcelain painters', and 'by far the best, of the artists employed', then

Colour Plate 11. *A fine cylindrical mug, with the late form of handle, inscribed 'A Trifle from Bungay'. This type of border motif is known as the 'Bungay border' and is found applied to teawares of the 1790s. 4½ ins. high. c.1790.* Godden Collection.

Thomas Rose is an obvious contender for the honour of being the anonymous 'Tulip painter' (pages 180-8) but Jewitt's information was certainly not first hand and is suspect on several counts and no dates are given.

Thomas Rose was apparently at Lowestoft before July 1778, when a son, also Thomas, was born to Thomas and Ann Rose.

The son, born in July 1778, married Mary Andrews in February 1800, and the couple remained at Lowestoft, producing children between 1801 and 1811. In 1841, Thomas Rose, junior, was described as a Fisherman, and his widow apparently later gave information to Jewitt and William Chaffers. This information could not have been very reliable for the widow was married to Thomas Rose, junior, only in 1800, and it would appear from Jewitt's account that Thomas Rose's, senior, eyesight had failed before the closure of the factory, at this period. Thomas Rose, junior, could hardly have decorated much Lowestoft porcelain, presuming that he was employed at the factory, as he was only about twenty-one at the time when it was closed.

Mrs. Simpson

Chaffers listed Mrs. Simpson as a blue painter at the Lowestoft factory, but I have been unable to trace any further information about her.

John Sparham

Another artist mentioned by Chaffers was 'John Sparham — artist'. He was born of Matthew and Mary Sparham in June 1758, so that he would have been of working age by about 1770. He married Susanna Mullinder in December 1783, and then the registers record the birth of sons in 1784 and 1786 (the spelling of Sparham then given as 'Sparrum'). The entry relating to the christening of William on May 29th, 1786, is particularly interesting as the father is referred to as 'late' suggesting that he had recently died:

'William, of late John and Susanna Sparrum.'

The date of death can be reasonably fixed as taking place between 1784, when a son, also named John, was born, and the christening entry of May 1786, when he is described as 'late'.

Being so young, John Sparham (or Sparrum), junior, who married Margaret Colby in 1807, could not have been usefully engaged at the factory.

John Stevenson

Chaffers lists John Stevenson as a Lowestoft modeller who went to Worcester but, as I have explained under 'William Hughes', on page 157, the term 'modeller' may perhaps have included the manufacture of the basic standard undecorated objects rather than modelling of new shapes.

One John Stevenson was buried on September 3rd, 1777, having died at the age of fifty-seven and this person may have been the father of the Lowestoft 'modeller' referred to by Chaffers. He was seemingly born in 1720. Mrs. Elizabeth Adams has traced a John Stevenson who married Sarah Shaw at Wolstanton in the Staffordshire Potteries in May 1740. It would appear that this person then moved down to London and was employed at the Bow porcelain factory by 1750. Baptismal register entries for John Stevenson's children describe him as a 'Potter'.

It seems almost certain that this Staffordshire born 'potter' who later worked at the

Plate 202. *Part of a Lowestoft tea and coffee service attractively painted in black enamel with slight gilding. Other pieces from this fine crested and initialled service are shown in Colour Plate 9. This set is known as the Ludlow service (page 110). Coffee pot 10¾ ins. high. c.1785.* Author's Collection.

Plate 203. *A rare form of fluted teapot of barrel shape painted with the Redgrave-style 'House' pattern (page 105). 4¾ ins. high. c.1785-90.* Sotheby's (Hollond Collection).

Plate 204. *A rare Lowestoft custard cup and cover, decorated with the Redgrave-style 'House' pattern (page 105). Note the thick leaves and flower knob. 3½ ins. high. c.1785-90.* City of Norwich Museums.

Plate 205. *A rare Lowestoft teapot stand, decorated with the Redgrave-style 'House' design. Glazed, flat base. This form of stand was for a teapot of the shape shown in Plate 218. 7¾ x 6½ ins. c.1790-5.* Victoria and Albert Museum (Crown Copyright).

Bow factory became a key hand at Lowestoft. Mrs. Adams has discovered a further fire insurance policy dated April 1771 which includes a dwelling in the occupation of 'John Stevenson, China Maker' and covered by Obed Aldred.

John Stevenson senior and his wife Sarah had a child, John born to them at Bow and baptised in November 1752. This person was also known to have worked at the Lowestoft factory having moved with the family at an unknown period between the establishment of the factory in about 1757 and June 1760 when a John Stevenson was apprenticed to Robert Browne of the Lowestoft factory. However, if there was only one young John Stevenson and if he was baptised soon after his birth, he was apprenticed at the very early (but not impossible) age of eight.

John Stevenson certainly married Susanna Barret at Lowestoft in February 1776, having been already employed at the porcelain factory for some sixteen years. He was to remain there until the closure or until September 1799 when John Stevenson with his brother William were taken on, with other Lowestoft hands, by the management of the Chamberlain factory at Worcester.

Plate 206. *Three views of a rare, relief-moulded scent bottle (page 212), dated on the base 1784. 2¾ ins. high.* Sotheby's (Hollond Collection).

Plate 207. *A charming teabowl and saucer, the Curtis-style formal floral design heightened with gilding — a rare feature. Inscribed in gold 'Ann Gouge'. Saucer diameter 4¾ ins. c.1785-90.* Author's Collection.

Plate 208. *A fine inscribed and dated teapot painted in the Curtis style, also found on Chinese porcelains made for the European market. The reverse side is shown in Plate 210. 6½ ins. high. 1787.* Formerly Godden Collection (Sale record 170, page 247).

Plate 209. *A fine inscribed and dated mug, by the same hand as the 'John Harm' teapot shown in Plate 208, that is probably by Thomas Curtis (page 152). The same style of numeral is found on the George Gall birth tablet dated 1797. 5½ ins. high.* Photograph, Sotheby's (Elliot Collection). Fitzwilliam Museum, Cambridge.

Plate 210. *A teapot and covered vase painted in the style traditionally associated with Thomas Curtis (page 152). The teapot is inscribed and dated '1787' on the reverse side (Plate 208). Note the typical formal rose motif, seen also in Plate 207, left. Vase 8¼ ins. high. c.1785-90.* Formerly Godden Collection.

Plate 211. *A superb mug, with extremely rare turned foot, painted in the Curtis style, but according to the form of lettering and numerals by a different hand (compare with Plates 208-9 and see page 189). 4¾ ins. high.* Formerly Godden Collection.

Plate 212. *Two views of a fine mug, painted and inscribed by the same hand as the Bobbet mug (Plate 211) and relating to the same date. 4½ ins. high.* Sotheby's (Hollond Collection, Sale record 194, page 248).

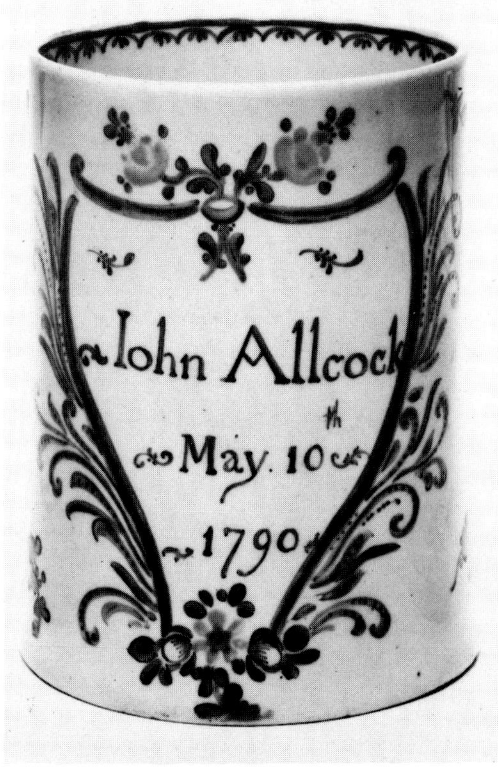

Plate 213. *A very rare, moulded cream or milk jug (a similar form was made at the Caughley factory), painted in the Curtis style. 3½ ins. high. c.1790.* Messrs. T.C.S. Brooke (Wroxham).

Plate 214. *A fine teapot painted in the Curtis style (also found on Chinese porcelains made for the European market). Most examples of this basic type are* not *inscribed. 5½ ins. high.* Sotheby's (Hotblack Collection, Sale record 157, page 246).

William Stevenson, Senior

Chaffers' assertion that he went to Worcester is borne out by the Chamberlain wage records, for payments are recorded to William Stevenson, 'Potter', from September 28th, 1799, the same commencement date as that for John Stevenson (page 170). On January 25th, 1800, a Sarah Stevenson was taken on the Worcester payroll as a

William Stevenson, senior, married Jane Dinmore of Lowestoft on July 16th, 1767, so that if we can assume that he was married at about twenty, we can arrive at a date of birth of about 1747, and his wife was born in about 1745, a fact gleaned from her recorded age at death.

William and Jane Stevenson bore the following children, the dates being those of the christenings as recorded in the local registers:

May 29th, 1768	William
November 6th, 1769	Ann
April 13th, 1771	John
July 22nd, 1772	Thomas
September 1774	Jane (died an infant)
October 1775	Jane (died an infant)
April 7th, 1777	Sarah
September 29th, 1779	Deborah
June 23rd, 1781	Thomas

William's wife, Jane, died at the age of forty-six and was buried on August 9th, 1791. The burial entry is most interesting for she was then described as 'widow of William'. William Stevenson therefore died between 1780 (a child was born in June, 1781) and August 1791. It is possible that he was employed at the china factory, perhaps as a 'finisher' like his son, from about 1765.

William Stevenson, Junior

As we have seen from the previous entry relating to William Stevenson, senior, the son of the same name was born in May 1768. He could have been employed at the china factory from the early 1780s, and we have no reason to question Chaffers' statement that he was a 'finisher'.

Chaffers' assertion that he went to Worcester is borne out by the Chamberlain wage records, for payments are recorded to William Stevenson, 'Potter', from September 28th, 1799, the same commencement date as that for John Stevenson (page 170). On January 25th, 1800, a Sarah Stevenson was taken on the Worcester payroll as a burnisher of gold, as were other Lowestoft wives and children, and we can, I think, safely assume that this person was William's younger sister, born at Lowestoft in April 1777.

It should be noted that in most cases the Worcester wage records give the alternative phonetic spelling 'Stephenson'.

* The term 'finisher' probably relates to a workman who trimmed seams and joints after wares had been taken from the moulds, or after handles had been applied. He could also have turned or trimmed the footrims of articles, and in general he would 'finish' the unglazed objects.

Plate 215. *A teabowl and saucer bearing the arms, crest and motto of the Rev^{d}. Robert Potter, Vicar of Lowestoft and Prebendary of Norwich (page 109). Saucer diameter 4 ¾ ins. c.1785-90. See Sale records 117 and 199, pages 243 and 249.* L. Godden Collection.

Plate 216. *A fine cylindrical mug, with the late form of handle used in the 1790s. Apart from the slight floral sprays, the decoration is in black enamel and gold (page 110). 4 ½ ins. high. c.1790.* Formerly Godden Collection. Christchurch Mansion Museum, Ipswich.

Mrs. Stevenson and Daughter

Chaffers noted that Mrs. Stevenson and daughter were blue painters at the Lowestoft factory.

To find a Mrs. Stevenson with a daughter of employable age, we have to go back to Jane Stevenson (née Dinmore) who was married to William Stevenson, senior, in July 1767. They had daughters Ann (born November 1769), Sarah (born April 1777) and Deborah (born September 1779). Jane (Mrs. Stevenson) died in August 1791, aged forty-six, at a time when her eldest daughter, Ann, would have been about twenty-two.

Mrs. Jane Stevenson's daughter Ann married John Redgrave on July 15th, 1792, and the couple had children at Lowestoft in 1794, 1795, 1797 and 1799. On the occasion of the birth of their first child, Ann, on January 2nd, 1794, a Lowestoft porcelain birth tablet was made. Ann's husband, John Redgrave, was also employed at the factory and he was one of the work people who were taken on by Chamberlain of Worcester in 1799 (page 170).

I believe that Chaffers' blue painters, Mrs. Stevenson and daughter, were Jane and Ann, as described above, but this is not to say that the wives of John Stevenson and William Stevenson, junior, were not employed in like capacity, for it would appear that the Lowestoft works gave employment to the wives and children of most of their male hands.

In the preceding pages of this Chapter, I have given details of the artists and other work people employed at the Lowestoft factory, but it is very doubtful if the list is complete (or can ever be completed unless some undiscovered factory records are

Plate 217. *A very rare form of cup and saucer, enamelled in the French taste taken up by the English potters in the 1790s. Saucer, diameter 5ins. c.1790-5.* Author's Collection.

Plate 218. *A very rare form of Lowestoft teapot of the 1790s. Note handle form which was also used on mugs (Colour Plates 10 and 11 and Plate 216). The form of stand is shown in Plate 205. 5½ ins. high.* City of Norwich Museums.

brought to light). However, we can perhaps assume that we have the names of most of the foremost decorators of the later Lowestoft porcelains.

It remains to try to link these names with known types or styles of decoration — a most dangerous, but fascinating, pastime. The Oriental styled landscape designs with underglaze blue used in conjunction with overglaze enamel, and sometimes with gilding (Colour Plate 7 and Plates 143-6 and 203-5) have always been associated with the Redgraves but, for the reasons given on page 163, I consider that these simple patterns were completed by Mary Redgrave and the female members of the Redgrave family rather than by James, or the two John Redgraves.

There is, however, another style of decoration that can perhaps be linked with the Redgraves. This comprises some charming, leafy, festoon ornamentation, often in puce, framing panels of initials or names, and overglaze blue enamel line borders are often found with these pieces, which belong to the 1790s. This style of decoration is seen to advantage in the unique tea caddy illustrated in Colour Plate 12 and Plate 228, and in the birth tablets of January 2nd, and April 9th, 1794, shown in Plates 227 and 229. It will be seen that these birth tablets record the birth of Redgrave children, and it is reasonable to assume that a member of the family decorated them, for they are distinctly better than average in the quality of the painting, and one can imagine a father regarding their painting as a labour of love. But who was the father? If we attempt to list the male members of the Redgrave family who reached maturity in the late 1780s or early 1790s (the style is not found on earlier pieces) we have the following candidates, and as it happens all are brothers, and the sons of John and Mary Redgrave (page 160).

Plate 219. *A small waste bowl and a teabowl of a rare form, occasionally used in the mid-1790s and also found on Chinese porcelains and on Caughley porcelain. Note the late, simple enamelled designs. Large bowl, diameter 4 1/10 ins. c.1795-9.* Author's Collection.

Plate 220. *A very rare covered preserve jar (page 211), enamelled and gilt with French taste sprig pattern. 4ins. high. c.1795-9.* Author's Collection.

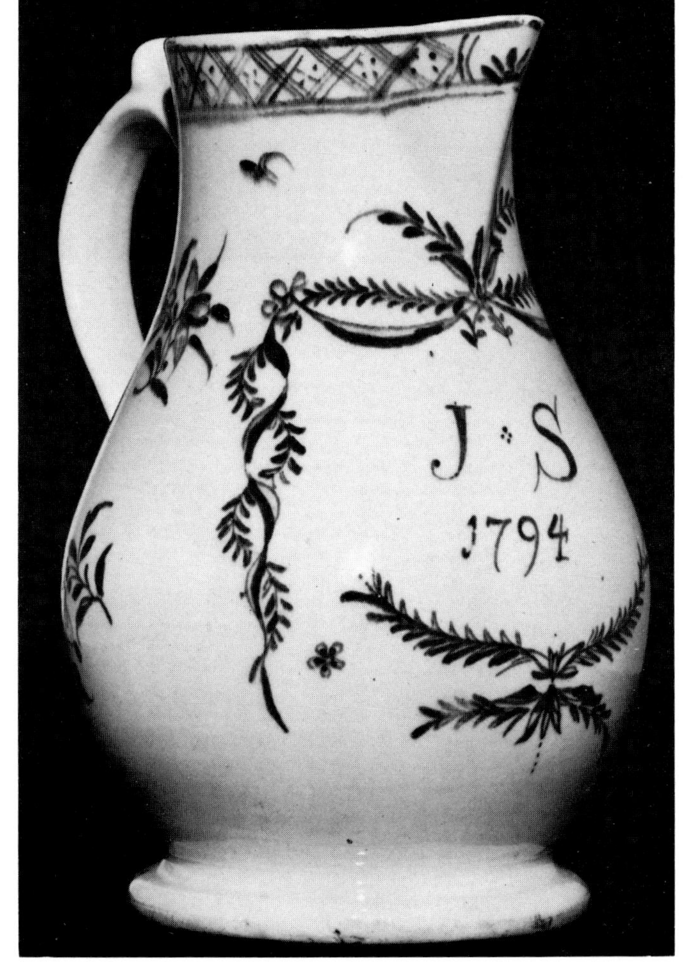

Plate 221. *A fine and typical Lowestoft jug, dated 1794, showing that such underglaze blue designs were continued until the closing years of the factory's history. 5 ¾ ins. high.* Formerly Godden Collection (Sale record 166, page 246).

Plate 222. *A typical teabowl and saucer with coffee cup decoration in a bright underglaze blue, typical of that used in the 1790s. Note also the late form of cup handle. Saucer, diameter 5ins. c.1795.* Author's Collection.

Edmund Redgrave, born March, 1770. We have no evidence that Edmund was employed at the factory, but he may well have been, as sons tended to follow their fathers' calling. Edmund Redgrave married Elizabeth Welton and a tablet commemorating the birth of their daughter, Susanna, on April 9th, 1794, is shown in Plate 227, the whole style of painting, including the floral reverse, being the same as the caddy shown in Colour Plate 12, but in the case of a further tablet made to commemorate the birth of their daughter, Ann, on November 4th, 1795, the decoration appears to be by a different hand.

John Redgrave, junior, who was born in 1775, married Ann Stevenson on July 15th, 1792. Their first child, Ann, was born on January 2nd, 1794. John Redgrave and his wife moved to Worcester in the later part of 1799.

James Redgrave, born August, 1778. Chaffers wrote of a flower painter of this name but the date of birth makes him rather an unlikely candidate for the decoration of a typical birth tablet dated January, 1794, when James would have been only about sixteen years old.

On balance, I regard John Redgrave, junior, as the most likely person to have decorated these fine commemorative pieces, but it is just possible that one of the female members of the family, listed on page 164, was responsible.

The traditional attribution of the formal floral designs in the Chinese manner (Plates 198, 200, 208-10, 213 and 214) to Thomas Curtis is probably correct. I have certainly not been able to discover any evidence to cast doubt on the attribution, although it appears that more than one painter worked in this style, for the style of lettering on inscribed pieces can be seen to differ (compare Plates 208-9 with 211-2).

The outstanding decorator of post-1770 Lowestoft porcelains was undoubtedly the person who, for very obvious reasons, was known as the 'Tulip painter' (Plates 147-53). Although this painter by no means limited his subjects to tulips, his naturalistic style of enamel painting is quite unmistakable. Apart from the characteristic style of painting, it is noticeable that his designs are not spoilt by elaborate borders, and many examples lack even the simplest of line edges; handles and spouts of teapots and coffee pots are also normally devoid of ornamentation (Plate 147).

The enamel painting is thinly applied, with highlights achieved by avoiding the use of enamel, so allowing the white porcelain body to serve the purpose, a technique used by some other painters, but none so delicately as our subject. The enamel is often rather dry, unlike the full, wet enamel colours found with the Curtis-style formal flower painting, and a peculiarity sometimes seen on some 'Tulip painter' examples is the overlaying of two colours to achieve the green, rather than the premixing of the pigments before application.

Apart from the prominent full blown tulip which is featured in so many (but not all) of this artist's floral compositions, a further characteristic is to be found on most examples. This comprises two lily-like flowers, often spotted, but with extremely long, trumpet-like stamens. A typical flower of this sort is shown in Plate 149, and this

Plate 223. *A very rare dated 'Trifle from Lowestoft' mug with typical late, enamelled border design. 3½ ins. high.* Sotheby's (Hollond Collection, Sale record 192, page 248). Messrs. T.C.S. Brooke (Wroxham).

Plate 224. *A rare form of late Lowestoft barrel shaped mug (page 208) painted by the same hand as that seen in Plate 223. 3⅞ ins. high. c.1795.* Sotheby's (Hollond Collection, Sale record 193, page 248).

Plate 225. *A rare blue painted pounce pot (page 211) with unusual (perhaps unique) inscription and a rare, but typical, 'Trifle' inkpot. Pounce pot 2¾ ins. high. c.1790-5.* See Sale records 251 and 252. Ex Henry Levine Collection.

feature occurs in several colours, sometimes as part of the main composition but more often alone on the cover or reverse of a piece.

Dated examples of the 'Tulip painter's' work fall within the period 1774-1776, and although he probably worked for a period after 1776 his style is not found on porcelains after about 1780. Although this painter's work is associated with flower painting, I believe that he was also responsible for some of the figure patterns, especially those painted in puce monochrome (Plates 155-7), for the treatment of the pigment and border design is similar on the floral pattern shown in Plate 154. Some few pieces of the Tulip painter's art also bear armorial bearings; a teapot and a sugar bowl (Plates 147 and 152) are perhaps the sole remnants of complete services, and the treatment of these arms suggests that these features were also painted by the so-called 'Tulip painter'. The celebrated mug bearing the Arms and motto of the Blacksmiths' Company is possibly by the same hand, and this specimen is inscribed under the base, 'James and Sarah Hacon, 1775', in the style of lettering and numerals found on the typical floral painted pieces by the 'Tulip painter'.

Although this artist will probably always be known to collectors as the 'Tulip painter', I cannot resist the temptation to try to identify him more positively. The starting point of research into this problem must be the period of his work, because his characteristic hand is not found on documentary dated pieces before 1774.

Plate 226. *A fine dated presentation mug, decorated in the French taste and inscribed by the same hand as that seen in Plates 223-5, see also Colour Plate 11. 5ins. high.* See Sale record 271. Ex Henry Levine Collection.

Colour Plate 12. *A unique, inscribed, tea canister (the reverse side is shown in Plate 228). Painted by the same hand as the Redgrave birth tablets illustrated in Plates 227 and 229. Note the blue enamel edges found on several pieces of the 1790s. Dated, on flat, glazed base — 1797. 4ins. high.* Author's Collection.

Plate 227. *A finely enamelled Lowestoft birth tablet (page 197) dated April 1794, commemorating the birth of one of the Redgrave children (page 180). Note the style of lettering and numerals and compare with Plate 228 and Colour Plate 12. Diameter 4¼ ins.* Lowestoft Borough Library.

Plate 228. *A unique presentation tea canister decorated by the same hand as that shown in Plates 227 and 229. The other side of this canister is shown in Colour Plate 12. Dated, on flat, glazed base — 1797. 4ins. high.* Author's Collection.

Plate 229. *The reverse side of the 1794 birth tablet shown in Plate 227. The flower painting is by the same hand as on the tea canister. See Plate 228 and Colour Plate 12.* Lowestoft Borough Library.

Plate 230. *A late teabowl and saucer of a rare shape, attractively decorated with a gold design. Diameter of saucer 5ins. c.1795.* Author's Collection.

I have listed below the known Lowestoft painters and have added brief comments on their eligibility or otherwise for the position of Tulip painter. Further details of these artists are given earlier in this Chapter.

Robert Allen. No, he continued painting Lowestoft porcelains long after the Tulip painter's hand had ceased, i.e. c.1780.

James Balls. No, dates do not fit.

John Bly, Senior. No, he did not die until 1792, and if he was a painter (there is no evidence that he was) he should have continued after the Tulip painter's style ceased.

John Bly, Junior. No, not born until 1779.

Thomas Curtis. Unlikely, as this painter was not born until 1759 and he remained at Lowestoft until after the factory's closure.

James Mottershead. A distinct possibility. We have learnt (page 158) that this man, who may be assumed to have been a painter, was at Bow in the 1765-7 period. Overglaze enamel painting was, of course, widely practised at the Bow factory, and Mottershead may have learnt his trade there, and perhaps been responsible for introducing this branch of painting to the Lowestoft painters in the late 1760s. It is not known when he left Lowestoft, but certainly by the later part of 1793, when he wrote from Hanley in the Staffordshire Potteries advising the Lowestoft management on his methods

Plate 231. *A fluted teabowl and saucer, with coffee cup decorated with gilt floral sprays in the French taste. Note the rare and late cup handle form. Saucer, diameter 5ins. c.1795-9.* Author's Collection.

Plate 232. *A very rare and attractive Lowestoft teapot, of a shape that would have accompanied tea and coffee cups of the form shown in Plate 231. 6ins. high. c.1795-9.* See Sale record 265. Ex Henry Levine Collection.

of preparing gold. The period of the Tulip painter could fit Mottershead's stay at Lowestoft but we have no direct evidence to link him with our 'Tulip painter'. At least one Bow flower painter of the 1750s and 1760s had a rather similar style to that found on Lowestoft porcelains of the 1770s, but the comparison is not conclusive.

Richard Phillips. Unlikely, as this blue painter was working in the 1760s, and pieces attributed to him are quite unlike the style of the 'Tulip painter'.

Richard Powles. Unlikely, although at one time I was inclined to the opinion that the Tulip painter was Richard Powles, an artist better known for his scenic views, as he was apparently not born until 1764 (he was christened on October 15th, 1764, and his age at death in 1807 was recorded as forty-four) it is unlikely that he could have painted the several fine presentation pieces by the Tulip painter that bear the date 1774.

James Redgrave. No. Although referred to by Chaffers as a 'Flower painter', I cannot trace a James Redgrave in the local Church registers before August 1778, when the christening is recorded of James, son of John and Mary Redgrave.

John Redgrave. No. Born 1721, and probably employed from the factory's establishment, he died in 1801, although the Tulip painter's hand is seen only on pieces of the period c.1774-80. His son of the same name was not born until 1775.

Thomas Rose. A possibility. Chaffers wrote of Rose as a flower painter who had fled from France before the Revolution. Thomas Rose was at Lowestoft before 1778, for a son was born, also Thomas, to Thomas and Ann Rose in July 1778.

John Sparham. A possibility. John Sparham was born in about 1758, so that he could have been usefully employed at the factory in the 1770s, but the first dated pieces decorated by the 'Tulip painter' are of 1774 and they appear too accomplished in style and finish for a painter aged only about sixteen. There is also the point that John Sparham's wife, Susanna, gave birth to children in 1784 and 1786, later than the period tentatively ascribed to the Tulip painter's work. John Sparham, however, died at a date between about September 1785 and May 1786.

To sum up, of the Lowestoft artists known to us, the following three painters could have been responsible for the finely enamelled floral compositions which so often feature a prominent, full blown tulip (Plates 147-53), James Mottershead, Thomas Rose and John Sparham.

On the available evidence I favour James Mottershead, but there is much that is unknown, especially about Thomas Rose. It would be a strange situation if our 'Tulip painter' was really a 'T Rose'!

A study of the lettering and numerals found on inscribed and dated examples of post-1774 enamelled Lowestoft porcelains indicates that at least four different persons were employed decorating these pieces, and the differing styles help to segregate the work of individual painters.

The dates of the very rare examples of dated porcelain decorated by the 'Tulip painter' show a J-like number 1, a characteristic shared by other painters, but the number '7' is readily identifiable in that the top horizontal bar is heavy or accentuated, whereas the stem runs down at an angle in a nearly straight line without curve or accent (see the drawing below and Plate 147).

J774

This style of numeral and lettering which is found also on a floral painted mug by the 'Tulip painter', with the name and date 'Katherine Farquhar', 1774', is also found on the Gooch jug of 1775 (Plate 158) and it seems that at least the long inscription on this fine figure painted piece was by the 'Tulip painter'. The important Blacksmith's Arms mug in the Castle Museum, Norwich, is inscribed by the same hand and the figure supports to the armorial bearings suggest (with Plates 155-7) that our 'Tulip painter' also, on occasions painted figure subjects.

On the charming pieces which I have attributed tentatively to John Redgrave, junior (page 180), that is, the inscribed tea canister (Colour Plate 12), and the Redgrave birth tablets (Plates 227-9), the numerals '1' and '7' are different from the 'Tulip painter's' versions. The top of the J-like 'I' runs upwards from left to right like a barb, the seven has pressure thickening, as if written with a quill pen, and the down stroke is slightly curved. These points can be clearly seen in the drawing below and in Plate 227.

1794

Two hands evidently lettered the inscribed pieces painted with Oriental styled formal floral motifs associated with Curtis. One painter dated his pieces in the manner drawn below (Plates 211-2). His small 'e' has the inward return very high. The formal rose in the centre of the charming 'Ann Gouge' teabowl and saucer is a characteristic of this painter and is found on most examples.

1790

Some collectors may perhaps consider that the lettering and numerals on the examples illustrated in Plates 208-9 were painted by the same hand as those discussed above, and shown in Plates 211-2, but the 7 is delicately shaped and accentuated, and it is apparent that at least two painters worked in the so-called Curtis style.

1787

Several of these pieces show 'S'-like scrolls surrounding the inscription (Plates 208-9).

Plate 233. *A rare small mug, inscribed and painted in late, bright underglaze blue. Note the late handle form also seen in Plate 222. 2⅖ ins. high. c.1790-5.* Author's Collection.

Plate 234. *A late, but typical, Lowestoft birth tablet (page 197), painted in underglaze blue. The flat reverse shows a Chinese-style house on an island. Diameter $2\frac{4}{5}$ ins.* Author's Collection.

Plate 235. *A rare late Lowestoft milk jug enamelled in a typically late sparse style, in pink and brown. 4ins. high. c.1795-9.* Author's Collection.

Plate 236. *A charming earthenware small jug painted by a Lowestoft hand, probably Robert Allen (page 145). c.1795-1800.* Formerly Godden Collection.

Plate 237. *A pottery jug, painted by a hand seen also on Lowestoft porcelain (compare numerals and letters with Plates 223-6). This artist was perhaps Robert Allen, who had a decorating establishment and retail shop at Lowestoft from the 1790s (page 145). It is significant that this jug, dated November 1799 — two months after some of the staff had left the factory for Worcester — is of pottery, not of Lowestoft porcelain, suggesting that the factory had, in fact, closed (page 31).* Lowestoft Borough Library.

Plate 238. *A small pottery mug, inscribed to continue the birth tablet tradition (Plates 227 and 229). Probably painted by Robert Allen (page 145). Note the hook-like numeral '1' and compare with Plates 223, 226 and 237.* Sotheby's.

Plate 239. *A rare and attractive pottery 'Trifle' mug, probably decorated by Robert Allen (page 145). The lettering is similar to that found on Lowestoft porcelain 'Trifles' (Plates 223-6). 3⅝ ins high. c.1799.* City of Norwich Museums.

Plate 240. *A French hard-paste reproduction Lowestoft 'Trifle' mug (page 253). 5¼ ins. high. Late nineteenth century.* Sotheby's 'rogues gallery'.

Plate 241. *A French hard-paste reproduction of the Abraham Moore mugs (Plate 82). Note the crazed glaze, not found on true Lowestoft porcelain (page 253). 5⅞ ins. high.* Sotheby's 'rogues gallery'. Another example is in the Godden Reference Collection.

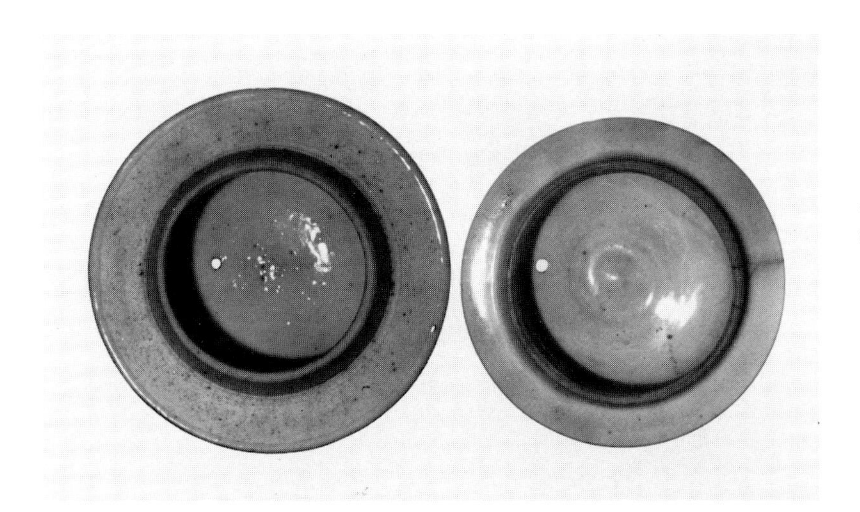

Plate 242. *A Chinese porcelain teapot cover (left), showing the underside with the flange devoid of glaze and with faults in the body. Compare with the Lowestoft soft-paste porcelain teapot cover (right) with glazed flange and rim (page 115).* Godden of Worthing Ltd.

Plate 243. *A Chinese porcelain saucer (left), upturned to show the thin footrim, with the sharp edge partly devoid of glaze. The right-hand example is true Lowestoft with the thick, fully glazed, footrim (page 115).* Godden of Worthing Ltd.

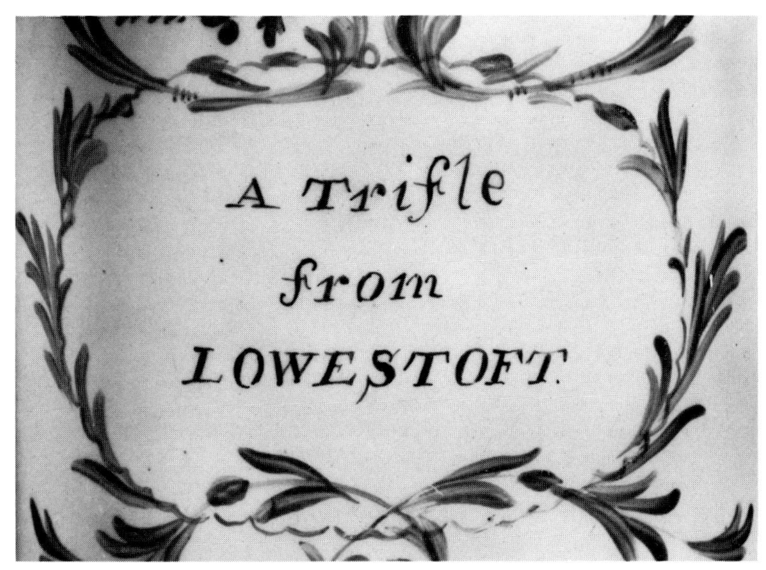

Plate 244. *Detail from a 'Trifle' mug, showing the inscription which appears to have been written by the same hand as all such pieces (page 146). Detail 2¼ x 3½ ins.* Godden Collection.

Plate 245. *Detail from a blue printed jug (Plate 135), showing the printed design washed-in with hand applied blue, a Lowestoft feature. Detail 2¼ x 3¼ ins.* Author's Collection.

CHAPTER V

Lowestoft Forms

The previous chapters have been concerned with the history of the factory, the styles of decoration and the work people employed there. We can now turn to the basic forms manufactured at the Lowestoft factory between c.1757 and 1799. While most pieces found today comprise parts of tea services, the factory produced a wide range of other articles, and these are listed in this chapter, in alphabetical order.

Over sixty basic articles are listed, many of which, such as teapots, are to be found in several different shapes, so that the range is quite considerable and varied, over two hundred different articles or separate forms being illustrated in this book.

Animals

Lowestoft animal moulds, so far discovered, comprise cats, dogs, sheep, rams and swans, and to this short list we could perhaps add the very rare cow cream jugs (Plate 163).

The cats are, like all other Lowestoft animals, extremely rare; they are quite small, on average two and a quarter inches high. The hand painted markings vary from example to example but, of course, the moulded shape shown in Plate 166 is constant. This also shows parts of a plaster of Paris mould from which such pieces were formed, together with an impression from these moulds. Examples feel solid and heavy, with the base flat and glazed over, but there is the normal conical vent hole, such as will be found on most Lowestoft animals and figures (Plates 161 and 174).

Dogs have only recently been attributed to Lowestoft. The standing model shown in Plate 165 has, in the main, been identified by the flat, concave curved base, of which matching unglazed counterparts were found on the factory site. The underside of these bases is, characteristically, glazed over. At present very few of these standing dogs have been traced. A reclining dog of a very similar type is shown in Plate 162, and has been claimed as a further Lowestoft model. The author has not examined this piece.

The inclusion in this book of the dogs shown in Plate 161 will surprise many readers, for these and similar examples have until recently been considered as being undoubtedly of Longton Hall make, and they are illustrated as such in nearly every reference book. However, tests on some have shown that the porcelain is phosphatic, indicating a Bow or Lowestoft origin. Armed with this surprising evidence, we can re-examine these dogs and discover that they exhibit other Lowestoft features, particularly the flat, glazed over base with conical vent hole (compare Plate 161 with Plate 174). The use of manganese on the body of these dogs is admittedly unusual, but it occurs again in the rare cow cream jugs (Plate 163) with the strange flat base which, in turn, links with the standing dogs and fragments found on the factory site (Plates 164 and 165).

The small pairs of sheep and ram figures come in two varieties, both of which are very rare. The larger ones, shown in Plate 167, are approximately two inches long, and have solid, flat bases, glazed over, with the normal vent hole. A second variety is of smaller size, only an inch and a half long, with recessed bases, as shown in Plate 168.

The little swans are, again, solid, with flat, glazed over bases and have a simple charm. Like the other rare amimal models, they are variously coloured and, curiously, the completely white examples are even rarer than those with enamelled features.

The cow cream jug shown in Plate 163 is modelled on a silver prototype, and similar examples in pottery are quite well known, but porcelain jugs of this type are excessively rare. In the past they have been attributed to the Longton Hall factory but, for the reasons given on page 195, they are now thought to be of Lowestoft origin.

The factory site yielded moulds for a pair of reclining deer and hind (see 1907 Catalogue of the Crisp Collection) but as yet no completed specimens of these models have been recorded.

The reader is referred to Peter Danks' brief report 'The Lowestoft Site' (*Transactions of the English Ceramic Circle*, Vol.7, part 3, 1970) but unfortunately the animal pieces mentioned are not illustrated.

Baskets

The earliest recorded type of Lowestoft basket is shown in Plate 43. These rare pieces vary in size for, although most baskets were formed in a mould, these early ones were thrown on the wheel by hand, as if one were making a bowl, the plain sides being then marked out with compasses and the openwork design cut out by hand. The example shown in Plate 43 shows clearly on the outside the rather random way in which the compasses were used to mark out the design, and it is glazed with the wonderful, soft, oil-like glaze found on a small class of Lowestoft porcelains of about 1760 (page 20). Known baskets are approximately four, five and a half, or six inches in diameter, but fragments from the factory site suggest that a larger size was also made.

It would appear that no other baskets were made at the Lowestoft factory until the 1770s, when copies were made in imitation of the popular Worcester oval baskets, with applied rosettes at the junctions of the basketwork sides. These oval baskets (Plate 133) were made in different sizes, and were normally decorated with underglaze blue prints, again in imitation of the Worcester examples, and those from Lowestoft often bear a copy of the Worcester crescent mark (page 50). It is possible that some of these baskets were decorated with overglaze enamel colours, but none has so far been recorded, although it is clear that some examples were decorated to special order, as I have had baskets with panels in the side painted with the owner's initials.

Apart from the standard, rather deep, oval basket there is a further very rare model which may have been made at Lowestoft. This is again a copy of a Worcester original, low and oval in shape, with circular, openwork walls.

Another basket model is circular with floral rosettes applied to the exterior at the junction of the openwork sides (Plate 134). These are small, with a diameter of four to six inches, being close copies of Worcester originals and are normally decorated with Worcester styled floral prints in underglaze blue. Examples are rare.

Beakers

Conical beaker-like objects, a typical example of which is illustrated in Plate 106, were made at Lowestoft during the first ten years of the factory's life, painted, of course, in underglaze blue. An early fragment from the factory site is shown in Plate LIX of Spelman's *Lowestoft China* (1905).

There is a possibility that these articles were intended as vases, perhaps to accompany the covered vases of the type shown in Plate 48, for later sets show a development of these flare topped vases, but I personally regard them as beakers.

A small beaker, or handleless mug, was also made in the 1760-70 period and this may be found painted, in underglaze blue, with a young satyr astride a barrel of beer, and ears of barley spaced around the body (Plate 107).

A straight-sided, beaker-like object with circular banding near the rim and the foot is inscribed in blue, 'Olney Harvey, 1798', but the author has not handled this piece and is therefore unable to vouch for its origin.

Birth Tablets

Birth tablets are small, circular objects, flat on one side, and recessed on the other, and having one or two holes at the top so that the tablet can be suspended. The flat side is normally painted with a Chinese-style scene, although many other motifs occur, while the recessed side is inscribed with a child's name and date of birth. These objects are unique to the Lowestoft factory and several were made for the children of workers at the factory.

At the present time thirty-three examples are known and they are highly prized by collectors. In date they range from 1765* to 1799. Of the known total, twenty-six are painted in underglaze blue and seven are decorated in overglaze enamel colours. The finest of these are of very fine quality, painted by a hand whose work is found on other late wares (Plates 227-9 and page 177).

Exactly how these tablets were used is uncertain, for although most authorities believe that they were hung on the cottage walls, if this were the case, it is difficult to see why the reverse was decorated, as this side would not have been seen. Other collectors have suggested that they were hung in the window. However, if they were intended to be hung on a wall or in a window, they might well have been larger, for the average diameter is only about three inches, and often only two and a quarter inches. My purely personal belief is that they were originally hung round the child's neck as a type of identify disc, a theory which would explain the circular shape, the relatively small size and the often amusing motifs on the reverse side. On the other hand, it can be argued that some few tablets are too large to have been hung round a baby's neck, and the one example has on the back a memorial to the mother (page 234). Whatever was the original use of these tablets, they are unique personal mementoes, quite typical of the factory's products.

The combined birth and memorial tablet, mentioned above, and listed on page 234, shows that some of these tablets were not necessarily made directly after the birth of the child, for this example is decorated in underglaze blue, halfway through the manufacturing process and, while one side records the birth of Martha Liffin in August 1794, the reverse side, which must have been painted at the same time, records the death of Mary Liffin on May 4th, 1795. It follows, therefore, that this tablet was made after May 4th, 1795, that is, some nine months after the birth recorded on the other side. The tablet made for Mary Redgrave and dated 1761 is, for the reasons given on page 220, also thought to have been made some time after the event it commemorates.

* One of 1761 is recorded but, for the reasons given on page 220, this is believed to have been antedated.

Bottles, see **Water Ewers**

Bowls

As these objects were hand thrown on the potter's wheel, it follows that they vary slightly in size, shape and in the thickness of the walls and footrim. Few bowls exceed twelve inches in diameter and remarkedly few were made after the 1770s and decorated in overglaze enamel colours, probably because the imported Chinese examples were so plentiful and inexpensive. One or two exceptions are recorded painted with special commemorative scenes, but there is a dearth of large bowls with standard overglaze designs. A rare shallow bowl (or dish) is finely painted with Eastern figures and is insribed 'Elizabeth Buckle, 1768' (Plate 100).

Bowls ranging downwards in size from about six and a half inches in diameter are really slop bowls from tea services, and some of these are much smaller. The rarest and, to me, the most attractive, are those decorated with relief-moulded motifs, in the Hughes style (Plate 55 and page 54) but a wide range of plain bowls was painted with different underglaze blue designs. After about 1770 some were decorated with underglaze blue prints and from about 1768 some overglaze enamelling was practised.

Small, rather high, bowls with an outswept rim are really the bases of covered sugar bowls of the type shown in Plate 187B, but a rather similar form of bowl was issued with some rare teasets of the 1790s (Plate 219).

Butter Boats

Butter boats have the appearance of miniature sauce boats, but measuring only about four inches long and standing less than two inches high. Typical examples are shown in Plates 9 and 71. They are often mistaken for cream boats, but accounts relating to similar vessels made by other firms show that they were intended to hold molten butter. Some are scaled-down versions of full size sauce boats, and these might even have been originally sold with their larger counterparts.

Several early, pre-1770 butter boats have Hughes-type relief moulding surrounding the blue painted panels, which normally depict Chinese-style scenes. They can be quite charming and are very collectable items, being issued in many basic shapes and with various added patterns, and furthermore they take up very little space. They were rarely made at Lowestoft after about 1780.

'Butter Pots'

Small, oval, covered tureens, with matching stands, were probably 'butter pots'. On the example from the early 1760s shown in Plate 52, it will be observed that the ribbing on the cover runs down from the central bird knob, while a variation in the Castle Museum, Norwich, has the ribbing running lengthwise along the cover. Other variations occur in the added underglaze blue border and in the form of knob (Plate 11), and all are now very rare.

In the 1760-8 period some charming covered butter tureens were made, with Hughes-type raised motifs (Plates 60 and 61 and page 66). These range in size from about six and a half to four and a half inches long, and also vary in the pattern of the raised designs and, as I have stated on page 68, sometimes the moulds were inverted, so that the sunflower motifs may grow downwards (Plate 60).

In the 1770s copies of Worcester oval butter tureens (Plate 126) were made, with applied leaves and flowers at the ends of the twig handles (ornaments which are quite typical of the Lowestoft factory, leaves from the same moulds being found on the rare figure models) and normally decorated with imitations of Worcester underglaze blue printed designs. A further version of a Worcester butter pot is circular in plan, with a floral knob, again bearing blue printed designs, such as the popular Worcester fence design (Plate 127).

Cabbage-Leaf Jugs (see **Jugs**)

Candlesticks

The Lowestoft factory does not appear to have made tall, standing candlesticks, but one model of a hand, or chamber, candlestick is recorded. This is shown in Plate 117, and an unglazed fragment from the site was found recently.

Cane Handle

One early Lowestoft cane handle amusingly painted in underglaze blue has been discovered and is now in my collection. One view is shown in Plate 2. The reader is also referred to Christopher Spencer's book *Early Lowestoft* (1981). The hollow portrait-type object shown in Plate 168 is probably also a cane (or other) handle terminal.

Chestnut Baskets

The covered basket (or tureen) shown in Plate 130 is a rare Lowestoft version of a well-known Worcester model, the Worcester original being also copied at Caughley. The porcelain body itself is vastly different from the harder, more compact, Worcester soapstone porcelain, and the applied leaves once again show clearly the Lowestoft origin of this rare specimen. Parts of moulds for such a piece were found on the Lowestoft factory site.

Chocolate (or Caudle) Cups

Tall cups, perhaps with handles at each side, were apparently made during the early days of the factory's history, for some very rare 'trembleuse' saucers were made, with a central high rim to hold the cup, and similar saucers from other factories have matching, tall, two-handled cups, sometimes with covers. These tall, covered cups were for hot chocolate, or sometimes for caudle.

Chocolate Pots

The fine covered pot (Plate 35) with the handle at right angles to the spout is most probably a chocolate, rather than a coffee pot. The body and style of painting show clearly that this specimen, with others of the same type, was made in the earliest years of the factory's existence, between 1757 and 1760. These are of extreme rarity and I do not know of any later Lowestoft chocolate pots.

Cider Mugs

The attractive bulbous bodied mugs shown in Plate 66 are known as cider mugs. They were made over many years, those shown being early, crisply moulded examples, but they were also made in the later 'floury' body, and these are thicker in the body, with blurred relief moulding, the handles also becoming simpler and more circular in section (Plate 250). Several variations of handle are known, even the two cider mugs shown in Plate 66 having slightly different handles, one without the return on the inside of the loop, and yet these two examples were made within a short period of each other.

A very rare variation of the cider mug shape has a lip applied to the rim, turning it into a form of jug.

Coasters

The quite early (c.1765) circular object shown in the new illustration Plate 102, may well have been produced as a stand for a bottle or decanter, in other words it could have been a porcelain coaster, in the silver fashion. I do not know of any such object from other English factories but Gilbert Bradley's collection contained two examples, one of which is that now illustrated.

Coffee Cans

Coffee cans are small, straight-sided mugs, standing about two and a half inches high. Lowestoft examples are very rare and the management appears to have favoured the shaped-sided coffee cups rather than these can shaped articles.

Small, can-like objects were apparently sold individually as small mugs, perhaps for children and, although these are nearly always called 'coffee cans', I do not believe that the Lowestoft ones were made for this purpose, and they are not found with tea and coffee services made at this factory.

Some rare little mugs of the 1790s are inscribed in underglaze blue 'A Trifle from Lowestoft' (Plate 233) and these seem to have been sold singly in their own right as mugs, not as coffee cans. Others are decorated with standard patterns.

Coffee Cups

Coffee cups have a shaped profile, as opposed to the straight-sided, cylindrical coffee cans, or small mugs. Very attractive coffee cups were made to go with the relief-moulded Hughes-type tea services (Plate 54 and page 59) and others have various flutings. Apart from these the coffee cups were thrown by hand and the shapes show individual differences. However, some handles were moulded and, except for the simple loop handles often with a return at the lower end (Colour Plate 9), they indicate a late date, in the 1790s (Plates 217, 222 and 231).

Coffee Pots

Early Lowestoft coffee pots are very rare, perhaps because they are so liable to damage but Christopher Spencer in his 1981 book shows both sides of a splendid example of about 1760, from his own collection. This piece is badly damaged with a large piece missing but I fancy that this does not unduly worry its discriminating owner.

I do not know of any coffee pots with Hughes-type relief moulding but if any were made they must have been magnificent articles. A known early type is that decorated with powder blue ground (Plate 95) which was in vogue from at least 1763 to the early 1770s, and this shows an early basic shape of coffee pot, with a rather wide top half of the body, surmounted by a rather flat cover (Plates 95, 148 and 190). The covers may have the standard plain knob or an open flower knob (Plates 147-8). The spout is often of a top heavy 'S' form with the pouring end well away from the body (contrast Plates 95 and 148 with the later shapes shown in Colour Plates 7 and 9). As with other objects, these coffee pots were made in different sizes.

From about 1775 a different form of coffee pot came into favour, taller than the rather squat earlier examples, with a gracefully shaped body, of which the cover tends to be high and may be surmounted by a standard globular knob or, rarely, by a floral one (Colour Plates 7 and 9, Plates 141 and 192). The spout appears longer than the earlier ones and points upwards, rather than to the front, and the end of the spout may now be shaped, instead of cut across in a straight line.

The tall, fluted, coffee pot shown in Plate 15 represents a very rare form, indeed it is the only example known to me. This is as well as I do not find the shape or balance to be successful.

The blue printed coffee pot shown in Plate 132 represents another very rare form of the 1775-85 period which, both in shape and added pattern, seeks to emulate the Worcester wares, but the handle form and applied leaf below are Lowestoft innovations, but perhaps not unique to this factory. Teapots rarely occur with this handle form.

Coffee pots were included in 'full' tea services but perfect examples are now very scarce and are hardly ever still found with a complete service. As with the Lowestoft teapots, the coffee pot covers have a glazed flange, contrasting with the Chinese, the Worcester, or the Caughley pots.

A class of covered jug (Plates 135, 140 and 158) is often referred to as a coffee pot, but they have a lip instead of a spout, and, as they are not found with tea or coffee services, I regard these articles as jugs (page 206).

Cream (or **Milk**) **Jugs**

It is often difficult to decide if the several small jugs were originally intended as cream or milk jugs. My own general rule is to term all upright jugs as for milk, restricting creamers to low examples of the type shown in Plates 120 or 138. This may well be too extreme a view suggesting that the vast majority of the owners of Lowestoft tea services used milk not cream, for all services that I have seen had high-type jugs. You may perhaps favour a rule that jugs under three and a half inches in height were creamers, taller examples for milk.

The earliest basic form of tea service jug was upright, with a sparrow beak spout (Plates 72, 73 and 88); the body is sometimes ribbed, or fluted (Plate 20), but normally plain. These utilitarian objects, which may be found in several rare moulded forms (Plate 72) and with various styles of added ornamentation, have a simple grace and are delightful items to collect. The plain, hand thrown examples with slightly different handle shapes (Plate 88), also to be found with many different forms of painted decoration, have a spontaneous charm and appeal.

The early blue and white examples are often thinly potted, while the later, post-1774 creamers with overglaze enamel decoration are rather heavily potted but can still be charming with their simple, scrolled handle (Plate 197).

Quite apart from these upright sparrow beak creamers, we have several different moulded creamers of rather squat form. An early variety of this class is of barrel shape (Plate 118), rather similar to a Worcester and Caughley form. This model was made for several years from about 1765 and, as with other basic shapes, slightly different designs of handle were added from time to time.

An attractive and rare form of creamer having on each side relief-moulded panels of cows and goats, is rather inadequately shown in Plate 138. A further charming, but again rare, little creamer is of shell shape (Plate 120), the basic shape being made at

Worcester and at Caughley, where it was known as a 'Dolphin ewer', on account of the dolphin handle on the originals, but which is replaced on Lowestoft specimens by a simple loop handle, perhaps rather small for the size of the body. The moulding on these shell-shaped creamers varies, some having crossed dolphins moulded under the lip, others only shell-like motifs.

In the eighteenth century the low creamer shown in Plate 150 was called 'low Chelsea ewer'. The shape was a very popular one, made at Worcester, Caughley, Bristol, New Hall and at some later factories. Most Lowestoft examples were painted with overglaze enamels, some by the 'Tulip painter' (page 107), but they were also decorated with underglaze blue designs and even, but rarely, with Redgrave patterns.

A very rare variation of the 'low Chelsea ewer' is a 'high Chelsea ewer', examples of which stand about 3½ inches high. These were also made at the Worcester and at the Caughley factories and, of course, earlier at Chelsea.

A very rare shape of creamer with double curved handle is shown in Plate 145, but most creamers bearing the standard blue and enamelled Redgrave patterns are of the standard upright 'sparrow beak' variety. An even rarer creamer of the 1780s painted with Curtis-type flowers (page 152) is illustrated in Plate 213, and is perhaps based on a similar Caughley jug shape. A further form of creamer has an enlarged lip rising from a globular vase-like body, and this, too, would appear to have been adapted from a Worcester model. Yet another very rare form is represented in the British Museum collection, of 'helmet' shape and closely following a popular design employed by the Chinese potters in the 1775-1800 period. This Lowestoft example is illustrated in Plate 77C of Dr. B. Watney's *English Blue and White Porcelain of the 18th Century* (1963). An unglazed base from such a jug was found on the factory site.

Cress Dishes

Pierced circular dishes are normally called cress dishes and should, of course, have an underplate to catch the drained water from the pierced dish above. A typical example of this rare article is shown in Plate 136, the basic design and the blue printed pine cone pattern being copied from a Worcester original. Examples were also made at the Caughley factory.

Cups (see **Chocolate Cups, Coffee Cups** or **Tea Cups**)

Custard Cups

The charming, small, covered, globular custard cups (Plate 204) are very rare but were sometimes decorated with the standard 'Redgrave' patterns (page 105).

Dessert Services

The Lowestoft factory does not appear to have made dessert services, for I do not know of any centrepieces or side dishes such as are found with dessert services from the other eighteenth century porcelain factories. As a general rule the Lowestoft management would appear to have steered clear of dishes and plates.

There is, however, a possibility that some Worcester styled, blue printed dessert services were made between 1775 and 1785, as the oval baskets and stands (Plate 133) may have been part of such sets and some plates with the same blue printed pine cone design are recorded (Plate 128), but these are of dinner service size, rather than the smaller dessert size.

Dinner Services

Very few dinner services can have been made at the English Lowestoft factory for only two large tureens from such services appear to be recorded, but these and some some matching large octagonal dishes (Plate 97) suggest that some sets were made during the 1765-70 period. Shaped edged plates very rarely occur.

After 1775 some dinner sets may have been made and decorated with Worcester-type printed designs, for a few plates are known (Plate 128) and these may originally have been part of dinner services. No true Lowestoft sets are known with overglaze enamel decoration.

The dearth of true Lowestoft dinner services is in marked contrast to the abundance of so-called 'Chinese Lowestoft', or 'Oriental Lowestoft', sets imported from China and often made to European design. These hard-paste dinner sets were the fashionable wares of the period and were surprisingly cheap, underselling our native products, see my standard work *Oriental Export Market Porcelain*.

Dishes

Lowestoft dishes are extremely rare, and I have already stated that no dessert dishes are known, but some large dishes, presumably originally from dinner services, were painted in underglaze blue. A typical example is shown in Plate 97 and this can be found in various sizes.

Egg Cups

Three typical egg cups are shown in Plate 109, the left-hand example being the earliest, dating from the mid-1760s. The tall one in the middle is decorated with an underglaze blue print, while the low variety shown on the right is painted in the late bright blue, and is of the 1785-95 period. All Lowestoft egg cups are rare.

Egg Drainers

Circular, small, saucer-like objects, some two inches in diameter, were pierced with numerous small holes and fitted with a loop handle. These are sometimes called tea strainers, but the accounts of other factories, where these objects were also made, show that they were egg drainers, and that they were sometimes sold with matching egg cups. Lowestoft specimens are extremely scarce.

Egg Stand

A small octagonal stand on four paw feet is in the Victoria and Albert Museum and has been called an egg stand. It has a central depression (painted with the Arms of Great Yarmouth, and inscribed 'A Trifle from Yarmouth') with around the edge four circular depressions interspersed with four oval depressions — which are too small for hens' eggs.

It appears to have been made in the 1790s, but this is the only example known to me.

Ewer and Basins (see **Water Ewer and Wash Basins**)

Eye Baths

All eighteenth century English porcelain eye baths are rare, the Lowestoft examples being especially attractive as they are relief moulded in the Hughes-style (see Plate 78 and page 54). Some slight variations may be found in the raised designs and in the style of the underglaze blue painting.

Feeding Cups

Feeding cups, or 'pap boats', are rare articles, especially the early hand painted examples produced before the underglaze blue printed designs were introduced in the 1770s. A perhaps unique miniature, or toy feeding cup, painted in black with a local view, is shown in Plate 113, while the full size standard shapes are illustrated in Plates 122A and B, the straight-sided one being the commonest and those with shaped sides are rare. Several different handle forms are recorded.

Figures

Contrary to popular belief, the Lowestoft factory did make porcelain figures, for four models are known (two pairs), and there is a possible fifth model (Plate 170) while others may well await discovery.

As stated on page 139 the Lowestoft figure models are found in two varieties, one with typical body and glaze, and with raised leaves and flowers which match those found on other Lowestoft porcelains. Figures of this type are shown in Colour Plate 8 and Plates 173, 180, 181 and 184. The other earlier class is made from a harder body and glaze, with applied flowers of quite a different type — with thin leaves and flowers. The style of painting, as described on page 140, is also different from that on the first mentioned class.

A charming pair of putti are shown in Plate 173. A head from such a figure occurs as a knob on a Lowestoft lid, and an unglazed arm was found on the factory site; the porcelain, glaze and flat, glazed over base links with other wares from this factory. The small putti shown in Plate 169 are not Lowestoft (page 135).

The finest Lowestoft figures are standing musicians, one playing a triangle, the other a mandolin or lute, although these instruments are now often missing. These figures are found on four footed bases (Plates 175 and 176) and on low mounds, the problem class being found both coloured and in an undecorated, white state. A related standing pipe player is shown in Plate 170, this example, the only one as yet recorded, having been discovered by the writer in 1954 and now to be seen in the Christchurch Mansion Museum, Ipswich (see also page 139).

The later versions of the triangle and mandolin players are mounted on shaped mound bases (an unglazed fragment of which was recently found on the factory site), encrusted with the typical thick Lowestoft leaves and flowers seen on many covers, baskets and similar Lowestoft objects (Plate 179). An unglazed arm from the female mandolin player was found on the factory site, and also the mould for the top half of her body (Plates 172, 182 and 183). Only five or six pairs of these figures are known, and these are as the pair shown in Plate 181, with one exception, a pair in the author's collection has a low floral encrusted 'bocage' of the typical Lowestoft flowers and leaves (Colour Plate 8 and Plate 180). One of these female figures is known mounted on a high circular base (Plate 184) and the style of this perhaps unique example indicates a late date, for this, and the related figures with the typical thickly applied leaves. This example, originally from the Aldred family, then from the Norman Baker and the author's collections, is now in the Christchurch Mansion Museum, Ipswich.

The final attribution of true Lowestoft figures was first published by the author in *The Connoisseur Year Book* (1957), in an account including additional supporting material, such as that provided by chemical analysis. The figures illustrated in Spelman's *Lowestoft China* of 1905 are now seen to be of Staffordshire origin, not Lowestoft, as believed at that time.

Flasks

The Lowestoft factory made several slim flasks (Plate 185) which seem to have been made to special order, for they are found inscribed with names and dates, or painted with special views, and do not appear to have been made with standard, impersonal patterns.

Appendix I lists dated examples of these (Plate 246), which are found ornamented both with underglaze blue and with overglaze enamels, although their production appears to have been limited to the post-1770 period. Unglazed 'wasters' of flasks were found on the factory site, and one very small, perhaps toy, flask is recorded.

Hors-d'Oeuvre Set

The circular, segmented dish (Plate 91) on a low foot is believed to be an hors d'œuvre dish. Other factories produced individual fan-shaped dishes that could be placed together to make a whole, similar to this Lowestoft example. A similar segmented dish, without foot, has recently been sold.

Individual hors d'œuvre dishes were also made, for a six-sided centre component is known and small fan-shaped dishes would originally have been grouped around this.

Inkpots

Inkpots were a popular form of gift and several inscribed examples are recorded (pages 220 and 221). Early examples, one dated 1766 being shown in Plate 84, are eight or nine sided, while later ones are circular, in each case having holes placed round the edge to hold the quills.

Most Lowestoft inkpots are painted in underglaze blue (Plates 247-8), but some enamelled examples are recorded, and these include some 'Trifle' pieces (see Plate 225 and page 242). The factory site has yielded several fragments of these inkpots which were seemingly made in large quantities but all examples are now very rare.

Jars

A tall, open jar, ten inches high, in the Castle Museum, Norwich, catalogue number 196, is of barrrel shape. This rare, and perhaps unique object bears a central panel of the owner's initials, but its original purpose is not known.

Other, rare, smaller, jar-like objects are perhaps tobacco jars.

Jugs

The Lowestoft factory made a fine array of jugs which may, in fact, be regarded as one of their special lines. In this section the open jugs (without covers) will be discussed first, and no account will be taken of vessels of jug form less than six and a half inches high, as these are regarded as milk (or cream) jugs.

One of the earliest recorded types of relief-moulded jug is illustrated in Plate 56, formed in a three-part mould rather than the normal two, and also most unusual in that the reliefs are spaced all over the body without space for a painted panel.

Later versions of relief-moulded jugs had, in most cases, a plain central band running round the body, normally painted with Chinese-style landscapes in underglaze blue (Plates 57 and 79). The relief-moulded borders vary quite considerably, but the motifs often included the popular sunflower-like device. These moulded jugs were made from the 1760s onwards, the post-1770 ones being of the later 'floury body' and some rare specimens painted in overglaze enamel colours rather than the earlier underglaze blue. At least five quite different varieties were made.

A later, quite rare version of the moulded jug is a copy of the well-known and popular Worcester cabbage leaf jug (Plate 123), a half mould for which was found on the factory site, and these may be found with, or without, the mask head spout, the Lowestoft version of this feature being far larger and fatter than those of Worcester and Caughley. The Lowestoft examples are nearly always decorated with Worcester-style printed patterns and, like other jugs, these cabbage leaf moulded specimens were made in different sizes. A similar jug shape lacks the cabbage leaf moulding on the body.

As a contrast to these jugs, with their relief-moulded embellishments, we have a series of noble, hand thrown jugs. Two early specimens are shown in Plates 39 and 44, and two, rare, larger examples are illustrated in Plates 45 and 46, showing the variations that can occur when the same basic design is painted by different work people. The jug shown in Plate 46 is rare, in that there is no footrim showing, and the examples depicted in Plates 44-6 belong to the 1760-5 period.

A very rare form of small jug is a bell-shaped mug, with a lip set in the top edge, opposite the handle, an example of 1773 being shown in Plate 111.

From about 1770 a class of jug, of which typical examples are shown in Plates 140, 158 and 189, was made without any foot showing on the outside, and this shape is found with underglaze blue designs as well as enamelled decoration. These jugs, apparently unique to the Lowestoft factory, were originally sold with covers (which are, however, often missing today) and the lip is normally fitted with a pierced straining wall.

There is a related class of covered jug which differs only in that there is a turned foot (Plate 135). All these jugs were hand thrown on the potter's wheel, so that the outline of the body varies quite considerably and, of course, they may be found in different sizes.

Several of both types were decorated to order for presentation, but their original use is open to some doubt; they are often classed as coffee pots, but are not found with tea and coffee services, nor are the patterns those found in such sets, and the existence of the strainer holes indicates that they were not water jugs. They certainly appear to have been made as individual articles, not as part of a service, and they could well have been punch, or perhaps cordial jugs, for one, bearing the owner's name, John Ward, has a long verse on the front, which includes the line:

Then give me Punch and tell me why

Knife and Fork Handles

Unglazed 'wasters' found on the factory site show that two types of knife and fork handles were made at the Lowestoft factory. One is attractively relief moulded in the Hughes tradition, see drawing below but I have never seen a complete and glazed example.

Of the second, unembellished, pistol handle type, two fine and early specimens of the period, c.1757-60, are shown in Plate 40. A few other examples of this type have come to light but these are rather smaller than the Godden specimens.

Knife Rests

A pair of 'knife rests' from a private collection was included in the Catalogue of the *Lowestoft China Bicentenary Exhibition* held at Ipswich in 1957, and although I have not seen these examples two comments could be made. Firstly, as contemporary accounts clearly show, objects which are so often called 'knife rests' were really made as asparagus servers; these servers are of fan shape, with open ends and with turned up sides. Secondly, they were popular articles made at several factories including Caughley and Derby. I have not seen a Lowestoft one and feel that the examples cited as Lowestoft could be of Derby make.

Leaf Dishes

Leaf dishes, of which three extremely rare examples of the 1757-60 period are shown in Plate 33, were made from the earliest days of the factory. The body and covering glaze is as described on page 51; two of the illustrated examples are reversed and show the characteristic veining — one with these features relief moulded, the other impressed into the body. (See also Colour Plate 1.)

Plate 103 shows three different types of leaf dish, the middle specimen being that most commonly found but, of course, the same basic shape was made at several other factories. The other two relief-moulded examples are very rare and probably unique to this factory. Christopher Spencer in his book *Early Lowestoft* illustrates another rare version of that shown in Plate 103, right, with three relief moulded leaves and sprays of blackcurrants. This is Mr. Spencer's Plate 112.

Other leaf dishes are illustrated in my Plate 116, the smaller of the deep ones of a form made also at Caughley, Derby and Worcester, and the other also a variation of a Worcester (and Caughley) form, the Lowestoft version being, however, longer and narrower than the original and lacking the relief moulding found under the base of the Worcester dishes. The small, flat leaf dish would appear to be of a design restricted to the Lowestoft factory. As with most other basic shapes these leaf shape dishes may be found in various sizes.

Milk Jugs

Jugs over three and a half inches, and less than six and a half inches high, may be regarded as milk jugs, as opposed to the smaller cream jugs. See my comments on cream jugs, page 201. They are normally of the sparrow beak variety and are sometimes found with matching teawares (Plate 142). It would appear that such milk jugs were originally fitted with covers (Colour Plate 9), although these are seldom found today. These large milk jugs are mainly found with post-1770 services and all specimens are rare (Plates 131 and 197).

Another rare form of jug, with bulbous body and straight-sided neck, is painted in enamel colours with the Arms of Monro of Bearcroft, and is illustrated in *The Connoisseur* magazine, October 1937. One of similar form, but painted in underglaze blue, with the inscription 'A Trifle from Lowestoft', was in the Wallace Elliot Collection, and would appear to belong to the 1785-95 period.

Miniature or 'Toy' Wares

One of the most charming of the Lowestoft lines is the miniature tea services made as playthings for the children, and it is surprising that any specimens of these porcelain toys exist today.

In fact, they may be found in several hand painted patterns, often scaled-down versions of stock designs; some miniature teawares were painted in overglaze enamel, but most were painted in underglaze blue.

These fascinating wares, of which a typical toy teapot is shown, with two creamers, in Plate 87, are dealt with fully by the late D.M. Hunting in an article contained in *The Antique Collector* magazine of November 1949.

The standard type of toy teapot measures only some three inches high, but there are some very rare examples which are a little larger, standing between three and three-quarters and four inches high. These are obviously too small for normal use, as they contain less than a cup of tea, and the fact that one of these middling pots in my own collection is inscribed 'A Trifle from Lowestoft' (see Colour Plate 2), suggests that they were sold as mementoes.

Mugs

It would appear from a few surviving sets, as Plates 17 and 160, that these articles were originally made in sets of graduated sizes, and from the number of inscribed mugs that are recorded it would seem that they made a popular presentation gift. Others were, of course, painted with stock patterns without any special embellishment.

While most of them made before 1775 are of a graceful bell shape (some of which, of the 1760s, are illustrated in Plates 81, 82 and 98), a few early examples, such as those shown in Plates 83 and 108, with typical handles, are cylindrical, and after about 1775 this shape largely replaced the earlier bell form. Typical examples are shown in Plates 147, 151 and 160. Until about 1785 the handle is of simple loop form, with thumb rest, but some later examples, and most inscribed 'Trifle' mugs, have the handle form shown in Colour Plate 11 and Plate 216, though a very rare form of double curved handle occurs on a 'Trifle' mug in the Victoria and Albert Museum. A cylindrical mug, of a type very rarely encountered, is shown in Plate 211, having a turned foot, and there also exists a tall, slender mug with a slight 'waist', and an attractive barrel-shaped mug which was occasionally employed in the 1790s (Plate 224). These may have a simple loop handle or, rarely, a double curved one.

Mustard Pots

Mustard pots are very rare in all eighteenth century porcelains, two Lowestoft shapes being shown in Plate 114.

Mustard pots were made for two quite separate kinds of mustard — wet, that is, mixed mustard that could be spooned on to the plate, and dry, that is, in powder form. The low mustard pots were for wet mustard, and a still rarer vase-shaped pot, an outline drawing of which is reproduced here, was intended for the dry.

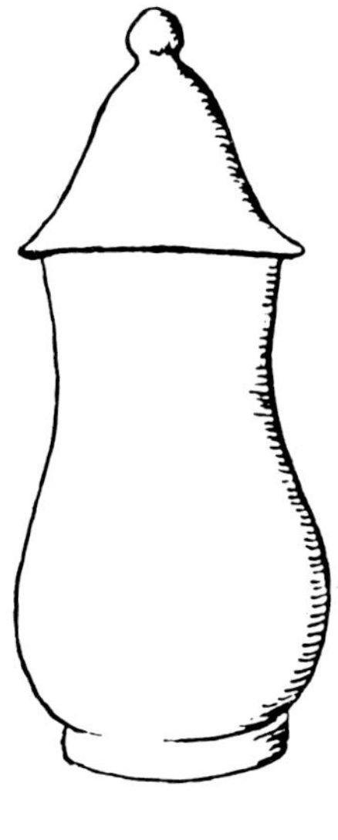

Oil-Bottles

The graceful, small, lipped, bottle-like object shown in Plate 90 — quite an early piece, of about 1765 — is believed to be an oil (or vinegar) bottle. A peculiarity of these rare bottles is the piercing of the handle, which was perhaps done so that the stopper or cork could be fixed by string to the handle, and could be kept from soiling the table.

Pap Boats (see **Feeding Cups**)

Pap Warmers

These rare objects, a typical example of which is shown in Plate 104, are the most intricate large wares to have been made at the Lowestoft factory, seemingly between 1760 and 1775. The main body is in three parts: a cylindrical body, with an opening in the front for the insertion of the burner; a bowl, in which the pap was held for warming, and a cover which is surmounted by a candle holder.

All known examples are decorated in underglaze blue and are, of course, very rare, showing signs of usage in the form of damage. The oil holder is nearly always missing, but an example is also shown in Plate 104, together with an unglazed factory 'waster' of the wick holder, with pierced knob.

While these pap warmers are well known in Continental porcelain and in earthenware (the Wedgwood factory made many in undecorated creamware), the only examples recorded in eighteenth century English porcelain are these blue and white Lowestoft ones, and some rare Chelsea examples of the 1755-60 period. The name often given to food and drink warmers of this general type is *Veilleuse*, and the standard work on these objects is *Veilleuses* by Harold Newman (1967).

Patty Pans

Circular patty (or tart) pans were made at Lowestoft from the early 1760s, the earliest being of the compact body, the later ones of the 'floury' porcelain. The standard shape of patty pan, typical examples of which can be seen in the Victoria and Albert Museum, had straight, angled sides as drawn below, and these were made in graduated sizes ranging from about three inches in diameter to six inches. A fragment of a very early example is shown by Spelman in his *Lowestoft China* (1905), Plate XLIX (see also Plate 31 of the present work).

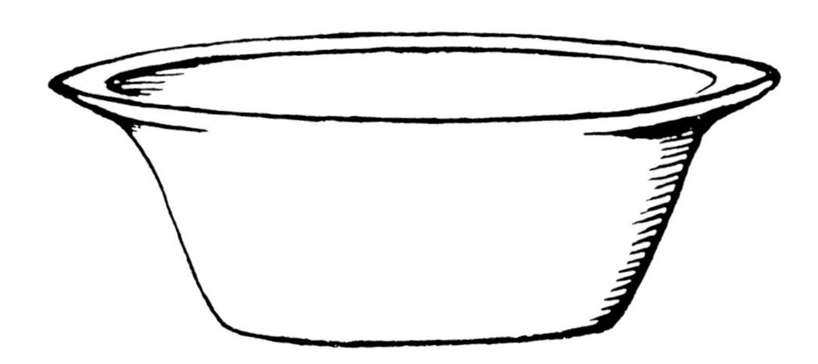

A rarer form has shaped sides, like the example illustrated in Plate 137, and these, too, were made in different sizes but the patty (or tart) pans were always painted in underglaze blue.

Pickle Dishes (see **Leaf Dishes** or **Shell-Shaped Dishes**, pages 207 and 212)

Pipe Stoppers

One of the rarest objects made at the Lowestoft factory must have been the pipe stopper, illustrated in Plate 182, which was intended to compact the tobacco in the bowl of the pipe. This Lowestoft example is in the British Museum and is here shown with a cast taken from the mould found on the factory site. The only other recorded example is in the Godden collection.

Plates

Dinner services were seldom made at the Lowestoft factory, so that plates are quite rare, although as some were inscribed and dated we may assume that these were made for presentation. The standard shape of large plates is shown in Plates 85 and 110, the flower painted example of 1766 probably being unique, for the decoration is certainly so uncharacteristic that this plate remained in a Brighton shop for several weeks with a price tag of under fifteen pounds! While most plates are circular, an octagonal variety was probably made to match the dish shape shown in Plate 97.

Saucer-shaped plates, without a condiment flange, were the bread and butter (or cake) plates originally sold in pairs, with a 'Full' teaset (Plates 95 and 202) but even these are now rare, although they must have been made during the whole length of the factory's existence. Relief-moulded Hughes-style plates are very rare. There is, in the Bernard Watney collection a fine, early, saucer-like bread plate with a wide, inner border of relief-moulded flowers, very similar to those round the rim of the jug shown in Plate 56.

Some small plates, with a diameter of about six inches, are occasionally found, normally with one of the blue printed designs. However, I have a charming blue painted small plate slightly more than five inches in diameter. Apart from the bread and butter plates sold with tea services, I do not know of any Lowestoft plates with overglaze enamel decoration.

Some rare late plates should have a shaped edge moulded with basketwork border, unglazed fragments of these French-styled plates having been found on the site, and are to be seen in the Castle Museum, Norwich.

Plaques

A circular plaque (5¾ inches in diameter) similar to an enlarged birth tablet is in the Castle Museum, Norwich. Painted in enamel colours with a scene from La Fontaine's fables, and having the initials R.P. on the back, this plaque is attributed to Richard Powles (page 159) and is probably a unique piece. It is illustrated in *The Connoisseur* magazine, October 1937, and in *English Porcelain, 1745-1850* (1965), Plate 47A.

A further plaque-like object is in the Fitzwilliam Museum at Cambridge, and this has a relief-moulded edge, partly hidden by the decoration.

Porringers

One of the most attractive of the Lowestoft forms is the rare, double handled porringer (Plate 153). A fine early example of about 1760-5, painted in underglaze blue, was included in the sale of the Hunting Collection in 1961, but the form appears again in the 1770s, as is evidenced by the porringer of the same basic form, shown in Plate 153, with overglaze enamel painting by the 'Tulip painter' (page 180).

Pounce Pots

Tub-like pounce pots, with pierced tops from which the pounce was sprinkled as a drying agent before the days of blotting paper, were made at Lowestoft and they are recorded with underglaze blue decoration as well as overglaze enamelled patterns.

All examples are now rare, and those inscribed 'A Trifle from Lowestoft' are especially desirable, but that shown in Plate 225 seems to be unique.

Preserve Pot

The conical pot shown in Plate 200 with its overlapping cover is believed to be a preserve (or honey) pot. This example, from the Christchurch Mansion Museum at Ipswich, is enamelled in the formal floral Curtis style and could well have been used with tea services decorated in a similar style. These conical pots are extremely rare.

The covered pot illustrated in Plate 220 is probably also a preserve pot. It has the unusual overlapping cover found on the pot discussed above, but appears to be the only example of this shape recorded.

Salad Bowls

The lobed-edge bowl shown in Plate 101 is probably a salad bowl. The style of decoration belongs to the 1768-72 period but the shape is extremely rare.

The later salad bowl illustrated in Plate 127 is a copy of a popular Worcester model. The outline form is the same, as is the blue printed decoration, but in some examples the relief moulding found on the inside of the Worcester (and Caughley) salad bowls does not not occur in the Lowestoft copies.

I do not know of any Lowestoft salad bowls bearing overglaze decoration.

Salts

An extremely rare and attractive six-sided, footed salt, with relief-moulded sides, is shown in Spelman's *Lowestoft China*, Plate LXII, and this is the only specimen of this type known to me. This is illustrated by Christopher Spencer, figure 130.

The attractive salt cellar illustrated in Plate 119 is based on a well known and popular silver shape. It is one of a pair, dating from about 1770 to 1775 and represents one of the rarest utilitarian table articles ever made at Lowestoft. A very rare earlier example of the 1758-60 period was sold in 1970. This specimen is illustrated by Christopher Spencer, figure 129.

Other shapes of salt cellar may have been made but they are not, as yet, positively identified. For example, an oval shaped cellar may have been made but the attribution to the Lowestoft factory is open to some doubt.

Sauce Boats

Many relief-moulded sauce boats were made from the earliest days at Lowestoft, all of which are most attractive and a collection could be formed of these articles alone. They were originally sold in matching pairs but pairs are seldom found today.

One cannot hope to illustrate all moulded forms of sauce boat, but typical specimens are shown in Plates 37, 38, 58, 59, 68, 69 and 70. The sizes differ slightly, ranging in overall length from eight to six inches (Plate 68), those of smaller dimensions being butter boats (page 198). One early and very rare moulded design incorporates four strutting birds, see Plate 10.

While most sauce boats were attractively relief moulded in the Hughes style (page 54), some, very rare, examples are devoid of any relief ornamentation (Plate 89). With the exception of some small boats, which were perhaps for butter, these articles were painted in underglaze blue, rather than with overglaze enamel colours.

The earliest were of the compact body, permitting good relief moulding such as can be seen in Plate 59, but some examples of the 1770s and early 1780s are of the 'floury' body with rather blurred moulding (Plate 131).

A wide, shallow form of fluted sauce boat, which is rare, is shown in Plate 124, with the basic shape copied from Worcester and also occurring in Caughley and Derby porcelains. The Lowestoft examples date from about 1770 and are normally decorated with underglaze blue prints.

Sauce boats do not appear to have been made at Lowestoft in the 1790s, but then nor were they made at Worcester at this late period.

Scent Bottles

Two distinct forms of porcelain scent bottles were made at the Lowestoft factory but examples are exceedingly rare.

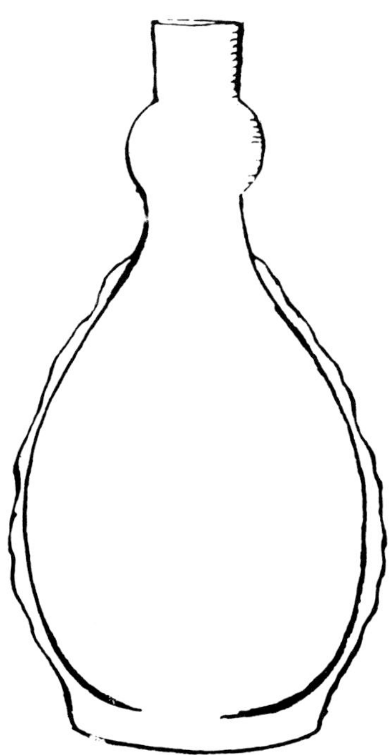

One moulded specimen, dated 1784, is illustrated in Plate 206. The outline of a further shape is reproduced above, a unique enamelled example of which is reproduced in the Crisp Collection Catalogue (1907) and is inscribed with the initials R.B. and decorated with a scene of the inside of a grocer's shop.

Shell-Shaped Dishes

One of the earliest Lowestoft productions comprised small dishes modelled on an oyster, or scallop, shell (Plate 32). These, now extremely rare, specimens of the 1757-60 period, are realistically shaped and the mould (or even each individual article) could well have been produced by the simple expedient of employing a real shell. The earliest versions were mounted on two or, sometimes, three conical feet as shown in Plate 32.[1]

The same basic form was employed in the 1760s but these are mounted on triangular feet (Plate 92) and are painted in the later dark blue.

A still later version, of the 1770s, has a standard, continuous footrim. These are in the 'floury' body and the moulding is not nearly as sharp as the earlier shell dishes, nor are the later ones as thinly potted (Plate 105). A part mould for such a late shell dish was found on the site.

Spittoons

Squat, globular, vase-like articles with a wide, open rim are often referred to as spittoons or cuspidors, but they could have been used for bulbs, as some accounts feature saffer pots.[2] Whatever their original use, the Lowestoft management produced these articles, the post-1775 examples were seemingly modelled after Worcester originals, and the rare Lowestoft examples normally bear a blue printed Worcester-type printed design. Some were equipped with a handle, but this is the exception rather than the rule.

Spoons

It is difficult to identify Lowestoft spoons with certainty. Some small examples must have been made to fit the mustard pots (Plate 114) and Dr. Watney, in his *English Blue and White Porcelain of the 18th Century* (1963), illustrates in Plate 82B a form of spoon which was copied from the Chinese, and produced at several English factories. These are very difficult to identify with certainty.

Spoon Trays

Spoon trays, on which the hot, wet teaspoons were placed, were originally included in some eighteenth century 'Full' tea services.

The earliest recorded Lowestoft shape is illustrated in Colour Plate 5 and this is of the 1758-60 period. Some few spoon trays of the 1760s are recorded. These are slightly smaller and a simplified version of the earliest variety; one is in the Hove Museum in Sussex.

I do not know of any spoon trays with relief-moulded Hughes-type decoration to match the teawares shown in Plates 54-5, 63-5, 72, 77, but examples were probably made. The attractive, small, shaped-edged, square tray shown in Plate 96 was probably intended as a spoon tray, as examples bear patterns found in tea services. The raised sides of these rare trays vary in the degree of the shaped edge, some being finely shaped.

The standard form of Lowestoft spoon tray is shown in Plate 139, having flat, glazed over bases, without any footrim. An extremely rare form, with a low footrim, is shown with the Ludlow teaset in Plate 202. All Lowestoft spoon trays are now extremely rare, and it is likely that originally these objects were included only in the most expensive 'Full' services, not with the less expensive standard, or 'short', sets.

---

1. A very similar form was apparently made at the short-lived works of Bonnin and Morris, at Philadelphia, U.S.A. (c.1769-1772) and such rare examples may bear the initial mark 'P' in underglaze blue. See *The Social History of the Decorative Arts Pottery and Porcelain, 1700-1914* by Bevis Hillier, Plates 124 and 125.
2. See the author's *Caughley and Worcester Porcelains, 1775-1800.*

Sugar Bowls or Sucriers

The covered bowl, with bird knob, illustrated in Plate 47, was probably the sucrier, or sugar bowl, from an early teaset of about 1760, and the relief-moulded one shown in Plate 53 is also possibly a sugar bowl from an early Hughes-type tea service (but see page 68). The relief-moulded Hughes-style, sucrier and cover shown in Plate 74 is a very rare example, even rarer than the few surviving teapots, of about 1764, and would have accompanied teawares illustrated in Plates 75 and 76.

Some attractive Lowestoft sugar bowls, including the toy sucriers belonging to the miniature teasets, are copied from a Chinese model and these have an inverted saucer-like cover (Colour Plate 9 and Plate 187B). A further standard shape of the 1775-85 period has a high cover with floral knob. This form was made either fluted (Plate 142) or plain, and each is found with underglaze blue patterns, or with enamelled designs.

As stated on page 198 most inexpensive services were sold with open sugar bowls — a scaled-down version of the waste bowl — not with the more expensive covered sugar bowl.

Some late teasets of the 1780s and the 1790s have fluted open sugar bowls, to match the objects shown in Plates 231 and 232.

Tankards (see Mugs)

Tea Bowls

Simple tea bowls, that is, handleless tea cups, were thrown, individually, on the potter's wheel, so consequently the shape varies greatly, and apart from noting the triangular footrim there is little to say about these simple little bowls, which were made at all periods of the factory's history.

The tea bowls, of course, follow the basic design of the tea service so that, apart from the simple, hand thrown examples, one finds moulded, ribbed or fluted bowls (Plates 73 and 142) and relief-moulded Hughes-type designs (Plate 76), and several fragments of these were found on the factory site as well as parts of the plaster moulds from which they were formed. An unusual form of teabowl occasionally used after about 1785 has a shaped profile, as shown in Plate 219.

Tea Caddies or Canisters

The large-sized relief-moulded canisters shown in Plate 67 are perhaps the most magnificent made at any English porcelain factory. Similar specimens were made for eight or nine years from c.1760. An early example is shown in the late D.M. Hunting's paper *Early Lowestoft*, published in the *Transactions of the English Ceramic Circle* (Vol.3, Part 1, 1951) and others are in the Castle Museum, Norwich, and in the Victoria and Albert Museum. They were originally sold in pairs but today the collector is lucky to find even one, and the covers are nearly always missing. Different initials occur in the panels at the end of these caddies indicating the class of tea, for example, 'H' for Hyson. It is probable that these large caddies were not sold (and used) with tea services, but that they were in a fitted wood tea caddy with a bowl for mixing the types of tea according to individual taste. The moulding on each side of the canister is slightly different.

Small, attractive, eight-sided tea canisters were sold with tea services of the same pattern, and may be found with Hughes-type raised motifs (Plates 64 and 65) or with only the underglaze blue painting, both types being now very rare. A squat, vase-shaped tea canister was included in powder blue decorated teasets of the 1760s, and may also have been included in other sets of this period.

From the 1770s the standard tea canister form is as that shown in Plates 129, 142, 146 and 228, the ribbed form is rare, but the plain version is found with many different forms of decoration, both in underglaze blue and in overglaze enamel colours.

A rare type of Lowestoft tea canister is of an attractive vase form (Plate 193), normally decorated with overglaze enamel colours, while a further, rare, taller, vase-like caddy has a hat box type cover.

Tea Cups

Tea cups were very rarely made at Lowestoft, most tea services being equipped with handleless tea bowls (page 214) or with narrow, upright coffee cups (page 200), but nevertheless some handled tea cups were occasionally provided, see page 24 and Plate 8.

Tea Services

A 'Full' tea service would have comprised:

Teapot and cover
Teapot stand
Coffee pot and cover
Sugar bowl and cover
Slop bowl
Spoon tray
Tea canister
2 bread (or cake) plates
12 saucers
12 tea bowls
12 coffee cups

However, customers could order services to their individual requirements, and many people would choose the less expensive 'short' sets, with fewer cups and saucers and without the coffee pot, tea canister or spoon tray. Inexpensive sets had open bowls rather than covered sugar bowls. All units were made in several forms, some plain, others with moulded ribbing or fluting.

The component parts of two tea services are shown in Colour Plate 9 and Plates 142, 146 and 202. In this section the separate units are listed separately in the alphabetical order of their names.

Teapots

The majority of Lowestoft teapots are globular with a simple loop handle (Plates 112, 144, 147, 159, 187, 188, 202, 208, 210 and 214) but most early, pre-1763, examples have an attractive handle with a thumb rest at the top and a return 'kick' at the lower end (Plates 49 and 94). No pre-1760 pots are recorded but many must have been made, and will display the characteristics listed on page 81, perhaps having the open flower knob similar to that shown on the chocolate pot in Plate 35, and as the fragment shown in Plate 31.

Some rare early teapots are relief-moulded, with closely spaced ribbing (Plate 49), while others, also rare, have Hughes-type relief moulding (Plates 63 and 75). The 1764 versions of these, with the blue key border (Plate 75 and page 62) normally have an angled tapering spout, as opposed to the shaped spout found with the earlier pots (compare Plates 49 and 94 with Plates 75 and 77) and also the plain loop handle without thumb rest or 'kick' (compare Plate 63 with 75). The early pots have a ribbed, conical knob (Plate 63). Some, from 1764, have an acorn knob, others an open flower, as the sugar bowl (Plate 74), while some early plain ones have a turned mushroom-like knob.

One form of relief-moulded teapot with carnation motifs is of barrel shape (Plate 77), and some rare, plain teapots are also of this form, having underglaze blue (or enamelled) designs but no relief decoration.

The standard form of Lowestoft teapot from about 1770 into the 1790s is globular, with a plain loop handle and a plain ball knob to the cover, found with two types of spout, one slightly curved (Plate 142, 144, 188 and 208), the other nearly straight, but tapering (Plates 112, 147 and 159). Some seventy-five per cent of all Lowestoft teapots are of these two related types. Two rare variations of knob occur, one having an open flower with rather flat leaves, (Plate 19), the later version having a closed flower with thickly moulded leaves (Plate 142).

These plain globular teapots were individually formed on the potter's wheel so that the shape varies slightly, some specimens being low and rotund, others rather tall and narrow by comparison, and some late examples of about 1790 have a high dome cover. The size also varies greatly, ranging from seemingly miniature specimens to those of mammoth proportions, which are normally called punch pots. The globular teapot is also found with ribbing (Plate 142) and these are moulded, not hand thrown.

Several new forms of teapot were introduced in the late 1780s and 1790, but all these are very rare, and the simple globular shape remained popular until the last days. The rare forms are illustrated in Plates 203, 218 and 232, and a further form exists with a mushroom-like knob and a type of handle found on late mugs, and also on the rare ribbed diamond-shaped pot rather similar to the popular New Hall form of teapot (Plate 218). A further rare pot is shown in Plate 203, of a ribbed barrel shape, perhaps emulating a Worcester and Caughley form. A most attractive teapot is shown in Plate 232, and this shape would probably have accompanied cups of the type shown in Plate 231. A teapot occurs with a handle similar to that shown in Plate 132.

The potting characteristics of the Lowestoft teapots are recorded on page 81, and further information is contained in an interesting article by the late D.M. Hunting in *The Antique Collector* magazine, December 1951, illustrating many types of Lowestoft teapot.

Teapot Stands

The orthodox shape of the Lowestoft teapot stand is octagonal (Plate 146) and, like the spoon trays, these had a flat, glazed over base. A very rare variation, however, had a very low rounded footrim (Plate 202).

Some stands were relief-moulded in the Hughes style, but these are very rarely found today.

A late diamond-shape stand (Plate 205) was introduced in the 1780s to go with the silver-shape teapot form (Plate 218) but all forms of teapot stand are very rare and were perhaps sold only with the most expensive 'Full' tea services.

Tea Strainers (see **Egg Drainers**)

Trays

All known tray-like objects were probably intended as spoon trays or as teapot stands (pages 213 and 216).

Tureens

As previously stated, few dinner services were made at the Lowestoft factory and only two large tureens appear to be recorded; these are oval in form and bear the underglaze blue Chinese landscape design shown on the dish in Plate 97. A tureen, from a private collection, is illustrated as Plate 78A in Dr. B. Watney's *English Blue and White Porcelain of the 18th Century* (1963).

Some tureen-like objects are really butter pots (Plate 126 page 198), but a number of Lowestoft tureen shapes probably await discovery.

There are some rare, small-sized tureens or covered bowls, which are sometimes decorated with underglaze blue Worcester-type prints, and these may have been cream and sugar tureens from dessert services, one variety of which is recorded with a pierced cover.

Vases

Blue and white vases were made from the earliest days of the factory, the covers normally having bird knobs (Plates 36 and 48). These vases were hand thrown on the potter's wheel, so that slight variations of form and size occur, with appreciable differences also in the style of decoration. Five different examples are illustrated by the late D.M. Hunting in the *Transactions of the English Ceramic Circle*, Vol. 3, Part 1 (1951), and an attractive early specimen is shown in Plate LIX of Spelman's *Lowestoft China* (1905).

Several other vase forms were made and decorated in underglaze blue, but these are usually of small size, under six inches high (Plate 99), but see Colour Plate 1.

Other forms were made after about 1775 and these are enamelled in overglaze colours. Garnitures of five vases were made (Plates 198 and 201) most of which, however, have been split up over the years. Nearly all were decorated in the style of imported Chinese porcelain vases (Plate 199), but the Lowestoft soft-paste examples are smaller than the Chinese hard-paste versions. Exceptions to these Chinese-styled enamelled designs are the rare vases decorated by the 'Tulip painter' (page 105). We should note that some small covered 'vases' are in reality tea caddies from tea services (Plate 193).

Veilleuses (see **Pap Warmer**)

Wall Pockets

Wall pockets, of cornucopia shape, which were originally sold in pairs, are amongst some of the most attractive and rarest articles made at the factory. They also are some of the very few Lowestoft shapes which seem to have been copied from the Bow factory. A pair of Bow wall pockets is shown in Plate 15B of Dr. B. Watney's *English Blue and White Porcelain of the 18th Century* (1963), and it is noteworthy, first, that both the examples shown face the same way, whereas the Lowestoft ones are true pairs, the 'tails' turned in opposite directions and, second, that the outline of the top, front, edge of the Bow version, is much more shaped than that of the gently curved Lowestoft examples.

These rare wall pockets are, strangely, of two different mouldings. That illustrated in Plate 42, an early example of about 1760, shows a charming restraint of decoration and is covered with the wonderful, clear, warm, liquid glaze (also found on the articles shown in Plates 43 and 44), the relief decoration appearing in several places to have been sharpened up or chiselled by hand. Slightly later examples have the normal glaze and are thickly potted, showing none of the hand tooling displayed in the early pocket. Several unglazed fragments of these cornucopia-like wall pockets were found on the factory site. All completed specimens are decorated in underglaze blue and predate 1770.

Water Ewer and **Wash-Basin**

The purely utilitarian, simple ewers and basins have great charm. All appear to have been made before 1775 and are painted in underglaze blue, except for one ewer and basin which are undecorated apart from the name and date, 'Maria Ann Hoyle, 1770', inscribed under the base.

Most ewers and basins are decorated with Chinese-style landscape motifs or with floral pattern and even these with the standard designs are now very rare. The specimen shown in Plate 80 illustrates the standard shape but, of course, the scenic panels depicting local views are of extreme rarity. These pieces are now in the Castle Museum, Norwich, and are inscribed under the bases 'E.A. Lowestoft. 1764'. An early basin, of the 1757-60 period, is recorded, and others, with matching ewers, must have been made.

Additional forms

Other forms may well have been produced and await discovery, several covers having been recorded which do not fit any known object, and subsequent years may witness the discovery of new animal, or even figure models. I should always be pleased to hear from anyone who may have, or find, articles not in the preceding account.

APPENDIX I

Dated Lowestoft Porcelains

Inscribed and dated porcelains, made to individual order and often depicting local scenes or even events, have rightly a special appeal to collectors, for such pieces are, of course, rare and highly prized.

There are two published lists of such individual pieces (sometimes, though rarely, found in sets). The first, compiled by Mr. A.J.B. Kiddell, is incorporated in a paper read to the English Porcelain Circle[1] in 1929, and printed in that Society's *Transactions*, No. III (1931), while in 1968 Mr. George J. Levine published an alphabetical list of 'Inscribed Lowestoft Porcelain'. The author is indebted to both of these sources, although the following list includes several corrections and additional material.

Every named, initialled, inscribed or armorial piece is of interest and of special commercial value, as it is rare and reveals individuality of design but to the serious student the dated pieces are of even greater importance, as the sequence of changing shapes and styles of decoration can be studied, and dated within a very few years.

On the following pages the reader will find a chronological list of dated Lowestoft porcelain, with added notes. Where the pieces listed are in Public Collections the whereabouts[2] is given so that the pieces can be studied. All blue and white pieces listed as being in the Castle Museum, Norwich, are illustrated in Sheenah Smith's 1975 catalogue of that collection. Several of the examples listed are illustrated in this book (and other works) and in these cases cross references are given; cross references are also given, where applicable, to the priced sale records given in Appendix II. To make reference easy to pieces included in this list, each article is numbered with the prefix 'D' (for dated). This prefix avoids confusion with the numbered list of items sold by auction and given in Appendix II. Examples new to this revised edition have the suffix 'A' to preserve the original numbered sequence.

Such a list as this cannot be complete, for from time to time hitherto unrecorded examples are brought to light. Indeed, I should be most grateful to hear from readers who may own (or know of) dated examples not listed on the following pages.

---

1. Renamed and continued as the 'English Ceramic Circle'.
2. Some pieces listed as being on display in Public Museums are on loan from private collectors and these present notes do not necessarily indicate the *ownership* of pieces included in this list.

1761

D.1. *Teawares* bearing relief-moulded ornamentation sometimes have the date 1761 worked into the design (page 54 and Plates 54 and 63). See also sale records 59, 60, 106, 148, 203, 212.

D.2 *Birth tablet* (diameter 3⅛ ins.) circular and blue painted, to be found in the Castle Museum, Norwich, is inscribed,

MARY REDGRAVE
born Nov.19th
1761

but it is thought that this specimen was made and decorated some years after 1761, as it is out of character with other early Lowestoft porcelains. Furthermore, it has on the back a rough note of the same date that appears on the front and it would appear unnecessary to have noted '1761' on the reverse if the front was decorated in this year, and it seems possible that the tablet was made and inscribed in 1765, at the same time as the one made for Martha Redgrave, who was born on August 12th, 1765. The styles are certainly very much alike and both have undecorated backs, a most unusual characteristic, perhaps unique to these two Redgrave birth tablets.

This birth tablet (with the Martha Redgrave 1765 example) is illustrated in Dr. B. Watney's *English Blue and White Porcelain of the 18th Century* (1963), Plate 75C.

1762

D.3 *Inkpot* (2¼ ins. high), nine sided, painted in underglaze blue and inscribed with the initials and date,

R B
1762

Painter's number '5'.
See sale record 85, page 241.
This inkpot was included in the *Catalogue of Lowestoft China in the possession of Frederick Arthur Crisp* (1907), with the following note:

> bought 3 February 1896, of William Rix Seago of Lowestoft. This is the Ink Pot made for Robert Browne, one of the original partners (of the Lowestoft China Factory). It was sold to Mr. Seago, by his great-grandson, also a Robert Browne, and is referred to in his affidavit as 'Ink Pot with initials R B 1762. This was the original ink pot of the originator and manufacturer of the factory.'

It is illustrated in F. Litchfield's *Pottery and Porcelain* (1912), in *The Connoisseur* magazine, September 1937, and in Dr. B. Watney's *English Blue and White Porcelain of the 18th Century* (1963), Plate 74A, and may be seen in the Castle Museum, Norwich.

1763

D.4 *Punch Pot* (or enlarged teapot), very large pot 18½ ins. long, decorated with powder blue ground. Incised initials and date,

H C
1763

under the spout. This mammoth pot is on view in the Castle Museum, Norwich.

D.4A. *Tea Pot* (5½ ins. high) decorated with powder blue ground (similar to Plate 94 but with floral panels) and inscribed under the base,

1763
B
R + E

Sold at Christie's in November 1975.

D.5. *Cup*, painted in underglaze blue with flowers and inscribed,

J C
1763

1764

D.6. *Mug* (4⅖ ins.) of typical bell shape, painted in underglaze blue and inscribed, within a cartouche,

Ann Hammond
Woodbridge
April 9. 1764

The name 'Richard Phillips' appears below the handle and the painter's number '3' is placed inside the footrim (page 158 and Plate 81).

This mug is also illustrated in Dr. B. Watney's *English Blue and White Porcelain of the 18th Century* (1963), Plate 76B, and is to be seen in the Castle Museum, Norwich.

D.7. *Bowl* (diameter 8¼ ins.), painted in underglaze blue. The interior design is of a wagon approaching an Inn. The centre is inscribed,

Thos Bonner
Halsworth
Carrier
1764

Painter's number '3'.
This specimen is illustrated in *The Connoisseur* magazine, September 1937, and also in the *Transactions of the English Porcelain Circle,* No. III (1931), Plate V, and is now on display in the Castle Museum, Norwich.

D.8 *Pair of vase-shaped water bottles (9⅜ ins. high) and a basin,* painted in underglaze blue, with shaped-edge panels containing local views — e.g. St. Margaret's Church, Lowestoft. Inscribed under the bases,

E A
Lowestoft
1764

Painter's number '3'.
See sale record 136, page 244.

These rare pieces from the Colman Collection are now on view at the Castle Museum, Norwich, and the two water bottles or ewers are illustrated in *The Connoisseur*, September 1937, page 130. See also Plate 80 of this book.

1765

D.9 *Mugs*, a set of three bell-shaped, painted in underglaze blue with birds and foliage, and inscribed, under the base,

Abrm Moore
August 29th 1765

Painter's number '3'.
See sale record 178, page 247.

Two mugs from this set are illustrated in Plate 82, and a further example is in the British Museum.

N.B. Mugs bearing this inscription were copied on the Continent (see page 253 and Plate 241).

D.10. *Bowl* (diameter 9½ ins.), decorated in a similar style to the above mugs, and inscribed in the same manner.
Painter's number '3'.
This bowl is in the Castle Museum, Norwich.

D.11. *Bowl* (diameter 5ins.), painted in underglaze blue, with Chinese-styled scenes, and inscribed,

S C.
1765

Painter's number '5'.
Two bowls with this decoration and inscription are recorded.

D.12. *Bowl* (diameter 8ins.), painted in underglaze blue, the exterior painted with fishing boats, the interior with chained swan device, and also inscribed,

M P.
1765

This bowl is in the Castle Museum, Norwich.

D.13. *Birth Tablet* (diameter 3⅛ ins.) decorated in underglaze blue and inscribed,

Mar^tha^ Redgrave
born Augt ye 12th
1765

Illustrated in Dr. B. Watney's *English Blue and White Porcelain of the 18th Century* (1963), Plate 75C, it is to be seen in the Castle Museum, Norwich.

1766

D.14 *Mug* (4⅜ ins. high) of cylindrical form, painted in black, with Chinese figures and landscape, and inscribed, under the base,

Is Hughes
Lowestoft
Sep^br^ 4th 1766

Painter's number '3'.
See sale record 104, page 262.

This mug, which is illustrated in Plate 83, is a rare early example of black 'pencilling' (see page 28) and also of the cylindrical form of mug, for most early examples are of bell shape (Plates 81, 82 and 98).

This specimen is in the Christchurch Mansion Museum, Ipswich.

D.15. *Mug* (3½ ins. high), cylindrical, painted in underglaze blue, with birds and foliage, and inscribed, under the base,

John Waters
Fulmerdiston
1766

A larger mug with the same decoration and inscription is recorded and most mugs were originally sold in sets of three, of different sizes.

These inscribed examples have given the name 'Fulmerdiston birds' to designs of this general type (Plates 66 and 89). This mug is in the Castle Museum, Norwich.

D.16. *Low footed bowl*, or tazza (diameter 5½ ins., height 2ins.) painted in underglaze blue, with a standing figure (perhaps hoeing tobacco plants), inscribed round the inside of the rim,

Trulls. Best Virginia. Norwich.
October 14th, 1766.

Painter's number '3'.

This unique article is in the Castle Museum, Norwich, and is illustrated in *The Connoisseur* magazine, September 1937, and in the *Transactions of the English Porcelain Circle*, No. III (1931), Plate V.

D.17. *Cream* (or milk) *Jug*, painted in underglaze blue in the Chinese style, inscribed, under the base,

C
W M
1766

D.18. *Saucers* (two are recorded) painted in underglaze blue, with Chinese styled garden scenes and inscribed on the reverse,

M R
1766

Painter's number '3'.
One saucer is in the Cheltenham Museum.

D.19. *Inkpot* (2½ ins. high) of octagonal form, painted in underglaze blue and inscribed under the base,

John Mills *
July the 4th. 1766

Indistinct painter's number, perhaps '3'. The painting of the inscription is very similar to the floral plate described in D.21 and illustrated in Plate 85.

This inkpot is in the British Museum and is illustrated in *The Connoisseur*, June 1927.

D.20. *Inkpot* (2½ ins. high) octagonal, similar in general style to the John Mills inkpot listed above but inscribed,

* The name ends with an s-like flourish and could equally well be 'Mill' or 'Mills'.

S.A. Curties
July 4th 1766

Painter's number '3'.

This example (Plate 84) from the Wallace Elliot Collection is now in the Victoria and Albert Museum and is illustrated in *The Connoisseur*, June 1927.

D.21. *Plate* (9ins. in diameter), the front painted with a large single flower in underglaze blue (Plate 85). The reverse inscribed,

Charles Ward.
July the 5. 1766

with 'doodle'-like decorations in the form of e.g. scrolls. The style of the inscription is very similar to that on the John Mills inkstand, dated only a day previously, but the single flower motif appears to be unique and so unusual that it was on offer in a Brighton shop for several weeks at a price below twenty pounds but within three months was sold at Sotheby's for six hundred pounds.

1767

D.22. *Mug* (5¾ ins. high) of typical early bell shape, painted in underglaze blue with flowers and birds and inscribed,

Jno Stacy
Little Fransham
1767

Painter's number '5'.

D.23. *Teapot* (4¼ ins. high) of standard globular form, painted in underglaze blue, with a view of St. Margaret's Church, Lowestoft, and inscribed,

S.C.
1767

See sale record 82, page 241.
Painters number '5'.

Illustrated in the Catalogue of the F.A. Crisp Collection (1907), page 1, and in *The Antique Collector* magazine, December 1951, fig. 3.

D.24. *Teapot*, of standard globular form, painted in overglaze enamel colours and a canary yellow ground. Inscribed,

J.G.
1767

It is very likely that this inscription was added later, the style of decoration being that of the late 1770s or 1780s. This piece also shows the normal signs of a refired piece and it is to be seen in the Victoria and Albert Museum.

1768

D.25. *Mug* (4⅝ ins. high) of typical early bell shape, painted in underglaze blue with hunting scenes and inscribed,

Ed. Adams.
Brandeston
1768

This example is in the British Museum.

D.26. Set of *Mugs* (in graduating sizes 6, 4⅝ and 3¼ ins.) painted in underglaze blue with a rising sun device and the inscription,

Ed. Amond.
Wymondham
1768

Painter's number '5'.
See sale record 150, page 245).

Examples from this set of mugs are in the British Museum, the Castle Museum, Norwich and the Victoria and Albert Museum. One is illustrated in *The Connoisseur*, June 1927.

D.27. *Mug* (5¾ ins. high) again of typical bell shape, painted in underglaze blue with floral sprays and inscribed,

James Bullard
R.A.
1768

Painter's number '3'.
See sale record 151, page 246.
This example is illustrated in Plate 98.

D.28. *Mug* (4⅕ins. high) of typical bell shape, painted in underglaze blue, the front panel showing a figure hanging herrings over smoking fires, above the inscription,

John Cooper
1768

The initials R.P. are placed under the handle (see page 158) and the painter's number '3'.

This mug, in the Great Yarmouth Museum, is illustrated in Dr. B. Watney's *English Blue and White Porcelain of the 18th Century* (1963), Plate 76C, and was sold for £11 in 1902!

D.29. *Mug*, of typical bell shape, painted in underglaze blue with two stags and human head crest and the inscription,

John Cottingham
1768

D.30. *Mug*, of typical bell shape, painted in underglaze blue with face and sun rays device and inscribed,

Micl. Jaye
Norwich

Dated under the base — 1768.
See sale record 80, page 241.

D.31. *Teapot* (6ins. high) of conventional globular form, painted in underglaze blue with Oriental landscape design and inscribed,

Elizth Iohnson [Johnson]
Norwich
Febr 5th 1768

See sale record 77, page 241.
Painter's number indistinct, '5' or '6'.

This teapot is in the Castle Museum, Norwich, and is illustrated in *The Antique Collector* magazine, December 1951, fig. 3.

D.32. *Shallow Bowl* or circular dish (with a diameter of 11ins.) very well painted in underglaze blue on the inside, with 'Chinese Priests and Monks' in Oriental landscape. Inscribed under the base,

Elizath Buckle
1768

Painter's number '5'. The decoration of these pieces made for Elizabeth Buckle is traditionally attributed to Robert Allen but this artist would have been aged only about twenty-three in 1768 (page 145). This superb bowl is illustrated in Colour Plate 'D' of Dr. B. Watney's *English Blue and White Porcelain of the 18th Century* (1963) and also on the jacket of that work. It is shown in Plate 100 of the present book.

The superb and interesting bowl is now in the Castle Museum at Norwich having been purchased in 1982 by the Friends of the Norwich Museum with the help of the National Art Collections Fund, for the sum of £2,500.

D.32A. *Bowl* (diameter 9½ ins.) the exterior painted with floral sprays in underglaze blue. The interior inscribed,

Ino. Welton
Badingham
1768

Painter's number '5' on inside of footrim.
On loan to the Castle Museum, Norwich.

D.33. *Bowl* (diameter 9⅝ ins.) painted in underglaze blue with flowers and butterflies, and inscribed,

Wlm Barton
Forncett
1768

Painter's number '5'.
See sale record 133, page 244.

D.34. *Bowl*, painted in underglaze blue with flowers and a bird, inscribed,

Edward Morley
1768

See sale record 13, page 238.
This bowl is in the Castle Museum, Norwich.

D.35. *Bowl* (diameter 8¼ ins.) painted in underglaze blue with female figure holding a parasol and flowers and inscribed,

John Wright
Wangford
1768

This bowl is in the Castle Museum, Norwich and the interior is illustrated in *The Connoisseur* magazine, September 1937, page 133.

D.35A. *Bowl* (diameter 8½ ins.) painted in underglaze blue with emblems of freemasonry, Latin mottoes and flowers. Dated 1768.

This bowl is listed in the Schreiber Collection catalogued as Bow, but it appears to be of Lowestoft origin.

D.36. *Plate*, painted in underglaze blue with typical Chinese styled landscape design and inscribed on the reverse,

R.W.N.
1768

This plate is in the Victoria and Albert Museum, number c 125. 1924.

1769

D.37. *Mug* (4½ ins. high) of typical bell shape, painted in underglaze blue and inscribed,

'Add to Knowledge Temperance (II Peter)
James Last of Saxmundham
1769'

Painter's number '5'.
See sale record 190, page 248.

D.38. *Mug* (6ins. high) of typical bell shape, painted in underglaze blue with flowers and inscribed,

Ann Stockdale
1769

D.39. *Mugs* (4½ ins. high) of typical bell shape, painted in underglaze blue with flowers and inscribed,

Phill Tricker
1769

Painter's number '5'.
See sale record 78, page 241.

Two examples are recorded, one being in the Castle Museum, Norwich, the other in the Fitzwilliam Museum, Cambridge. One, from the Crisp Collection, is illustrated in F. Litchfield's *Pottery and Porcelain* (1912), page 258.

D.40. *Teapot* (4¾ ins. high) of typical globular form, painted in underglaze blue and inscribed,

Jeas Fisher
1769

Painter's number '5'.
See sale record 189, page 248.
This interesting teapot is in the Castle Museum, Norwich.

N.B. A polychrome decorated flask exists with the inscription,

'A Trifle from Lowestoft 1769'. This is not of Lowestoft make, nor is it of the 1769 period.

1770

D.41. *Mug* (5½ ins. high) of typical bell shape, painted in underglaze blue with flowers and inscribed,

Bridgit Turner
in Mullbarton Decem^r
the 12 1770

Painter's number '5'.

D.42. *Jug*, painted in underglaze blue, and inscribed.

James Green,
Wroxham,
1770

Painter's number '5'.

D.43. *Plate* (diameter 9ins.) painted in underglaze blue with floral sprays, and inscribed,

Willm & Mary
Ellis

The underside with the date 1770.

This plate is in the Christchurch Mansion Museum, Ipswich. See Plate 110.

D.44. *Sauceboat* (7½ ins. long) moulded in relief with sunflower-like motifs and inscribed in underglaze blue, on panels each side,

Made at Lowestoft, Sepr 6
in the preseence (sic) of J.S. Browne
Wardrobe Court
Doctors Commons, London
1770

Painter's number '5'.
See sale record 127, page 244.

This rare sauce boat from the Colman Collection is illustrated in *The Connoisseur*, September 1937, also in the *English Porcelain Circle Transactions*, No. III (1931), Plate VI, and is now in the Castle Museum, Norwich.

D.45. *Ewer and Basin* (water ewer 8½ ins. high) of typical shape but undecorated, except for the underglaze blue inscription, under the bases,

Maria Ann Hoyler
1770

See sale record 75, page 241.

D.46. *Sugar bowl* (of Chinese shape, as Plate 125) without cover, painted in underglaze blue with flowers and insects, and inscribed,

John & Elizh. Gibbs
1770

1771

It is in this year that we first find dated pieces with underglaze blue *prints*, as opposed to the hand-painted designs (D.51), although, of course, the hand-painted patterns were continued.

D.47. *Mug* (4½ ins. high) of typical bell shape, painted in underglaze blue with flowers, and inscribed,

A Maria Camm
Laneham
ex dono I H
Oldton
1771

Painter's number '5'.

A jug and teapot are recorded with the same inscription, see numbers D.52 and D.54.

D.48. *Mug*, of typical bell shape, painted in underglaze blue and inscribed,

Robt Crow
1771

D.49. *Mug* (4½ ins. high) of typical bell shape, painted in underglaze blue, and inscribed,

James & Mary Curtis
1771

See sale record 26, page 238.

This example is in the Castle Museum, Norwich, and is one of the pieces traditionally believed to have been painted by Thomas Curtis, but see page 152. It is illustrated in *The Connoisseur*, September 1937.

D.50. *Mug* (5ins. high) of typical bell shape, painted in underglaze blue and inscribed,

James Postans
Norwich
1771

Painter's number '5'.
See sale record 65, page 240.

D.51. *Mug* (5¾ ins. high) of typical bell shape, printed with floral sprays in underglaze blue, and inscribed,

Willm Mewse
Southwold
1771

This early example of underglaze blue printing is in the Bristol Museum.

D.52. *Jug* (7¾ ins. high) of typical form painted in underglaze blue, with flowers, and inscribed,

A Maria Camm
Laneham
ex dono I H
Oldton
1771

A matching mug and teapot are recorded, see numbers D.47 and D.54.

D.53. *Jug* (9½ ins. high) of typical form, painted in underglaze blue, and inscribed,

James Postans
Norwich
1771

Painter's number '5'.

This jug is in the Castle Museum, Norwich, and another, similar, one is recorded.

D.54. *Teapot* (6⅜ ins. high) of typical globular form, painted in underglaze blue with flowers, and inscribed,

A Maria Camm
Laneham
ex dono I H
Oldton
1771

Painter's number '5'.
See sale record 110, page 242.

A matching mug and jug are recorded, see numbers D.47 and D.52.
This teapot is illustrated in Plate 112.

D.55. *Bowl*, painted in underglaze blue and inscribed,

Ric'd Mason,
Jany 1st 1771

See sale record 1, page 237.

N.B. Some pieces of teaware are enamelled in overglaze puce colour with floral pattern and are inscribed J. Hoyler 1771. The author is personally not happy about the attribution and date, although they have been accepted by other collectors.

1772

D.56. *Mug*, of typical bell shape, painted in underglaze blue with an (inn sign?) depicting a negro in a shield, and inscribed,

John Harman
Beccles
1772

This example is in the Castle Museum, Norwich, and is illustrated in the *English Porcelain Circle, Transactions* No. III (1931), Plate 11A and in *The Connoisseur*, September 1937.

D.57. *Mug* (5¾ ins. high) of typical bell shape, painted in underglaze blue with a cross within a panel, and inscribed,

John Rolfe
Woodbridge

Dated under the base '1772'.
Painter's number '5'.
See sale record 135, page 244.

Illustrated in the *English Porcelain Circle, Transactions* No. III (1931), Plate 11B.

D.58. *Mug*, of cylindrical, straight-sided form, painted in underglaze blue and inscribed,

The Borlace
L: O: B:
1772

D.59. *Mug* (6¼ ins. high) of cylindrical form, painted in underglaze blue with floral sprays, and inscribed,

Timothy Turrall
Norwich
1772

This example is in the Castle Museum, Norwich.

D.60. *Jug* and cover, of typical form, printed and painted in underglaze blue with flowers, etc., and inscribed,

Jacob Shalders
Norwich
1772

This jug is in the Castle Museum, Norwich.

D.61. *Jug* (6½ ins. high) of typical form, *printed* in underglaze blue with floral sprays and butterflies, and inscribed,

John Baker
Yarmouth
1772

See sale record 130, and 248.

Illustrated in the *Transactions of the English porcelain Circle,* No. III (1931), Plate IVb. See also Plate 121.

D.62. *Jug* (5 ins. high) of typical form, painted in underglaze blue, with flowers and insects, and inscribed,

Sam[ll] Cubitt
Lowestoft
1772

This example is in the Fitzwilliam Museum, Cambridge.

D.63. *Jug* (7½ ins. high) painted in underglaze blue with flowers and butterflies, and inscribed,

Jers Smith
Claxton
1772

Painter's number '5'.

This example is in the Christchurch Mansion Museum, Ipswich.

D.64. *Teapot* (8½ ins. high) of large size, painted in underglaze blue with flowers and insects, and inscribed,

L.N.
1772

D.65. *Teapot*, of typical globular form, painted in underglaze blue with the Royal Arms and supporters, with also the initials and date,

G.R. 1772 on one side, and G.B. 1772 on the other

See sale record 31, page 238.
This example is in the Castle Museum, Norwich.

D.66. *Bowl* (diameter 9½ ins.) *printed* in underglaze blue, depicting a sportsman with gun, in landscape, and inscribed,

John & Ann Glasspool
Blundstone
1772

See page 102.

D.67. *Birth Tablet* (diameter 5ins.) painted in underglaze blue, the reverse with Chinese-styled houses, etc. The front inscribed,

Sarah Mason
born January 3rd
1772

See sale record 91, page 242.

Both sides of this tablet are illustrated in the Catalogue of the Crisp Collection (1907), page 14.

N.B. A low oblong salt, in the Castle Museum, Norwich, is inscribed under the base in underglaze blue.

M.S.
1772

but the present writer has reservations over the attribution to the Lowestoft factory. It is perhaps of Derby origin.

D.67A. *Feeding Cup* (3ins. high), the sides painted with flower sprays in underglaze blue, the anti-slop top inscribed,

Ann Smith.
Norwich
1772

1773

D.68. *Mug* (4½ ins. high) of typical bell shape, painted in underglaze blue, and inscribed,

Robert Feltum
Shottesham
1773

Painter's number '5'.

D.69. *Mugs*, set of three in graduating sizes, painted in underglaze blue, with floral sprays, and inscribed,

Willm Feltum
Shottesham
1773

See sale record 68, page 240.
One example from this set is in the Fitzwilliam Museum, Cambridge.

D.70. *Mug* (4½ ins. high) of bell shape, painted in underglaze blue with flowers and inscribed,

Ann Sawyer
1773

Painter's number '5' (rather indistinct).

D.71. *Jug* (5ins. high) painted in underglaze blue, with flowers and insects, and inscribed,

Willm Callow
Ludham
1773

Painter's number '5'.

This example is illustrated in *The Connoisseur*, September 1937, and the side-view in Plate 111 of the present work.

D.72. *Bowl* (diameter 7⅛ ins.) painted in underglaze blue, the interior with a ship, and inscribed below,

Robt. Harper
Cantley
1773

This bowl is illustrated in *The Connoisseur*, June 1927.

1774

This is the first year in which dated examples of overglaze enamel painting are recorded, although, of course, underglaze blue painting was also continued after this period.

D.73. *Jug* and cover, of typical form, painted in underglaze blue, and inscribed,

Willm Laddell
Crostwick
1774

This example is in the Castle Museum, Norwich.

D.74. *Inkpot* (2ins. high) painted in underglaze blue with scrollwork and crossed pens, and inscribed,

I (J) Heaton
1774

N.B. This example now does not appear to be Lowestoft, a Liverpool origin is more likely.

D.75. *Sauce boats* (4½ ins. long). A pair of small-sized moulded sauce boats decorated in black (or a very dark inky blue), and inscribed,

Miss de Vaux
1774

These sauce boats are in the Victoria and Albert Museum.

Enamelled Examples

D.75A. *Mugs* (6, 4¾ and 3⅝ ins. high). A superb set of three cylindrical mugs, painted in overglaze enamel colours by the 'Tulip painter' (see page 105), and inscribed,

J & E Tanton
Norwich
1774

See sale record 119, page 243.

This fine set of mugs is illustrated in *The Connoisseur*, June 1927, and is now on display at the Castle Museum, Norwich. One example is included in Plate 147.

D.76. *Mug* (6ins. high) of cylindrical form, painted in overglaze enamels, with flowers by the 'Tulip painter' (see page 105), and inscribed,

M Quinton
Norwich
1774

D.77. *Mug* (3⅗ ins. high) of cylindrical form, painted and slightly gilt, with floral sprays by the 'Tulip painter' (page 105) and inscribed,

Katherine Farquhar
1774

D.78. *Teapot* (6½ ins. high) of typical globular form, painted in overglaze enamel colours, with Chinese figures, pagodas, etc., and inscribed,

Maria Hoyle
Norwich
1774

This teapot is illustrated in Geoffrey Wills' *Country Life Book of English China* (1964), Plate 106.

D.79. *Teapot*, of small size but of typical globular form, painted in overglaze enamel colours and inscribed,

John of Thomas & Elizabeth Drake
Dec 6th 1774

D.80. *Bowl* (diameter 9½ ins.) finely painted in overglaze enamel colours, with a farmyard scene and inscribed,

John & Eliza Remmant
Success to the Jolly Farmer
1774

This bowl is illustrated in colour in W.W.R. Spelman's *Lowestoft China* (1905), Plate 1xxxix, and is now on display in the Castle Museum, Norwich.

D.81. *Creamboat* (4ins. long) of moulded 'Chelsea ewer' form (Plate 150) painted in overglaze enamel colours with flowers by the 'Tulip painter' (page 105) and inscribed inside,

G.G.M.H.
1774

See sale record 98, page 242.

This creamer is illustrated in *The Connoisseur*, October 1937, and is now in the Castle Museum, Norwich.

1775

D.82. *Birth Tablet* (diameter 2½ ins.) painted in underglaze blue. The reverse has a lady and gallant standing by a fence, and the front is inscribed,

Samuel Wright
Born January 30th. 1775

See sale record 97, page 242.

Both sides of this tablet are illustrated in the Catalogue of the Crisp Collection (1907), page 13.

D.82A. *Mug* (4½ ins. high) of cylindrical form, painted in underglaze blue with some overpainting in red enamel. The front inscribed,

Jacob & Mary
Bray
1775

This example also bears the painter's number '5' and is the latest example known to me with this feature.

D.83. *Mug* (4ins. high) of bell shape, painted in overglaze enamel colours, the front painted with the Arms of the Blacksmith's Company (perhaps by the 'Tulip painter', see page 105).
Inscribed under the base,

James & Sarah Hacon
1775

See sale record 103, page 242.

This unique mug is illustrated in colour in the Catalogue of the Crisp Collection (1907) page 7, and in *The Connoisseur*, October 1937. It is now on display in the Castle Museum, Norwich.

D.84. *Mug* (5¾ ins. high) of cylindrical shape, painted in overglaze enamel colours with floral sprays and rhyme, and inscribed,

Joseph Barker
Troston
1775

D.84A. *Mug* (4½ ins high) of cylindrical form, painted in overglaze enamels with floral sprays in the name of the 'Tulip painter' and inscribed,

Edwd. & Mary
Holley
1775

See Plate 124.

D.85. *Jug* and cover (9¾ ins. high) of typical form finely enamelled in overglaze enamels, the sides painted with figures in landscape, the front with rhyme and inscription,

Long may they live
Happy may they be
Blest with Content
and from Misfortune free
Manning & Elizebeth
Gooch
1775

See Plate 158.

1776

D.86. *Mug* (4⅜ ins. high) of cylindrical shape, painted in underglaze blue with flowers, and inscribed,

Robt. Howes
1776

See sale record 49, page 239.

D 87. *Jug*, of typical form, painted in underglaze blue with a verse, and inscribed,

Samuel Cubitt
Blofield
1776

This jug is in the Great Yarmouth Museum, and is illustrated in F. Litchfield's *Pottery and Porcelain* (1912), page 259.

D.87A. *Birth Tablet* (diameter 3ins.) of normal circular form with hole near top edge decorated on the reverse with floral prints in underglaze blue. Inscribed on the front,

E A
1776

(The sevens are painted in reverse!) Castle Museum, Norwich.

Enamelled Specimens

D.88. *Mug* (4½ ins. high) of cylindrical form, painted in enamel colours with Chinese figures, and inscribed,

Walter Snell
1776

This mug is in the British Museum.

D.89. *Jug* (5¼ ins. high) of typical shape, finely painted in overglaze enamel colours with flowers by the 'Tulip painter' (page 105) and inscribed,

C E
Heaman
1776

See sale record 57, page 240.

D.90. *Teapot* (5½ ins. high) of typical globular shape, painted in overglaze enamel colours with flowers on one side by the 'Tulip painter' (page 105) and inscribed on the other side,

Jane Wharlton
Gainsbrough
Lincolnshire
1776

D.91. *Teaset* (or rather part of a once complete teaset) of which the sugar basin, jug, and some cups and saucers are recorded. These pieces are decorated in red enamel and gilding, with grapes and trailing vines, and inscribed,

M & E
Calder
1776

See sale records 58, 61 and 198.

Some pieces are now in the Castle Museum, Norwich, but it appears likely from their form, as well as the style of decoration, that they were made and decorated in the 1790s rather than in 1776. The creamer is illustrated in *The Connoisseur*, October 1937.

D.92. *Creamer*, painted in overglaze enamel colours and inscribed,

M T
1776

1777

D.93. *Mug* (5½ ins. high) of cylindrical shape, painted in underglaze blue, and inscribed,

Simon & Presily Blaxhill
1777

This mug is in the British Museum.

D.94. *Bowl* (diameter 6¼ ins) painted in underglaze blue with Chinese-style scene, and inscribed,

Philip & Mary Browne
1777

D.95. *Birth Tablet*, painted in underglaze blue. The reverse is painted with flowers, the front inscribed,

Elizh. Lammon
Born June 29 1777

Enamelled Specimens

D.96. *Inkpot* (diameter 3¼ ins.) of waisted, circular form, painted with puce scale border and flower sprays, and inscribed,

B. Townshend
1777

See sale record 145, page 245.

1778

D.97. *Jug* (7ins. high) painted in underglaze blue with flowers, etc., and inscribed,

J Bayfield
1778

See sale record 67, page 240.

D.98. *Teapot** (5½ ins. high) of typical globular shape, painted in underglaze blue with Chinese landscape and garden scene, and inscribed under the base,

Mary Crowfoot
1778

See sale record 84, page 241.

D.98A. *Teabowl and saucer*, painted in underglaze blue to match the teapot listed as number D.98 and with the same name and date painted on the bases. It would appear that a complete tea service was originally made.
Ipswich Museums.

D.99. *Cup*, painted in underglaze blue in a similar style to the Crowfoot pieces, above, but inscribed,

* There was, apparently, originally a matching tea service, for two cups and saucers are to be seen with this teapot in the Christchurch Mansion Museum, Ipswich The teapot is illustrated in *The Antique Collector* magazine, December 1951, fig.4.

Mary Crowse
1778

This cup is in the British Museum.

D.100. *Flask* (shape as Plate 185) painted in underglaze blue with Chinese-style fence and trees, and inscribed,

I (J) B
1778

See sale record 74, page 241.
Illustrated in the Catalogue of the Crisp Collection (1907), page 10.

D.101. *Tablets*, a pair of tablets painted in underglaze blue, the reverse side showing Chinese-style houses in landscape, the fronts inscribed,

M.B.
1778

Enamelled Specimens

D.102. *Teapot*, of typical globular form, decorated in overglaze enamel colours with floral sprays, etc., and inscribed, above and below the spout,

Daniel Fountain
Ann Winson
1778

D.103. *Bowl* (diameter 6ins.) the exterior painted with Chinese figures in overglaze enamel colours, the interior inscribed,

George & Mary Ann Rouse
Uggeshall
1778

This bowl is in the Victoria and Albert Museum.

1779

D.104. *Teabowl and saucer*, painted in underglaze blue, with Chinese-style root pattern, and inscribed under the bases,

Jas Gray
1779

See sale record 122, page 243.

D.105. *Inkstand* (2ins. high) of circular form, painted in underglaze blue, with Chinese garden and river scene, and inscribed,

N M
1779

See sale record 128, page 244.

D.106. *Plaque* (6 x 4ins.) printed in underglaze blue with Chinese-style scene, and inscribed with verse and,

Ruthe Auckland
1779

This rare plaque is in the Fitzwilliam Museum, Cambridge.

Enamelled Specimens

D.107. *Teapot*, of typical globular form, painted in overglaze enamel colours with formal floral motifs in the Curtis style (see page 152) and inscribed,

J P. 1779
A Trifle from Lowestoft

This teapot is in the Castle Museum, Norwich, but the inscription would appear to have been added at a later date to enhance an otherwise standard teapot.

D.108. *Bowl*, painted in enamel colours with four harvesting scenes, and inscribed,

C J.
Harvest Home
Feldon Farm.
1779

This bowl, which was mentioned many years ago by William Chaffers in his *Marks and Monograms*. . . ., has not been seen by modern writers and the original attribution to the Lowestoft factory has not been checked.

D.109. *Creamer* (3¼ins. high) painted in overglaze enamel colours with formal floral design in the Curtis style (page 152) and inscribed under the handle,

E.W.
1779

See sale record 113, page 243.

1780

D.110. *Mug*, of typical bell shape, painted in underglaze blue, with flowers, and inscribed,

Sarah Smy
1780

This mug is in the British Museum.

D.111. *Mug* (4¼ins. high) of cylindrical form, painted in underglaze blue with floral sprays, and inscribed,

John & Mary Livock
Lowestoft
1780

See sale record 76, also 251.

D.111A. *Mug* (4½ins. high) of cylindrical form, the sides painted with flowers in underglaze blue and inscribed within a cartouche,

Ann Cotton
1780

In general style this mug is similar to number D.111, also the surname and date links with the following item, D.112.
Author's Collection.
Illustrated in Plate 186.

D.112. *Jug* (7½ ins. high) of typical form, painted in underglaze blue with flowers, and inscribed,

John Cotton
1780

This jug is in the Castle Museum, Norwich.

1781

D.112A. *Jug* (8⅞ ins. high) of moulded form with relief decoration and with mask head spout. The side is decorated in underglaze blue with a deer crest in a cartouche with the initial and date below,

T C.
1781

Floral sprays decorate the front and the panels.
This example is in the Victoria and Albert Museum (number c 89. 1977).

D.113. *Mug* (4¼ ins. high) of cylindrical form, painted in underglaze blue with floral sprays, and inscribed,

Robt Haward
1781

This mug is in the British Museum.

D.114. *Mug*, of cylindrical form, painted in underglaze blue, and inscribed,

Mary Pain
Shottisham
1781

1782

D.115. *Jug* (7⅛ ins. high) of typical form, painted in underglaze blue with floral sprays, and inscribed,

Thos Davy
Fressingfield
1782

See sale record 134, page 244.

D.116. *Plate**, painted in underglaze blue with floral sprays, and inscribed on the front, within a cartouche,

Jos Daniels
1782

D.117. *Teapot* (5½ ins. high) of typical globular form, painted in underglaze blue, and inscribed,

Robt & Mary Godfrey
1782

See sale records 81 and 222.
Illustrated in F. Litchfield's *Pottery and Porcelain* (1912), page 258.

D.118. *Inkpot*, painted in underglaze blue with flowers and insects, and inscribed,

S.A.
Sepr. 26. 1782

See sale record 11, page 237.

This inkpot is illustrated in *The Country Life Book of English China* (1964) by G. Wills, Plates 102-3.

D.119. *Flask*, of typical form (Plate 185), painted in underglaze blue with floral sprays, and inscribed,

John Moore
Yarmouth
1782

This flask is in the British Museum.

D.120. *Flask* (diameter 5¾ ins.) of typical form (Plate 246), painted in underglaze blue, showing Chinese-style scene, with floral sprays, and inscribed,

John Toake
Yarmouth
1782

See sale record 223.

D.121. *Birth Tablet* (diameter 3⅜ ins.) painted in underglaze blue, the reverse depicting a fox running in a simple landscape, the front inscribed,

Robert
Rope
Born
Febuary (sic)
13, 1782

See sale record 92, page 242.

This birth tablet is in the Great Yarmouth Museum, both sides are illustrated in the Catalogue of the Crisp Collection (1907), page 13.

D.122. *Birth Tablet* of large size (diameter 5¾ ins.) printed and painted in underglaze blue. The reverse is printed with the so-called 'pine-cone' design, and the front bears the following painted inscription,

Eliz Wyeth
Octr ye 10th 1782

Illustrated in Dr. B. Watney's *English Blue and White Porcelain of the 18th Century* (1963), Plate 81B.

1783

D.123. *Mug* (6ins. high) of bell shape, printed in underglaze blue, with sportsman and dog, and inscribed,

P
J M
1783

See sale record 64, page 240.

This fine mug is in the Castle Museum, Norwich, and is illustrated in *The Connoisseur*, September 1937.

* This plate, with two matching cups, is in the Fitzwilliam Museum, Cambridge.

D.124. *Mug* (3⅜ ins. high) of cylindrical form, printed in underglaze blue, with Chinese-style river scene, and inscribed,

Thomas Soulsby Rix
Sept. 1783

This mug is in the Castle Museum, Norwich.

1784

D.125. *Mug* (4½ ins. high) of cylindrical form, painted in underglaze blue with floral sprays, and inscribed,

Josh. Danels
1784

Two teabowls and saucers are also recorded with the same inscription, one being in the Castle Museum, Norwich.

Enamelled Specimens

D.126. *Mug* (6⅜ ins. high) of bell shape, enamelled in overglaze enamel colours, the sides painted with shipping, and the front inscribed,

John Drane
Moulton
1784

This fine mug is in the Fitzwilliam Museum, Cambridge, and is illustrated in the *E.C.C. 1948 Exhibition Catalogue*, Plate 108.

D.127. *Scent Bottle* (3ins. high) relief-moulded with fleur-de-lis and heart motifs, and inscribed, in overglaze enamel colours,

S.C.
1784

This scent bottle is in the Castle Museum, Norwich, and is illustrated in Plate 206.

D.128. *Scent Bottle*, inscribed in overglaze enamel colours,

W.J.S.
1784

1786

D.129. *Jug* (7½ ins. high) of typical form, painted in underglaze blue with a coach, drawn by four horses, and inscribed,

Willm Bevein
Lowestoft
Coachman
1786

This example, from the Colman Collection, which is illustrated in *The Connoisseur*, September 1937, in the *English Porcelain Circle Transactions*, No. III (1931), Plate IIIA, and in Dr. B. Watney's *English Blue and White Porcelain of the 18th Century* (1963), Plate 85D, now resides in the Castle Museum, Norwich, catalogue entry 209.

D.130. *Creamer* (3½ ins.) of typical form, painted in underglaze blue with floral sprays, and inscribed,

S.S.
1786

This jug is in the Fitzwilliam Museum, Cambridge.

D.131. *Birth Tablet* (diameter 2⅞ ins.) painted in underglaze blue, the reverse with Chinese scene, the front inscribed,

Thomas Page
born December 31st
1786

See sale record 221.

1787

D.132. *Mug*, of cylindrical form, painted in underglaze blue, and inscribed,

Sarah Duffield
1787

D.133. *Jug* and cover (10½ ins. high) painted in underglaze blue with flowers, etc., and inscribed,

John & Sarah Livock
Lowestoft
1787

See sale record 129, also 253.
This jug is illustrated in *The Connoisseur*, September 1937.

D.134. *Flask* (diameter 5½ ins.) of typical form, painted in underglaze blue with Chinese-style houses in landscape. The reverse is painted with floral spray and inscribed on the neck,

W.S.
1787

D.135. *Birth Tablet* (diameter 2¾ ins.) painted in underglaze blue. The reverse shows a Chinese-style landscape, and the front is inscribed,

John Teasel
born September 22
1787

Enamelled Specimens

D.136. *Mug* (5½ ins. high) of cylindrical form, the sides painted in enamel colours with flowers, the front inscribed,

Mary Sutten
1787

The lettering and general treatment are similar to the John Harm teapot listed next.
See sale record 118, page 243.

This fine mug, which is illustrated in colour in *The Connoisseur*, June 1927, and also in Dixon's *English Porcelain of the 18th Century*, Plate 60B, is now in the Fitzwilliam Museum, Cambridge. See Plate 209 of the present work.

D.137. *Teapot* (6½ ins. high) of typical globular form, painted in overglaze enamel colours, with formal floral pattern in the

Curtis style (page 152), inscribed on one side,

John Harm
1787

See sale record 170, page 247.
See also Plate 183.

1788

D.138. *Mug* (4⅞ ins. high) of typical cylindrical form, painted in underglaze blue and inscribed,

Philp Nuthall
Caister
1788

D.139. *Teapot*, of typical globular form, painted in underglaze blue, with flowers, and inscribed,

Ciscealea Carter
Lowestoft
1788

See sale record 30, page 238.
This teapot is in the Christchurch Mansion Museum, Ipswich.

D.140. *Toy Teabowl*, of very small size (only 1⅜ ins. high) painted with Chinese scenes, and inscribed in underglaze blue,

I (J) L
1788

A further example, inscribed S L / 1790 was made to match this example, see *The Connoisseur*, September 1937.

See also sale record 253.

D.141. *Birth Tablet* (diameter 3⅜ ins.) painted in underglaze blue, the reverse with Chinese house and garden, and the front inscribed,

Honnour (sic) Downing
born October 22 1788

See sale record 95, page 242.
Illustrated in the Catalogue of the Crisp Collection (1907), page 12.

1789

D.142. *Mug* (3¾ ins. high) of slightly waisted, cylindrical form, with blue printed border, and inscribed,

G C (joined)
Lowestoft
1789

D.143. *Birth Tablet* (diameter 2¾ ins.) painted in underglaze blue. The reverse side with Chinese-style scene, the front inscribed,

S.S.
1789

See sale record 87, page 242.

Enamelled Specimens

D.144. *Mug* (3¼ ins. high) of cylindrical form, painted in overglaze enamel colours, with pink scale border and Chinese-style formal floral pattern, inscribed,

Henry Drake Browne
1789

1790

D.145. *Teapot*, of typical globular form, painted in underglaze blue with floral sprays, and inscribed,

Remember Her, who gives this Trifle
E R. Lowestoft. Suffock. 1790

The cover inscribed, E.R. 1790.
This teapot is in the Castle Museum, Norwich.

D.146. *Toy Teabowl* (1⅜ ins. high) painted in underglaze blue with Chinese-style scene, and inscribed on the flat base,

S.L.
1790

A pair to the I L / 1788 example, (q.v.).

See sale record 253.
D.147. *Birth Tablet* (diameter 3¼ ins.) painted in underglaze blue. The reverse painted with flowers, the front inscribed,

Winifred Lemmon
Born March 18 1790

Smithsonian Institute, Washington. U.S.A.

D.148. *Birth Tablet*, painted in underglaze blue. The reverse with dove on a stump, the front inscribed,

Mary Ann Lifin*
Born November 4 1790

This birth tablet is in the Great Yarmouth Museum.

Enamelled Specimens

D.149. *Mug* (4½ ins. high) of cylindrical form, painted in overglaze enamel colours, and inscribed,

John Allcock
May 10th 1790

See sale record 194, page 248.
This mug is illustrated in Plate 212.

D.150. *Mug* (4¾ ins. high) of basic cylindrical form, but with the rare feature of a turned foot (Plate 211). Enamelled in overglaze colours with formal floral pattern in the Curtis style (page 152), it is inscribed in the front,

Willm. Bobbet
May 10th 1790

See Plate 184.

---

* Other pieces give the, perhaps correct, spelling 'Liffen'.

D.151. *Teapot* (5½ ins. high) of typical globular form, painted in overglaze enamel colours with Curtis style formal floral pattern, and inscribed,

William & Ann Cobb
Harleston.
1790

See sale record 157, page 246.

This teapot is in the Fitzwilliam Museum, Cambridge, and is illustrated in Plate 214.

D.152. *Flask*, of small size (diameter 3½ ins.) painted in overglaze enamel colours with Curtis-type flowers, and inscribed,

John Butcher
1790

1791

D.153. *Jug* (7ins. high) of typical form, painted in underglaze blue with floral sprays, and inscribed,

John Vince
Great Melton
1791

This jug is illustrated in *The Connoisseur*, September 1937.

D.154. *Bowl* (diameter 4½ ins.) painted in underglaze blue with Chinese-style scene, and inscribed,

S Abbot
1791

D.155. *Bowl* (4⅞ ins. high) painted in underglaze blue with Chinese pagoda pattern, and inscribed,

William Bennett
1791

This bowl is in the Christchurch Mansion Museum, Ipswich.

D.156. *Inkpot* (diameter 2¾ ins.) painted in underglaze blue with floral sprays, and inscribed,

A Trifle show Respect
J Hughes
1791

See sale record 48, page 239.
This inkpot is in the British Museum.

D.157. *Inkpot* (2½ ins. high) painted in underglaze blue, and inscribed,

John Salter
1791

The base is inscribed J.S.
See sale record 111, page 242.
Illustrated in A.E. Murton's *Lowestoft China* (1932) opposite page 50.

D.158. *Birth Tablet* (diameter 3¼ ins.) painted in underglaze blue, with floral sprays, and inscribed,

Robert Downin
Born January 19. 1791

See sale record 93, page 242.

D.159. *Birth Tablet* (diameter 3⅜ ins.) painted in underglaze blue. The reverse shows a Chinese-style scene, and the front is inscribed,

Elizabeth Ruthen
Born February 4 1791

See sale record 96, page 242.
This birth tablet is in the Christchurch Mansion Museum, Ipswich.

1792

D.160. *Mug* (5¾ ins. high) of cylindrical form, painted in underglaze blue, with a couplet and inscribed,

Mary Curtis
1792

This mug is in the Fitzwilliam Museum, Cambridge.

D.161. *Mug* (3½ ins. high) of cylindrical form, painted in underglaze blue, with flowers, etc., and inscribed,

Margaret Hodson
1792

D.162. *Birth Tablet* (diameter 2⅞ ins.) painted in underglaze blue, the reverse showing a sailing lugger, the front inscribed,

Susan Golder
Born May 20 1792

The reverse side of this tablet is illustrated in Dr. B. Watney's *English Blue and White Porcelain of the 18th Century* (1963), Plate 83B.

D.162A. *Flask*, painted in underglaze blue, and inscribed,

W.P. Downing
Sept. 1. 1792.

(This specimen has not been seen and verified by the author.)

Enamelled Specimens

D.163. *Mug* (3½ ins. high) of cylindrical form, painted in overglaze enamel colours with flowers, and inscribed,

Marta Garrad
1792

See sale record 55, page 240.

D.164. *Mug* (3¼ ins. high) of cylindrical form, painted in overglaze enamel colours, with floral sprays and inscribed,

Mary Warnes
1792

The last two mugs appear to be decorated by the same hand.

1793

D.165. *Jug* (8ins. high) painted in underglaze blue (with gilt mask head spout) and inscribed,

Robert Lewis
1793

D.166. *Plate*, or saucer dish, painted in underglaze blue, with two figures and inscribed within a heart,

Thos & Eliz.th Crafer
Downham
1793

See sale record 186, page 248.

D.167. *Birth Tablet* (diameter 2½ ins.) painted in underglaze blue, the reverse with a Chinese scene, and the front inscribed,

Johnathen Downing
Born December 27 1793

See sale record 94, page 242.
Illustrated in the Catalogue of the Crisp Collection (1907), page 12.

D.168. *Birth Tablet* (diameter 3ins.) painted in underglaze blue. The reverse with Chinese-style houses, etc., the front inscribed,

Ann Ruthen
Born June 30. 1793

See sale record 86, page 241.
Illustrated in the Catalogue of the Crisp Collection (1907), page 12.

D.169. *Birth Tablet* (diameter 2¾ ins.) painted in underglaze blue, the reverse depicting a vase of flowers, with the front inscribed,

Sam[l] Teasel
Born August 11th 1793

This birth tablet is in the Castle Museum, Norwich.

D.169A. *Creamer* or milk jug, painted in underglaze blue with basket of flowers and inscribed under the base,

A.H.
1793

Enamelled Specimens

D.170. *Mug* (3ins. high) of cylindrical form, painted with overglaze enamelled cornflower sprigs, and inscribed,

E (or F) R.
1793'

See sale record 224.
(A similar mug is believed to be inscribed F.H. 1793).

D.170A. *Mug* (3⅛ ins. high) of cylindrical form, enamelled with cornflower sprigs and inscribed,

M.A.R.
1793.

Formerly Henry Levine Collection, see sale record 268.

D.171. *Birth Tablet*, painted in overglaze enamel colours, with cornflower sprigs, and inscribed on the front,

John Gaul
Born April 22. 1793

This birth tablet is in the Castle Museum, Norwich.

1794

D.172. *Jug* (5¾ ins. high) of typical form, painted in underglaze blue, with floral sprays and inscribed,

J.S.
1794

See sale record 166, page 246.
Illustrated in Plate 221.

D.173. *Birth (and Memorial) Tablet* (diameter 2⅞ ins.) painted in underglaze blue, inscribed,

Martha Liffin
Born August 17 1794

and on the other side,

Mary Liffin
Died May 4 1795

See sale record 132, page 244.

This tablet, which must have been decorated in 1795, not 1794, is the only example recorded commemorating both a birth and a death. It is now in the Castle Museum, Norwich, and is illustrated in the *English Porcelain Circle Transactions*, No. III (1931), Plate VII.

Enamelled Specimens

D.174. *Creamer* (3⅜ ins. high) of rather squat shape, painted in overglaze enamel colours with floral sprays, and inscribed,

Catherine Sneath
Weston
1794

See sale record 52, page 239.
Illustrated in *The Connoisseur*, October 1937.

D.175. *Birth Tablet* (diameter 4¼ ins.) painted in overglaze enamel colours with flowers, the front inscribed,

Ann Redgrave
Born Jary (sic) ye 2d 1794

See sale record 138, page 245.
This attractive birth tablet is illustrated in *The Connoisseur*, October 1937.

D.176. *Birth Tablet* (diameter 4½ ins.) painted in overglaze enamel colours, the reverse showing flowers, the front inscribed,

Sush. Redgrave
Born April ye 9th 1794

The style of decoration of this fine birth tablet, which is in the Lowestoft Library and illustrated in Plate 227, should be compared with that of the tea caddy shown in Colour Plate 12, the flower painting on the reverse having been obviously painted by the same hand as the ends of the caddy.

D.176A. *Mug* (3½ ins. high) of cylindrical form enamelled with sprig design and inscribed,

David James
1794

D.176B. *Mug* (3½ ins. high) of cylindrical form enamelled with cornflower type floral sprays and inscribed,

J B.
1794

This most probably relates to John Barker who was born in January 1794.

1795

D.177. *Memorial Tablet* (see 1794 Martha Liffin — Martha Liffin birth and memorial tablet).

Enamelled Specimens

D.178. *Mug* (3½ ins. high) of cylindrical form, painted in overglaze enamel colours, and inscribed,

Ann Conway
1795
A Trifle from Lowestoft

See sale record 192, page 248.
Illustrated in Plate 223.

D.179. *Mug* (4½ ins. high) of cylindrical form, painted in overglaze enamel colours with cornflower sprigs, and inscribed,

M.D.
A Trifle from Lowestoft
1795

To be seen in the British Museum.

N.B. This inscription also occurs on Continental hard-paste fakes, see Plate 240.

D.180 *Mug* (4⅝ ins. high) of cylindrical form, painted in overglaze enamel colours and inscribed,

H.H.P.W.
1795

This mug is in the Castle Museum, Norwich, and is illustrated in *English Porcelain, 1745-1850* (1965), Plate 47A.

D.181. *Mug* (5ins. high) painted in overglaze enamel colours with cornflower sprigs, and inscribed,

D I
to H Gillman
1795

See sale record 269.
Illustrated in Plate 226.

D.182. *Birth Tablet* (diameter 4½ ins.) painted in overglaze enamel colours, the reverse with red flowers, the front inscribed,

Ann Redgrave
Born Novbr 4. 1795

See sale record 105, page

This example is in the Castle Museum, Norwich, and is illustrated in *The Connoisseur*, October 1937.

1796

D.183. *Jug* (9½ ins. high) painted in underglaze blue, and inscribed,

Thos Wright
1796

D.184. *Birth Tablet* (diameter 2⅞ ins.) painted in underglaze blue. The reverse has floral sprays, and the front is inscribed,

Mary Rushmer
Born Octr 29. 1796

D.185. *Birth Tablet* (diameter 3ins.) painted in underglaze blue. The reverse is painted with floral sprays, and the front is inscribed,

Mary Ward
Born Dec.r 4th 1796

See sale record 88, page 242.

This is in the Castle Museum, Norwich, and is illustrated in the Catalogue of the Crisp Collection (1907), page 12.

Enamelled Specimens

D.186. *Teapot* (5ins. high, to the rim) of typical globular form, painted in overglaze enamel colours, with slight cornflower sprays, and inscribed under the base (and cover),

Jn° Browne
January 27, 1796

This, with a matching cup and saucer, is in the Castle Museum, Norwich.

D.187. *Birth Tablet* (diameter 2¾ ins.) painted in overglaze enamel colours, the reverse bearing flowers, and the front inscribed,

Henriette Gall
Born April 18, 1796

See sale record 196, page 248.

1797

D.188. *Birth Tablet* (diameter 2¾ ins.) painted in underglaze blue, the reverse with Chinese-style house, the front inscribed,

John Lee
Born Augut (sic) 23. 1797

See sale record 131, page 244.

Enamelled Specimens

D.189. *Mug* (2⅝ ins. high) of low cylindrical form, painted in enamel colours with a view of a house, and inscribed,

Susannah Cullum
1797

This is in the Fitzwilliam Museum, Cambridge.

D.190. *Tea canister* (4ins. high) painted in overglaze enamel colours. The sides are painted with sprays of flowers, and the front and back inscribed, within typical feathery cartouche,

M M (joined)
Joy guide her footsteps
(and)
J D R (joined)

The flat, glazed base has the remains of the rubbed date 1797. This unique inscribed tea canister is illustrated in Colour Plate 12 and Plate 228.

The same hand is seen on birth tablets made for the Redgrave family (page 177 and Plates 227 and 229).

D.191. *Birth Tablet* (diameter 2¾ ins.) painted in overglaze enamel colours, the reverse with flowers, the front inscribed,

George Gall
Born 24th Octbr 1797

1798

D.192. *Beaker* (?) (4⅛ ins. high) painted in underglaze blue and inscribed,

Olney Harvey
1798

See sale record 66, page 240.

D.193. *Inkpot*, of octagonal form, painted in underglaze blue with floral sprays and inscribed,

John & Sarah Drinkald
Lowestoft
1798

This is in the British Museum.

D.193A. *Inkpot*, of circular form painted in underglaze blue with a cartouche and inscribed,

P. High
Lowestoft
1798

D.194. *Birth Tablet*, painted in underglaze blue, the front inscribed,

Eallathe Leggett Liffin
Born Decr. 9 1798

See sale record 90, page 242.

D.195. *Birth Tablet* (diameter 2⅘ins.) painted in underglaze blue. The reverse shows a Chinese-style house, and the front is inscribed,

Amelia Peel
Born Sepr 23rd 1798

See Plate 234.

Enamelled Specimens

D.196. *Flask* (diameter 5½ ins.) of typical form (Plate 158) painted in overglaze enamel colours with, on one side, the Arms of the Tylers and Bricklayers' Company, and on the other a naval battle. It is inscribed,

C.B.
1798

This is in the Great Yarmouth Museum.

D.197. *Birth Tablet* (diameter 2⅝ ins.) painted in overglaze colours, the reverse with flowers, the front inscribed,

John Butcher
Born May 21st 1798

This is in the Christchurch Mansion Museum, Ipswich.

1799

D.198. *Birth Tablet* (diameter 3¼ ins.) in underglaze blue. The reverse is painted with a Chinese scene, the front being inscribed,

John Ward
Born Febry. 15th 1799

See sale record 89, page 242.
This is in the Castle Museum, Norwich.

D.199. *Jug*, inscribed, in a hand similar to that found on Lowestoft 'Trifles',

Robert Beecroft
Born Novbr, ye 10th
1799

It is highly significant, to the discussion on the date that the Lowestoft porcelain factory closed, that this jug is of a pottery body, not porcelain (page 31).
See Plate 237.

D.200. *Small Mug*, inscribed and decorated in the style of Lowestoft birth tablets,

Susan Symonds
Born Jany 14
1802

by a hand found on much late Lowestoft porcelain but this specimen is of a pottery body, as purchased by Robert Allen for decorating and sale, after the porcelain factory had closed (page 145).
See Plate 238.

APPENDIX II

Sale Records

The following section is composed of extracts from auction sale catalogues of Lowestoft porcelain sold from 1873 onwards, for over a hundred years! Most of the great collections are featured in this selection, and from these sales present-day museum and private collections have been built up, and many well-known articles can be traced in sale after sale for a period of fifty or more years.

It is possible to include only some of the more interesting articles, several of which are illustrated in this book. The original sale prices have been given merely as a matter of nostalgic interest and, with the exception of the last records, these amounts must not be regarded as being current, for over the last few years the prices willingly given for these charming and interesting pieces have risen to a very great extent, as is evidenced by the records quoted on page 35.

The 'Lots' quoted have been numbered consecutively for easy reference.

A CATALOGUE OF THE HIGHLY INTERESTING COLLECTION OF LOWESTOFT PORCELAIN. . . BEING THE COLLECTION OF WILLIAM RIX SEAGO, ESQ. SOLD BY MESSRS. SPELMAN, AT LOWESTOFT IN AUGUST 1873

Part of the foreword reads:

Mr. Seago has employed many years and spared no means in forming his collection. It derives more than ordinary interest from the possession of many rare pieces — obtained from Families whose ancestors were connected with the Factory — illustrating the various styles of Lowestoft Porcelain, and forming, by a series of typical specimens, a complete history of the manufacture from its commencement. . . . *

1. A blue and white basin, after the Oriental; inside is 'Richard Mason, Jany 1st 1771'. Obtained from the Mason family. *7/-*

2. An elegant blue and white dessert dish [query, like the oval basket illustrated in Plate 106] with open basket-work sides and May blossoms in relief. Part of a service in the possession of Mr. Aldred, Yarmouth, the grandson of one of the proprietors of the factory of that name, from whom he inherited the same. *36/-*

3. A curious coffee jug [really a jug with a lip, not a spout] and cover, painted [in overglaze enamels] with figures in imitation of Oriental, and 'DL' at the bottom. Formerly the property of Daniel Landerfield, and made in the factory by an acquaintance of his sister, by whom it was painted. *80/-*

4. A curious teapot with Oriental figures, in the style of Worcester. Given to Mr. Seago by Mrs. Nicker, whose mother purchased it at the factory. *65/-*

5. Teapot with ruins and landscapes in pink. *24/-*

6. A fine coffee cup with coat of arms, crest and motto — '*In Deo Potero*'. Part of the service made for the Rev[d]. R. Potter. . . . *£6. 6. 0.*

[See also items 59, 117 and 199.]

7. Bowl with monogram J.S.S. between palm and olive branches, surmounted by a man holding a bowl, flowered border. Given to Mr. Seago by the widow of the son of John Sparham, a painter in the factory. *28/-*

8. A sketch of a coat of arms by Bly, at one time a workman in the Lowestoft factory and afterwards at Worcester. *12/-*

9. 2 Cups [in fact teabowls] and saucers with Venus instructing Cupid, painted in pink. *£5. 10. 0.*

[Part of at least one fine service, Plates 155 and 157.]

10. Pair of cups [teabowls] and saucers with pink flowers and gilt, [Plate 154], and another cup with figures angling and Cupid flying two doves. *46/-*

11. A curious blue and white inkstand, marked underneath 'S.A. Sept 26th 1782'. The initials of Mr. Samuel Aldred, one of the proprietors of the factory. *30/-*

[Resold in the Crisp sale of February 1935, for £19.]

12. A rare and extremely curious basin with pastoral figures

* The illustrations in this 1873 Catalogue show that much of this collection was of Oriental hard-paste porcelain, not true Lowestoft, so these Chinese porcelains have been deleted from this extract.

and landscape, outside birds and flowers, and at the bottom 'E. Buckle', all painted in blue. Part of the service painted for Elizabeth Buckle by her nephew, Robert Allen, (see page 145) the manager of the factory. The original drawing from which this subject was taken is now in the possession of Allen's grandson, Mr. R. Allen Johnson, who has the remainder of the service. *£6. 16. 0.*
[Resold in the Crisp sale, February 1935, for £15.]

13. A 10 inch blue and white bowl; inside is 'Edward Morley. 1768' with a bird and flowers outside. *£1. 16. 0.*

14. A fine 11 inch bowl; inside is a lugger in full sail with the name 'The Judas' beneath; rich borders and flowers. This lugger formerly belonged to Messrs. Peach.... *£3. 0. 0.*
[Subsequently sold in the Crisp sale, in February 1935, for £41.]

CURTIS SALE
8 WESTERN TERRACE,
LOWESTOFT
SEPTEMBER 1887.

Auctioneer's note:

> 'The following Lots of Lowestoft China deserve the particular attention of Collectors and Connoisseurs from the fact that the late Mr. Charles John Mann Curtis was a son of Mr. Thomas Curtis — 'porcelain painter' in the Lowestoft Manufactory, and thus became possessed of most of the unique and choice specimens now submitted for unreserved competition.'

Overglaze Enamelled Pieces

15. A teapot painted by Thomas Curtis, with scale border and festoons and cornucopia of flowers, a fine specimen. *£5. 10. 0.*

16. A pair of finely painted scale and festoon bordered Plates, by Thomas Curtis, 1775. *£3. 10. 0.*

17. A pair of very fine fluted cups and saucers with scale border. *£1. 5. 0.*

18. A pair of small plates with sprays of flowers, inscribed 'Averill Sibel'. *17/-*

19. A scale-border mug with vase of flowers and sprigs. [No price recorded.]

20. A double-twisted handle and fluted teapot, painted with pink roses — a rare specimen.* *£4. 0. 0.*

21. A unique and complete tea service, of fine transparent quality, decorated with flowers in cornucopias and scrolls, painted by Thomas Curtis in 1775 and intended as a wedding present for his son James, including — teapot and stand, sucrier and stand, cream ewer, stand and cover, caddy with cover, two cake plates, and 1 dozen cups and saucers. *£30. 9. 0.*
[Resold in the Sir Samuel Hoare sale, in November 1933, for £31.]

22. A beautiful 10 inch Bowl, splendidly decorated with groups, wreaths, and festoons of flowers, scale outside and gilt and flowered inside borders. *£3. 13. 6.*
Thomas Curtis. 1772.

23. Three rose pattern plates by Thomas Curtis, unfinished specimens. *£2. 5. 0.*

24. A very fine and rare 11 inch pencilled specimen bowl, with black and gold groups of roses, festoons of flowers, and inside border. *£4. 4. 6.*
[This bowl was almost certainly of Chinese make and decoration.]

Blue and White Patterns

25. A small teapot 'A Trifle from Lowestoft' and a pair of cups and saucers. *£2. 0. 0.*
[The teapot was resold in the Sir Samuel Hoare sale, in November 1933, for £34. See Colour Plate 2.]

26. A fine mug — inscribed 'James and Mary Curtis, Lowestoft, 1771'. Cracked. *£4. 0. 0.*
[Now in the Castle Museum, Norwich, being part of the Colman Bequest, it was sold for £28 in the Sir Samuel Hoare sale, in November 1933.]

27. A very rare open-work basket.

28. Large embossed (relief-moulded) jug — Willow pattern.

29. Four fans, with patterns of China decorations in use in manufactory.

THE INTERESTING COLLECTION OF OLD ENGLISH
PORCELAIN ....FORMED BY MERTON A. THOMS, ESQ.,
(LOWESTOFT SECTION ONLY) SOLD BY
MESSRS. CHRISTIE, MANSON AND WOODS,
ON FEBRUARY 10TH, 1910.

Blue and White

30. A teapot and cover, painted with flowers in blue, and with a panel inscribed 'Ciscaelea Carter, Lowestoft, 1788'. *£43. 1. 0.*

31. A large teapot and cover, painted in blue with the Royal Arms and cipher of George III and the date 1772, also on the reverse a scroll shaped panel, enclosing the initials 'G.B.' and the date 1772. *£26. 5. 0.*
[This example is now in the Castle Museum, Norwich.]

32. A teapot and cover, painted with panels of Chinese landscapes in blue, on a ground of raised white flowers and with initials 'I.H.' and the date 1761 in relief. *£65. 2. 0.*

33. Part of the same tea service, comprising cream-jug, basin, octagonal canister, three cups and two saucers. *£31. 10. 0.*

34. A large jug, painted with Chinese river scenes in blue, and modelled with formal flowers and foliage in low relief. 10 inches high. *£5. 5. 0.*

35. A tea service, painted with Chinese river scenes in blue, consisting of a teapot and cover, cream-jug, two bowls, a plate, five tea cups and saucers and one coffee cup. *£4. 14. 6.*

Overglaze Enamel Decoration

36. A cylindrical mug, painted with foliage in pink and brown, and green bands, the front inscribed

A TRIFLE FROM
LOWESTOFT

4¾ inches high. *£23. 2. 0.*

---

* The description of this teapot, with a double-twisted handle, would suggest that some 'Lowestoft' articles included in this sale were of hard-paste Chinese-export market porcelain, perhaps collected by the Curtis family as being similar in style to his father's painting, for this form of handle is well-known on Oriental teapots, but is not recorded on soft-paste, true Lowestoft pots. This floral-painted Chinese porcelain was often classed as Lowestoft at this period, an error which persists in some circles to the present day.

37. A cylindrical mug, painted with a view of a seaport, lighthouse and shipping, and the Arms of Trinity House in colours, on a white ground enriched with gilt dots. 5½ inches high. *£75. 12. 0.*
[This fine mug, or its companion, is now in the Victoria and Albert Museum.]

38. A beaker-shaped vase and three mugs, painted with Chinese figures in colours. *£11. 0. 6.*

39. A tea service, painted with Chinese figures in colours, consisting of two teapots and covers, sugar-basin and cover, bowl, two cream-jugs, seven tea cups, eight saucers, and two coffee cups. *£11. 11. 0.*

AN IMPORTANT AND EXTENSIVE
COLLECTION OF LOWESTOFT PORCELAIN,
(THE LEVINE COLLECTION) SOLD BY
MESSRS. SOTHEBY AND CO. ON
APRIL 30TH, 1925.

PREFACE. It is probable that since the dispersal of the major portion of the Seago Collection in 1873 there has not been such a large and important collection of the wares of this factory offered for sale by public auction....The collection is rich in specimens of polychrome decoration, which was produced from about 1770 onwards, and it contains a variety of decorative and utilitarian pieces finely enamelled with Chinese famille verte, famille rose, and Japanese Imari decoration, also a number of floral and classical patterns of great beauty, including the famous pink scale and Angouleme patterns, and some rare pieces with black and gold decoration.

Among the more important inscribed pieces for which the factory is famous are Trifles from Lowestoft, Bungay and Hingham, and a variety of named and dated pieces covering a period nine years after the commencement of the factory to nine years prior to its close, and bearing a number of old East Anglian names; of great interest also is part of an armorial tea service belonging to the poet, politician and scholar, the Rev. Robert Potter, Vicar of Lowestoft.

Blue and White

40. A pair of sauce boats, with raised fruit decoration and gadroon edges, one painted by No. 3 and the other by No. 5 and three other sauce boats, of varying shapes and sizes. *£10. 10. 0.*

41. A large jug, painted with Chinese lake scenes and figures, and moulded decoration 9 inches high. Painter's number 3. *£5. 5. 0.*

42. A large cylindrical mug, with scroll handle, painted with a figure holding a sunshade, and another smaller mug painted with butterflies and flowers. Painter's number 5 on the large mug. *£5. 10. 0.*

43. A cream jug, with typical scroll handle and bulbous body, painted with sprays of flowers, and inscribed within a cartouche 'A Trifle from Lowestoft'. 3¾ inches high. *£30. 0. 0.*

44. A circular butter dish, cover and stand with applied flower handle to cover painted [printed?] with flowers in blue, make an open crescent. *£4. 5. 0.*
[Probably similar to that shown in Plate 127.]

45. A fine ewer and basin, painted with scroll borders, insects and Chinese landscapes, and small detached sailing ships. Ewer 9½ inches high. Basin 11 inches diameter. Painter's number 2. *£9. 10. 0.*

46. A pair of cornucopiae with raised scroll ornament, painted with figures within cartouches, and another from a different mould, similarly painted. 7½ inches high. Painter's number 3. *£6. 0. 0.*

47. A pair of small tureens, covers and stands, of flat, oval shape, with applied rustic handles and small flowers, painted [printed?] in blue with butterflies and flowers, glazed all over. 7½ inches long, mark copy of Worcester crescent. *£11. 0. 0.*
[Probably similar to that shown in Plate 126.]

48. An inkstand of cylindrical form, the shoulders with three holes for pens, painted with sprays of flowers, and inscribed within a rococo scrollwork panel:

A TRIFLE SHOW RESPECT

and on the base:

J HUGHES, 1791.

2¾ inches diameter. *£54. 0. 0.*

49. A cylindrical mug, painted inside the rim with a trellis pattern border, and on the body with sprays of flowers, and inscribed within a cartouche:

ROBT HOWES. 1776.

4½ inches high. *£25. 0. 0.*
[This cracked mug was resold in the Colman sale in April 1948, for £27.]

Overglaze Enamel Decoration

50. A rare preserve jar and cover, of conical shape, painted with a scroll border and detached flower sprigs and insects. 3¾ inches high. *£20. 0. 0.*
[Plate 173.]

51. An interesting bowl and sucrier, painted within gilt and pink panels with quay scenes and figures, and the Oriental cup and saucer from which they were (or may have been) copied. *£23. 0. 0.*

52. A cream jug, with plain pointed spout, and scroll handle with unusual blue decoration, finely painted with sprigs of flowers in colours and inscribed within a puce coloured panel:

CATHERINE SNEATH.
WESTON. 1794.

3¼ inches high. *£33. 0. 0.*
[This creamer was resold in the Colman sale in April 1948, for £42.]

53. A large Punch Bowl, finely painted in imitation of Imari ware, the inside rim with trellis and lambrequin border, the outside of the bowl depicting Chinese landscapes and river scenes. 9¾ inch diameter. *£10. 0. 0.*
[Probably similar to that illustrated in Plate 143.]

54. A very fine tea and coffee service, painted in imitation of the Japanese style with flowering shrubs and birds [the decoration of this fine service, often termed the 'two bird pattern' is generally attributed to one of the Redgraves], comprising a globular teapot and cover, a cylindrical teapot, cover and stand, a coffee pot and cover, a slop basin, two sugar basins, a spoon tray, three circular dishes, four cream jugs, thirteen tea cups and thirteen coffee cups and saucers. [For pattern see Colour Plate 7, Plate 144.] *£34. 0. 0.*

55. A small mug of cylindrical shape, painted with bouquets of flowers, and inscribed within rococo scrollwork panel,

MARTA GARRAD. 1792.

3½ inches high. *£64. 0. 0.*

[Resold in the Wallace Elliot sale in May 1938, for £31.]

56. A fine coffee-pot and cover, decorated in black with an entwining border, and a landscape with a castle and bridge and a man fishing in the foreground, within a gilt and black diaper scrollwork panel. 9 inches high. *£8. 10. 0.*

[This example, a jug, is now in the Castle Museum, Norwich.]

57. A Jug, with plain spout and flat scroll handle, painted with sprigs and sprays of roses and tulips, and inscribed within a puce scrollwork panel:

C E
HEAMAN
1776

5¼ inches high. *£28. 0. 0*

[This cracked jug was resold in the Wallace Elliot sale in May 1938, for £48, and again in the Colman sale in April 1948, for the same sum. It is interesting to see that when this jug was sold in 1872, as part of the Owles' collection, it was sold as Chelsea.]

58. A cream-jug, of cup shape with narrow spout, double scroll handle and ribbed body, finely gilt and painted with festoons of grapes and vine leaves and gilt borders, inscribed on the foot within a gilt heart-shaped panel,

M and E
CALDER
NORWICH
1776

3 inches high. *£44. 0. 0.*

[Resold in the Colman sale in April 1948, for £42.]

59. A teabowl and saucer from the Rev^{d}. R. Potter service, painted with arms, crest and motto, within gilt line borders. [Plate 215.] *£19. 0. 0.*

THE INTERESTING
COLLECTION OF RARE
LOWESTOFT CHINA
....THE PROPERTY
OF THE RT. HON. SIR
SAMUEL HOARE, Bt., G.B.E.,
C.M.G., M.P. Sold by Messrs.
Sotheby & Co. on
November 17th, 1933.

This collection was started by the present owner's father in the year 1887, and was to a great extent completed in the subsequent two or three years. Its foundations were laid in 1887 at the sale of the effects of Charles John Mann Curtis, a son of Thomas Curtis, a painter at the Lowestoft China Manufactory (page 238). The collection was subsequently greatly developed two years later at the Reeve sale in May 1889. A few important pieces with inscriptions from the well-known collection of William Booth were added in 1906....

60. A miniature Garniture, of four vases, two with covers, and a pair of beakers, all painted with flower sprays in enamel colours, decorative pink scale, festoon and butterfly borders round the rims. 4¼ inches to 6 inches high. *£23. 0. 0.*

61. A tea cup and saucer, fluted, with wavy gilt rims, decorated with festoons of grape and vine pattern in gold and red, enclosing in the centre within a golden heart, the inscription, 'M and E Calder, Norwich, 1776'. Saucer badly cracked. *£9. 0.0.*

62. A rare cylindrical mug, inscribed within a feathery puce cartouche 'A Trifle from HOLT', within pale blue and coloured entwined borders round the neck and base, c.1795. 3½ inches high. *£84. 0. 0.*

63. Two fine mugs of cylindrical shape, perhaps painted by Thomas Curtis, with a Chinese design of a vase of flowers under a pink scale border and inscribed in monogram with the initials 'J.S.D.' at the sides. Pint and a half size 5½ inches high, pint size 4½ inches high. *£26. 0. 0.*

[Similar mugs with other initials are recorded.]

64. The 'Gamble' transfer-printed Sportsman mug of unusual bell shape, printed in underglaze-blue with a dog putting up a quaint parrot-like partridge on the left, the sportsman in eighteenth-century costume with his gun over his shoulder, holding it by the barrel, inscribed in front with the initials 'J & M P. 1783'. 6 inches high. Tradition states that this print, which is the most ambitious transfer-print recorded, was supplied by Mr. Gamble, of Bungay.... *£16. 0. 0.*

65. A bell-shape mug with cell diaper border in underglaze-blue round the rim, flower sprays and butterflies round the sides and in front, within a light rococo cartouche, inscribed 'James Postons, Norwich, 1771'. 5 inches high. *£14. 0. 0.*

66. A very interesting beaker or tumbler, painted in underglaze-blue with a border inside the rim, scattered sprigs in blue round the body and in front within a husk, draped panel inscribed, 'Onley Harvey. 1798'. *£21. 0. 0.*

67. A Jug painted in underglaze-blue with a lattice diaper border round the rim, flower sprays at the sides and inscribed in front 'J. Bayfield 1778', within a rococo cartouche. 7 inches high.

[Badly cracked.] *£10. 0. 0.*

68. A fine bell-shaped mug, inscribed in underglaze-blue within a thin rococo cartouche 'Willm Feltum, Shottisham, 1773', flanked by flower sprays, a lattice diaper border inside the rim, 4½ inches high. Painter's number 5. *£70. 0. 0.*

[Other examples, of different sizes, from this set are recorded.]

(Resold in the Colman sale, April 1948, for £78.)

THE CELEBRATED COLLECTION OF LOWESTOFT CHINA, THE PROPERTY OF THE LATE FREDERICK ARTHUR CRISP. SOLD BY MESSRS. SOTHEBY AND CO. LONDON. FEBRUARY 14TH, 1935.

69. A Lowestoft large jug with loop handle and dentate pattern round the base and shoulders, painted in underglaze-blue with

Chinese river scenes and vignettes in moulded panels round the neck. 8½ inches. Painter's number 3. *£3. 15. 0.*

70. A large family teapot of globular form, with loop handle and spout, marked at the junctions, painted in blue with Chinese pagodas and garden and river scenes, with elaborate diaper and butterfly borders. 7¾ inches high. *£3. 3. 0.*

71. A tea service decorated with a meandering grape and vine leaf pattern, in brown with gold-lined borders, comprising — milk jug, sugar basin, slop bowl, 13 cups and 12 saucers. *£8. 0. 0.*

72. A tea and coffee service, painted in blue with sprays of flowers between panels of wavy blue-scale whorls, comprising: coffee-pot and cover, teapot, cover and stand, tea-caddy and cover, two sugar basins and covers, hot-milk jug and cover, slop basin, cream-jug, 6 tea cups, 6 coffee cups and twelve saucers. Open crescent mark. *£16. 10. 0.*

73. The Browne wedding service, painted with flowers in pink on a white body, gilt arabesque border around the neck and rim of lid, comprising — a fine teapot and cover, sugar basin, slop basin, cream-jug, 8 tea cups and 8 saucers. *£18. 0. 0.*
[This service is mentioned in the affidavit of Robert Browne, dated December 12th, 1895, as the 'first thing in Mr. Seago's collection identified by me was my father's wedding tea service'. The description fits the teabowl and saucer illustrated in Plate 154.]

Inscribed and Dated Lowestoft, Blue and White

74. A Flask of round flat pilgrim form, painted in blue with a garden scene with trellis on one side, root ornament on the reverse, with lattice borders, the neck with the initials and date, 'I.B.' 1778. 4⅜ inches high. *£12. 10. 0.*
[Resold at the Hotblack sale in December 1955, for £31.]

75. An ewer and basin, in plain white, the former of bottle-shape with a slightly blistered neck, the latter with everted rim, the bases of both inscribed 'Maria Anne Hoyler. 1770'. Ewer 8½ inches high, basin 9½ inches in diameter. *£7. 0. 0.*

76. A cylindrical mug, painted with a lattice border inside the rim and sprays of flowers flanking a cartouche, inscribed 'John & Mary Livock, Lowestoft' 1780. 4¼ inches. Damaged. *£8. 0. 0.*
[Resold in the Hotblack sale in December 1955, for £16.]

77. A teapot of early form, with loop handle and typical spout, painted in blue with Chinese river scenes and landscapes, the base inscribed 'Elizth. Johnson, Norwich, Feb^{r}. 5th, 1768'. 4½ inches high. Painter's numeral 6. *£10. 0. 0.*
[This damaged teapot was resold in the Hunting sale of October 1961, for £70, and is now in the Castle Museum, Norwich.]

78. A mug of bell shape, with a lattice border in the interior, the exterior painted with two sprays of flowers, and in front with a cartouche, inscribed 'Phill Tricker, 1769'. 4½ inches. Painter's numeral 5. *£5. 0. 0.*
[Resold in 1938, for £35.]

79. The James Hughes teapot, painted with vignettes of Chinese river scenes in blue within floral panels, a flower spray under the spout and a diaper border round the neck, moulded in relief within small ovals under the vignettes, with the initials and date 'I.H. 1761' [moulded in relief]. 4½ inches high, the earliest dated Lowestoft specimen known... *£9. 0. 0.*
James Hughes, son of James and Susannah Hughes and grandson of Robert Browne, was baptised at Lowestoft March 1st, 1761.
[Resold at the Hotblack sale in December 1955, for £27.]

80. A mug of bell shape, with loop handle, well painted with two flower sprays on the side, and in front with an inn sign of bracket clock form, containing a representation of a human face in the form of a sun in splendour, inscribed below, 'Mic^{l} Jaye, Norwich', and dated on the base, 1768. 4½ inches high. Damaged. *£9. 10. 0.*
[Resold in the Hotblack sale in December 1955, for £20.]

81. A teapot and cover, slightly painted with flowers, butterflies and insects in blue, one side of the teapot inscribed within a cartouche, 'Robt and Mary Godfrey, 1782', the lid with the initials 'R.M.G.' and similar date. 5½ inches high. *£15. 0. 0.*

82. The Lowestoft Church teapot, decorated on one side with the view of St. Margaret's Church, walled churchyard, two windmills and Lighthouse, and on the other side with three ships, part of the side with the ship is missing, the base with the initials 'S.C.' and date '1767'. 5½ inches. Painter's numeral 5. *£12. 0. 0.*
[Resold in the Hunting sale, in October 1961, for £150.]

83. The Samuel Aldred coffee-pot [really a covered jug, see page 206], with loop handle and lip-spout inscribed underneath the spout with the initials 'S A' in a monogram, the rest of the body finely printed in blue with a dog putting up a quaint parrot-like partridge, on the left the sportsman in eighteenth century costume with his gun over his shoulder, holding it by the barrel. 7½ inches high. *£20. 0.0.*
...This fine print was supplied to Robert Browne by Mr. Gamble of Bungay, the Samuel Hoare mug similarly printed was dated 1783...[page 102.]

84. A teapot and a pair of cups and saucers, painted with a vignette of a landscape and trees, root ornament and fenced garden, the bases of the teapot, saucers and the cups, inscribed 'Mary Crowfoot, 1778'. *£16. 0. 0.*
[A teabowl and saucer are in the Christchurch Mansion Museum, Ipswich.]

85. Robert Browne's inkstand, of nine-sided form, with deep well, four holes for pens, the shoulders painted with small flower sprays, the sides with Chinoiseries and cartouche panels dividing the figures, the initials 'R B' and the early date '1762', divided by a column. 2¼ inches high. Painter's numberal 5. *£68. 0. 0.*
This is the inkstand of the originator and manager of the factory which passed from his collection to Mr. Seago and from him to Mr. Crisp. [See page 220, it is now in the Castle Museum, Norwich, being part of the Colman Bequest.]

Birth Tablets

86. A birth tablet, painted with Chinese houses and river scenes on one side, and on the other under pendant husks, inscribed 'Ann Ruthen, Born, June 30th 1793'. 3 inch diameter. *£15. 0. 0.*

The Crisp Collection included other blue and white birth tablets, inscribed as briefly listed below:

87. S.S. 1789. *£10. 10. 0.*
88. Mary Ward, Born Decr. 4th 1796. *£11. 10. 0.*
89. John Ward, Born Febry. 15th 1799. *£11. 0. 0.*
90. Eallathe Leggett Liffin, Born Decr. 9th 1798. *£11. 0. 0.*
91. Sarah Mason, Born January 1772. [large size 5 inch diameter]. *£13. 0. 0.*
92. Robert Rope, Born Febuary 13. 1782. *£30. 0. 0.*
93. Robert Downin, Born January 19. 1791. *£11. 0. 0.*
94. Johnathen Downing, Born December 27, 1793. *£28. 0. 0.*
95. Honnour Downing, Born October 28, 1788. *£33. 0. 0.*
96. Elizabeth Ruthen, Born February 4, 1791. *£29. 0. 0.*
97. Samuel Wright, Born January 30th, 1775. *£40. 0. 0.*

[For an enamelled birth tablet, see Item 105].

Overglaze Enamelled Specimens

98. A cream boat, painted by the well-known Tulip painter and with feather moulding round the base, the interior with a narrow diaper border and the initials 'G.G.M.H. 1774'. 4 inches. *£13. 0. 0.*
[Resold in the Colman sale in April 1948, for £29.]

99. A mug, of cylindrical form, painted with Angouleme cornflour sprigs, blue line border and a puce ribbon and husk panel, enclosing the legend 'A Trifle from Lowestoft'. 3½ inches high. Illustrated in Crisp's '*Lowestoft China*', p. 4. Damaged. *£9. 0. 0.*

100. An inkstand of slightly waisted cylindrical form, pierced with four holes for pens, with Angouleme cornflour sprigs and inscribed in front 'A Trifle from Lowestoft'. 2¾ inches high. Illustrated in Crisp's '*Lowestoft China*', p. 9. *£36. 0. 0.*
[Two other inkstands with the same inscription realised £30 and £29.]

101. A barrel-shaped mug, with grooved ribbing round the neck and base and sepia borders, Angouleme sprigs, and an oval medallion, inscribed 'A Trifle from Lowestoft'. 4 inches high. Illustrated in Crisp's '*Lowestoft China*', p.8. *£15. 0. 0.*
[Three other 'Trifle' mugs fetched £10 and £27, the latter being a pair.]

102. An interesting scent flacon of flattened bottle shape, painted on one side in colours with Robert Browne, the grandson of the original potter of that name, serving at the counter of his Grocer's shop and on the reverse inscribed with the initials 'R B' in monogram, on a pale green ground. 2¾ inches high. Illustrated by Crisp in '*Lowestoft China*', p.9, purchased from Robert Browne of Blackheath. *£12. 0. 0.*

103. The well-known bell-shaped mug. . . painted in colours with the Arms of the Blacksmiths' Company. . . motto 'By hammer and hand all Arts doth stand'. The base inscribed in red 'James and Sarah Hacon. 1775'. 4¾ inches high. Illustrated in Crisp's '*Lowestoft China*', p.7. Damaged. *£21. 0. 0.*
[Now in the Castle Museum, Norwich, being part of the Colman Bequest.]

104. The James Hughes mug etched in black with river scenes, pagoda, two Chinese boys and a dog, a typical Chinese *shan shui* subject with an inner lambrequin border, the handle with an exotic bird in black, the base inscribed also in black — '1s Hughes. . . Septr. 4th 1766. Lowestoft'.
4⅜ inches high. Painter's number '3' in black. James Hughes married, at Lowestoft in 1760, Susannah, daughter of Robert Browne — of the Lowestoft factory. *£54. 0. 0.*
[This mug, now at Christchurch Mansions, Ipswich, is illustrated in Plate 83.]

105. A fine large birth tablet, with blue rim and red sprays inscribed within feathery scrolls 'Ann Redgrave, born Novbr. 4. 1795'. The reverse plain except for a single flower spray in colours. 4½ inches high. *£49. 0. 0.*
[Now in the Castle Museum, Norwich, being part of the Colman Bequest.]

106. The Judas Lugger punch bowl, finely decorated on the exterior in Chinese 'famille rose' style with panels of flowers, pink scale and vermilion lattice diaper, the interior with an elaborate pink scale festoon and butterfly border, the centre with a medallion containing a view of a fishing boat and ribbon label with name 'The Judas'. 11½ inch diameter. *£41. 0. 0.*
[Resold in the Colman sale in April 1948, for £98.]

THE WELL—KNOWN COLLECTION OF. . . WALLACE ELLIOTT, ESQ. SOLD BY MESSRS. SOTHEBY AND CO. MAY, 1938.

Blue and White

107. A pair of Lowestoft salt cellars of silver pattern and circular shape, supported on three mask and paw feet and attractively painted with festoons of flowers round the sides, the lions' masks picked out in blue. 2⅞ inches. Rare. *£9. 10. 0.*
[Resold in the Colman sale, see Plate 119.]

108. A Pap Warmer and candlestick of usual cylindrical form, [Plate 104] moulded with grotesque masks, shell handles, the container surmounted by a domed cover with nozzle finial, painted with flowers in underglaze-blue, 9¾ inches high. Painter's number '5'. *£6. 0. 0.*
[Resold in the Hotblack sale in December 1955, for £25.]

109. The 'John Cable' Lowestoft jug with ovoid body, cylindrical neck, mask-lip spout and stout loop-handle, moulded on the neck and body with bands of leaf and floral ornament and painted with sprays of flowers in blue, the front painted within a simple cartouche with a stag trippant, inscribed below 'John Cable'. 10¼ inches high. Painter's number '5'. *£26. 0. 0.*

110. A Lowestoft inscribed and dated teapot, painted with flowers on one side and within a slight rococo cartouche, inscribed in the other —

A MARIA CAMM
LANEHAM
EX DONO I : H.
OLDTON
1771

. . . 6⅜ inches high. [Plate 85.] *£16. 0. 0.*
[A jug and a bell-shaped mug with identical inscriptions were sold for £19 and £26. The jug was resold in the Colman sale, in April 1948, for £72.]

111. The John Salter inkstand of tall wasted cylindrical form, the shoulders with sprays of flowers in blue and four holes for pens, the sides with floral branches and under an arch of pendant flowers inscribed 'John Salter 1791', the base with the initials 'I.S.' in blue. 2⅞ inches diameter. 2½ inches high. *£20. 0. 0.*

[Resold in the Colman sale in April 1948, for £30.]

112. An inscribed and dated bell-shaped mug with scroll loop handle, painted with flower sprays on either side and in front within a slight rococo cartouche inscribed 'Phill Tricker, 1769', a trellis border within the rim. 4½ inches high. Painter's number '5'. *£35. 0. 0.*

Overglaze Enamel Decoration

113. A Lowestoft cream jug of pear shape, with lip spout and loop handle, painted with flowers in so-called Curtis style and inscribed in red under the handle, 'E W 1779'. 3¼ inches high. *£10. 0. 0.*

114. A Lowestoft 'Trifle' mug of cylindrical form with typical handle, inscribed in front 'A Trifle from Bungay', within a puce oval panel and pendant husks, a turquoise and puce ribbon festoon border round the neck and base. 3⅝ inches high. *£21. 0. 0.*

115. A rare Lowestoft 'Trifle' pounce-pot of waisted cylindrical form, painted with conventional floral border, sprays of flowers and within a puce cartouche inscribed 'A Trifle from Lowestoft'. 2½ inches high. *£40. 0. 0.*

116. An interesting Lowestoft cylindrical mug, painted in sepia and gold with an ornate Chinese border round the rim, sprays of flowers and in the centre within an escutcheon the monogram 'W.T.T.C.' in gold, and below the words 'Sacred to Friendship' with a ribbon label. 4¼ inches high. (Cracked.) *£14. 0. 0*

[Resold in the Hunting sale, in October 1961, and purchased for the Castle Museum, Norwich, for £85.]

117. A Lowestoft armorial cup and saucer in plain white with gilt borders, painted with the arms of the Rev. Robert Potter, Vicar of Lowestoft and Prebendary of Norwich, the arms, or a chevron sable, between three mullets pierced gules, Crest: a horse's head holding in the mouth a sprig of oak, below the punning motto 'In deo Potero'. *£12. 0. 0.*

[A teabowl, coffee cup and saucer from this service fetched £200 when offered in the Holland sale, in October 1967, see page 249 and Plate 215.]

118. The Mary Sutten Lowestoft mug of cylindrical form with loop handle, painted with brick red lambrequin border within the rim, the sides painted with sprays of flowers in colours and inscribed within a puce rococo and floral cartouche, 'Mary Sutton, 1787' in red. 5½ inches high. [Plate 209.] *£48. 0. 0.*

119. The well-known set of three Tanton mugs of cylindrical shape, brilliantly decorated by the Tulip painter — with roses and other flowers including tulips and inscribed within ornate puce rococo cartouches in front

J & E
TANTON
NORWICH
1774.

The three sizes are 3⅝, 4⅝ and 6 inches high. *£125. 0. 0.*

[Now in the Castle Museum, Norwich, being part of the Colman Bequest, these mugs are by the Tulip painter; one is included in Plate 147.]

A COLLECTION OF FINE OLD ENGLISH PORCELAIN... LOWESTOFT CHINA WITH RARE PATTERNS AND INSCRIBED AND DATED SPECIMENS... THE PROPERTY OF THE LATE CHARLES A. KING, ESQ. SOLD BY MESSRS. SOTHEBY AND CO. ON JULY 14TH, 1938.

Blue and White

120. A Lowestoft miniature vase and a beaker originally part of a garniture, attractively painted in underglaze-blue with Chinese garden scenes and trees, under loop and dot borders round the rims, 5¼ and 5½ inches high. *£6. 0. 0.*

121. A Lowestoft moulded 1761 teapot, painted with reserved vignettes of Chinese landscapes and river scenes, within floral-moulded panels on either side, the cover and shoulders with trellis and 'S' scroll borders, on either side a panel with the letters and date 'I.H. 1761', stated to be for James Hughes, son of James and Susanna Hughes and a grandson of Robert Browne, partner and manager of the firm (and a cylindrical mug painted in blue with flowers). Painter's number '8'. *£21. 0. 0.*

122. A Lowestoft inscribed cup and saucer, painted in blue in Chinese style with a garden scene and root pattern within a trellis border, inscribed on the base of the cup and saucer 'Jas Gray. 1779'. *£9. 0. 0.*

Enamelled

123. A rare and interesting Lowestoft bowl, painted in colours with the Battle of Camperdown, October 11th, 1797, on the exterior, on one side the 'Active' cutter in Yarmouth Roads, and on the reverse the battle in progress with a dismasted Dutch ship in the foreground and numerous Dutch and British battleships firing broadsides, the interior of the bowl with a conventional puce, red and green border, the centre with a cornucopia of flowers. 9¼ inch diameter. *£30. 0. 0.*

[Resold in the Colman sale, April 1948, for £90.]

124. A Lowestoft 'Trifle' mug of cylindrical form, with rococo loop handle and green line border inside the rim, the front with a puce cartouche containing the legend, 'A Trifle from Lowestoft', feathery sepia and blue dot borders at the top and base and Angouleme sprigs at the sides. 3½ inches high. *£18. 0. 0.*

125. A Lowestoft teapot and cream-jug, painted in colours with cornucopia and flowers under festoons and pendant borders [5¾ inches high] and a bowl and cream-jug, painted with Chinese figures in colours, 6 and 3⅛ inches high. *£10. 0. 0.*

THE FINE COLLECTION OF RARE LOWESTOFT PORCELAIN, THE PROPERTY OF MRS. COLMAN, CROWN POINT, NORWICH, SOLD BY MESSRS. SOTHEBY AND CO. APRIL 20TH, 1948.

N.B. A Selection from the Colman Collection was bequeathed to the Castle Museum, Norwich, and many of these specimens are illustrated in *The Connoisseur* magazine of September and October 1937.

Underglaze-Blue Decoration

126. A small powder-blue jar and cover, with barbed reserved panels on a dark powder-blue ground, 5 inches, and a saucer dish with reserved vignettes of Chinese *shan shui* and flower sprays. 7 inch diameter. *£36. 0. 0.*

127. The 'Wardrobe Court' sauce-boat, with a typical moulded pattern of flower-heads, leaves and cartouches, painted in blue with floral meander round the incurved rim and sprays inscribed on one side:

Made at
Lowestoft, Sept 6
in the presence
of J.S. Browne

and painted in blue on the other side in similar script,

Wardrobe
Court
Doctors Commons
London
1770

the interior, with a floral spray, has been repaired, the lip spout with a floral medallion and trellis diaper, 7½ inches long. Painter's number '5'. *£48. 0. 0.*

128. A Lowestoft inkstand, with waisted cylindrical body and flat shoulders with four holes, pencilled in a light blue with a Chinese garden scene and peonies, the base with the initials and date N + M 1779 2 inches high. *£10. 0. 0.*

129. The 'John and Sarah Livock' coffee-pot of large size, with lip spout and ribbed scroll handle, painted with flowers and butterflies and in a rococo and floral cartouche under the spout, inscribed:

John and Sarah
Livock
Lowestoft
1787

the cover with a small panel with initials, J & S L 1787

sprays of flowers and a lambrequin border matching the neck. 10½ inches high. *£28. 0. 0.*

130. An inscribed coffee-pot [really a covered jug], with lip spout and scroll handle, transfer-printed with a cell-diaper border around the rim, flower-sprays at the sides and between two butterflies under the spout inscribed:

John Baker
Yarmouth
1772

One of the few inscribed and transfer-printed pieces known. 6½ inches high [Plate 121]. *£18. 0. 0.*

131. A Lowestoft small birth tablet, inscribed within a single line border:

John Lee
born August 23.
1797

with an insect and leaf motifs between, the reverse with a Chinese-cum-Lowestoft cottage, within a double line border. 2¾ inch diameter. *£28. 0. 0.*

132. A rare combined birth and memorial Tablet, painted in a light blue on the sunken side with the inscription:

Martha Liffin born August 17. 1794.

flanked by insects, the reverse with a loop and sprig border enclosing the memorial to the mother:

Mary Liffin, died May 4, 1795.

and flanked by flower-sprays, 2⅞ inch diameter. *£44. 0. 0.*
[This specimen was broken in half.]

133. A Lowestoft large inscribed bowl, the exterior painted in underglaze-blue with two large flower sprays and butterflies and insects between, the interior with another spray and a single butterfly, inscribed on the base:

Wlm. Barton
Forncett
1768

the interior with a lambrequin border, 9⅝ inch diameter. Painter's number '5'. *£46. 0. 0.*

134. A Lowestoft inscribed jug, with pear-shaped body, pinched lip spout and scroll handle, painted with two sprays of flowers and underneath the spout within a rococo cartouche inscribed:

Thos. Davy
Fręssingfield.
1782

the outside of the rim with a trellis diaper border, 7⅛ inches high. *£42. 0. 0.*
[This specimen was cracked.]

135. An inscribed Christening mug of large bell shape, with scroll handle, painted in dark underglaze-blue with two flower sprays and insects flanking a shaped cartouche enclosing a cross and above a panel inscribed:

John Rolfe. Woodbridge.

the base with the date 1772, the interior with a trellis and floral border, 5¾ inches high. Painter's number '5'. *£58. 0. 0.*

136. A rare early Lowestoft inscribed and dated ewer, with globular body, tubular neck with 'blistered' and flared mouth, finely painted with views of St. Margaret's Church, Lowestoft, flanked by the High Light and the Low Light on the beach, the neck with smaller vignettes and men-o'war and the lower part of the body with smaller views of the Lighthouse, the Low Light and the Battery on the Ness, under the base inscribed:

E & A
Lowestoft
1764

the neck rim with a blue rococo border, above a line, 9⅝ inches

high. Painted number '3'. *£115. 0. 0.*
[The companion ewer and basin is in the Colman Bequest at the Norwich Museum and is similarly inscribed and dated, see Plate 80.]

137. The well-known Lowestoft ewer and basin, both painted with views of the High Light, two Windmills and St. Margaret's Church, within a large cartouche, flanked by smaller panels with views of the Low Light, the Battery and ships in the Roadstead, with a lambrequin border. Ewer 9⅜ inches high. Painter's number '5'. *£80. 0. 0.*
[Slightly damaged.]

Enamel Decoration

138. A rare Lowestoft large coloured birth tablet, painted in colours on one side with a simple spray of flowers on a plain white ground, the reverse bearing the inscription in red:

Ann Redgrave
Born Jan^{ry} 2nd
1794

within an oval puce husk panel, puce pendant ribbons above and a leaf-spray tied with ribbon below, also in puce, blue enamel border round the rim. 4¼ inches diameter. *£60. 0. 0.*
[Resold in the Hotblack sale in December 1955, for £70. A further Ann Redgrave birth tablet (made for a cousin) is in the Castle Museum, Norwich, and a Susanna Redgrave tablet (Plate 227) is in the Lowestoft Museum collection, see also the Redgrave tea-caddy, Colour Plate 12.]

139. A finely painted Lowestoft teapot and cover, delicately decorated in puce camaieu with classic ruins and pillars on each side, a miniature view above the spout, the cover similarly decorated, gilt scalloped borders. 5¾ inches high. *£30. 0. 0.*

140. A Lowestoft cylindrical mug, painted with turquoise festoon borders and sprigs... Inscribed

A Trifle from Bungay,

within a puce shield-shaped cartouche, 4½ inches high. [Colour Plate 11.] *£68. 0. 0.*

141. A Lowestoft small cylindrical mug, with turquoise line borders, intertwined with floral meander, within a puce cartouche inscribed:

A Trifle from Holt

3½ inches high. Extremely rare, no other recorded. *£88. 0. 0.*

142. A rare Lowestoft inkstand, with four holes on the shoulders for pens, painted with sprays of flowers in colours and inscribed within a puce cartouche

A Trifle from Wangford

2⅞ inches diameter. *£62. 0. 0.*

143. A rare Lowestoft 'Trifle' pounce-pot, of waisted cylindrical form, the top pierced with numerous holes and painted with a puce florette, the sides with sprays and sprigs of flowers and a 'C' scroll and festoon border, inscribed with a feathery quatrefoil cartouche:

A Trifle from Lowestoft,

flat base. 2½ inches high. *£78. 0. 0.*

144. A Lowestoft armorial jug, with lip spout and floral festoon border round the rim, flower sprays at the side, painted with crest, arms and motto of Monro of Bearcroft. 3⅞ inches high. *£60. 0. 0.*

145. A Lowestoft inscribed inkstand of waisted cylindrical form, painted with sprays of flowers round the sides, the shoulders with six holes of pens and puce trellis-diaper, inscribed under the base in puce

B Townshend
1777

3¼ inches diameter. *£44. 0. 0.*

146. An interesting Lowestoft cylindrical mug, painted with views of the Windmill, Battery, High Lighthouse with new revolving lantern and ships in the roadstead, within a very elaborate feathery quatrefoil cartouche in puce, the monogram 'J.C.' in gold, the interior of the rim with a cell-diaper border. 4¾ inches high. *£90. 0. 0.*

147. A rare Lowestoft flask, attractively painted with a Hogarthian scene of two gentlemen 'in their cups' seated at a tripod table, with a punch bowl between them, the reverse with a sailor and his lass seated on some rocks, a wide green scale border, and puce feathery motifs round the neck. 5⅝ inches high. *£70. 0. 0.*

148. A fine Lowestoft cylindrical mug brilliantly printed with Chinese figures and vignettes of birds, flowers and landscapes, on a red and black trellis diaper ground, the inside of the rim with a red feathery scroll border, 5½ inches high. [Plate 191.] *£62. 0. 0.*

149. A very fine Lowestoft cylindrical mug superbly enamelled with a seated figure of a Chinaman under a tree, smoking a pipe, a dog at his feet, a youth wearing a sword and with a hawk on his wrist, standing in front of him, on a black trellis diaper ground. 5½ inches high. Brilliant and rare. [Plate 191.] *£150. 0. 0.*

A FINE COLLECTION OF LOWESTOFT PORCELAIN (SOLD ANONYMOUSLY BUT COMPRISING THE COLLECTION OF THE LATE G.F. HOTBLACK) OFFERED BY MESSRS. SOTHEBY AND CO. ON DECEMBER 6TH, 1955.

Blue and White

[N.B. Several 'lots', especially the inscribed and dated pieces, were known examples from earlier collections and are given in this list under the name of the first collection, for example, see item 74.]

150. A Lowestoft mug of bell shape, painted in blue with a sun in splendour and human face within an architectural panel, inscribed below:

Ed. Amond. Wymondham.

and flanked by flower sprays, the interior of the rim with a lambrequin border, dated 1768 on the base, 4⅝ inches high. Damaged. *£24. 0. 0.*
[Now in the Castle Museum, Norwich.]

151. A fine and interesting Lowestoft bell-shaped mug, with ribbed loop handle and lambrequin border inside the rim, inscribed within cartouche:

James Bullard
R.A.
1768

on either side of the cartouche two sprays of flowering plants. 5⅞ inches high. Painter's number '3'. [Plate 98.] *£70. 0. 0.*

152. A fine Lowestoft cylindrical mug, with trellis border inside the rim and within an elaborate cartouche painted with a typical and discreet Lowestoft bathing machine, and in the Stamford Roads two ships in full sail, beneath a ribbon label inscribed:

A Trifle from Lowestoft

flanked by sprigs of flowers and pendant husks. 5½ inches high. *£115. 0. 0.*

Enamel Decoration

153. A finely painted Lowestoft coffee-pot and cover, with scroll spout painted with a pendant spray, the one side painted with a seated Chinese lady talking to a man who carries a bird on his hand, the reverse with two girls, the one carrying a basket over her shoulder in a fenced garden. 7¾ inches high. *£34. 0. 0.*

154. A Lowestoft 'famille-rose' garniture, painted by Thomas Curtis with baskets of flowers in Chinese taste, the reverse with sprays and sprigs of flowers below pink scale borders, comprising: two baluster vases and covers, a pair of pear-shaped bottles and a flared beaker. 5, 4½ and 5½ inches high. [Similar to Plate 198.] *£58. 0. 0.*

155. A pair of rare, small Lowestoft cats, seated with their tails curled round the near side, both with tabby markings, supported on green oval bases. 2¼ inches high. *£62. 0. 0.*

156. A pair of rare Lowestoft white swans, with red beaks, dark crests and red and black eyes, finely modelled in swimming attitude. 2¼ inches high. *£52. 0. 0.*

157. A Lowestoft inscribed teapot, painted in colours with small sprays of flowers round the shoulders and neck with pink scale and festoon borders of husks and flowers, on one side within a puce shield-shaped cartouche, inscribed in red:

Willm & Ann Cobb
Harleston
1790

5½ inches high. [Plate 214.] *£82. 0. 0.*

158. A superb set of three Lowestoft coloured mugs of cylindrical shape, with loop handles and of pint and a half, one pint and half pint size, each finely painted with the same subject of two figures in European costume standing by the banks of a river, in the background sailing boats and a church, and to the right a castle enclosed within an elaborate rococo puce escutcheon, flanked by sprays of flowers in colours, the handles with brick red pendant sprays of flowers in colours, and the insides of the rims with line and loop dot borders in the same palette. 5¾, 5 and 3½ inches high. [Plate 160.] *£260. 0. 0.*

A SELECTION OF LOWESTOFT PORCELAIN FROM THE GEOFFREY GODDEN COLLECTION, SOLD BY MESSRS. SOTHEBY AND CO. JULY 17TH, 1959.

Blue and White

159. A Lowestoft moulded jug with scroll handle and thumbpiece, painted in runny blue with Chinese *shan shui*, pagodas and boats between moulded peony head and leaf borders round the shoulders and base, the cylindrical neck with underglaze-blue panels within moulded foliate borders. 9 inches high. *£10. 0. 0.*

160. A miniature teapot and cover painted with Chinese waterscapes and boats with lantern sails, within vandyck borders round the rims, the cover with acorn knob and matching vignettes. 3¼ inches high. Painter's number '7' and three teabowls and two saucers from the same service, one bowl with numeral '17'. *£15. 0. 0.*

161. A pair of octagonal dishes decorated in Chinese style with a figure on a hump bridge spanning a creek and with pagodas, willow and plantain trees and a fisherman, the rims with prunus sprays. 11¼ inches long; painter's number '5'; and a circular plate showing a Chinese figure with curious whip-like fishing rod and another at a table with a vase of flowers. 9 inch diameter. Painter's number '7'. *£23. 0. 0.*

162. A transfer-printed coffee-pot and cover of pear shape, the double-twist grooved handle with moulded leaf terminal [Plate 105], printed with a fenced garden with tree peony and two birds in flight, the cover with flower knob. 9 inches high. And a bowl printed on the exterior with a Pillement-style figure seated beside a squirrel perched on trelliswork in two panels divided by fern and flower sprays. 8⅞ inch diameter. *£16. 0. 0.*

163. A small, powder-blue teapot and cover decorated on the globular body with irregularly scalloped panels containing Chinese landscapes and *shan shui* reserved on a mottled powder-blue ground, the cover with two smaller vignettes. 5 inches high. [Plate 94.] *£26. 0. 0.*

164. An attractive powder-blue coffee-pot and cover painted on the pear-shaped body with Chinese waterscapes within irregularly shaped panels and on the cover the smaller round and kidney shaped medallions, reserved on a rich deep blue ground. 9½ inches high. Cover restored. *£18. 0. 0.*

165. A transfer-printed mug of bell shape with loop handle and thumbpiece printed with two sprays of chrysanthemums, rose, kingcup and other flowers divided by two insects below a printed cell diaper border round the rim. 5¾ inches high: and a pair of plates with shaped rims printed with flowers and fruit and with sprays round the border. 9⅝ inch diameter, simulated Worcester crescent marks. *£15. 0. 0.*

166. A Lowestoft rare inscribed jug of pear shape with scroll handle and thumbpiece and supported on a stout circular foot, painted in front with a cartouche of entwined ribbon and palm leaf festoons containing the inscription:

J.S.
1794

and decorated with flower sprigs on either side of the handle, which has vertical blue strokes at the junctures, a narrow diaper border round the rim. 5¾ inches high. [Plate 221.] *£46. 0. 0.*

Enamel Decoration

167. A fine Lowestoft teapot and cover with loop handle, attractively decorated on the globular body in sepia and gold on either side with Chinese pagodas beneath a pine tree and a junk sailing on the water, the slightly domed cover with button knob and matching decoration. 6¼ inches high. *£26. 0. 0.*

168. A pair of Lowestoft figures of a ram and a sheep, each lying down with heads looking sideways, white except for coloured eyes, muzzles and hoofs, the glaze fairly thick. 2¼ inches high. *£30. 0. 0.*

169. A rare Lowestoft figure of a cat, seated with its tail curled round its near side, marked with dark brown tabby striations, green mound oval base. 2¼ inches high. *£65. 0. 0.*

170. A Lowestoft inscribed teapot and cover of globular shape with plain loop handle, painted round the shoulders with pink and puce panels and festoons of flowers in the style of Curtis, inscribed on one side:

John Harm
1787

within iron-red scroll cartouche, the reverse with a bouquet of flowers, the cover, damaged, with matching trellis. 6½ inches high. [Plate 208.] *£46. 0. 0.*

A COLLECTION OF LOWESTOFT PORCELAIN, THE PROPERTY OF THE LATE D.M. HUNTING, ESQ. SOLD BY MESSRS. SOTHEBY AND CO. ON OCTOBER 31ST, 1961.

Blue and White

171. A Lowestoft cornucopia moulded with rococo scrolls and decorated in underglaze-blue with a panel of two oriental figures in a garden, with a bird flying above, all the scrolls heightened with rich blue. 8¾ inches high. Painter's number '3'. *£58. 0. 0.*

172. A fine early bell-shaped mug with ribbed double rococo handle with thumbpiece, well drawn and painted in Chinese taste with rocks and a branch of trailing tree peony. 6 inches high. Painter's number '2'. c.1758-1760. *£32. 0. 0.*

173. An early double-handled porringer with ribbed band round the lower half of the body, painted in light blue with flowering branches and birds in the half beneath the diaper border, below the rib, aquatic plants and on the conical foot stylised flowers, the double handles ribbed and with billets. 3¾ inches high. Painter's number '3'. c.1760. *£85. 0. 0.*

174. A very rare early chocolate-pot and cover of silver pattern with scroll spout and right angle ribbed handle, the high domed cover painted with a figure holding a floral spray on one side and a bird on a flowering branch on the other, flower finial, the body painted with a larger version of the same subject, the branch trailing round the side of the body...Chinese style diaper borders. 9¼ inches high. Painter's number '1' on the base. c.1757-1758. [Plate 35.] *£190. 0. 0.*

175. An early sucrier and cover of pre-1761 design, but probably used with 1761 services, circular vignettes in blue on a moulded ground with sprays and spandrels. 5 inches high. Painter's number '3'; and two slightly later cream jugs. 3½ inches high. *£82. 0. 0.*

176. The Elizabeth Buckle cream jug of barrel shape, with loop handle and lip spout, the body painted with a shepherd and shepherdess seated with sheep in the foreground and a man ploughing in the background, the base inscribed:

E Buckle

the neck and base with blue meander borders and a band of horizontal ribbing. 3¼ inches high. c.1768. *£54. 0. 0.*

177. A rare armorial bell-shaped mug of fine quality, the scroll handle with thumbpiece, the body without decoration except for a rococo escutcheon painted in underglaze-blue with the arms of Carysfort of Normans Cross in the County of Huntingdon. 4½ inches high. *£120. 0. 0.*

LOWESTOFT PORCELAIN, SOLD BY MESSRS. SOTHEBY AND CO. ON OCTOBER 25TH, 1966.

178. Two documentary Lowestoft mugs in two sizes, the bell-shaped bodies painted in blue with birds and flowers, the interior of the lips with scrolls, both inscribed under the foot:

Abr^{m} Moore.
August 29th
1765

Painter's number '3'. 6 and 4¾ inches high. *£90. 0. 0.*

[These damaged specimens represent two of a set of three, the smallest is in the British Museum. These mugs are shown in Plate 82, and they were copied on the Continent in the nineteenth century, see page 253 and Plate 241.]

179. An early Lowestoft blue and white patty-pan, or shallow bowl, with flared sides, painted with a primitive Chinese river scene in the centre with a drapery festoon border around the rim. Painter's number '3'. *£20. 0. 0.*

180. An early Lowestoft blue and white basket, painted with an Oriental figure fishing on the banks of a river with houses on the near and far shore, the sides formed of interlaced circles pierced and edged with an underglaze-blue border. Painter's number '3'. 6 inch diameter. *£33. 0. 0.*

[See Plate 43 for a similar but slightly smaller basket.]

181. A very rare Lowestoft spoon-tray of shuttle shape, with flat base with straight sides moulded with flutes and with underglaze-blue scalloped border, painted in the centre with a pagoda below a pine tree in a fenced garden with rocks. Painter's number '5'. 6¾ inches long. *£46. 0. 0.*

[Colour Plate 5 shows an earlier example of approximately this form.]

182. A fine Lowestoft powder-blue coffee-pot and cover with pear-shaped body, typical scroll handle and long spout, decorated with asymmetrical vignettes of Oriental landscapes in blue reserved on a powder-blue ground, the domed cover with matching panels and surmounted by an acorn knob. 9¼ inches high. *£260. 0. 0.*

[Illustrated in colour in S.W. Fisher's *English Blue and White Porcelain of the 18th Century*, 1947. A similar example is shown in Plate 95.]

LOWESTOFT PORCELAIN, THE PROPERTY OF THE LATE E.R. HOLLOND. SOLD BY MESSRS. SOTHEBY AND CO. ON OCTOBER 17TH, 1967.

Blue and White

183. A rare early small jar of baluster shape, painted in Chinese taste with a diaper border round the shoulders and with floral sprays, insects and a bird in flight above line borders round the base. 5½ inches high. Painter's number '2'; pre-1761 [no cover.] *£55. 0. 0.*

184. An oval moulded butter cooler, painted in dark inky-blue with Chinese vignettes within rococo leaf-bordered panels, divided by bold sunflower sprays, loop and ermine-tail border inside the rim. 5⅛ inches long. Painter's number '5'. [No cover. Of the same type as that shown in Plate 61.] *£55. 0. 0.*

185. A fine 'James Hughes' teapot and cover, the latter with rare acorn knob, the sides painted in underglaze-blue with Chinese river scenes beneath fret borders and surrounded by moulded floral decoration, bearing on either side of the base the letters 'I.H.' and date 1761, the loop handle and spout with simple floral sprays. 5½ inches high. [Plate 75.] *£160. 0. 0.*

186. A betrothal saucer dish bearing in the centre a heart-shaped panel inscribed:

THOS & ELIZ[th]
CRAFER
DOWNHAM
1793

flanked by figures of Thomas and Elizabeth, holding up the heart, within a Chinese trellis and floral border in unusually bright blue. [Broken in half.] *£80. 0. 0.*

187. A rare early sauce-boat, the loop handle with heart-shaped leaf terminal, the lobed body moulded in relief with pendant fruit, the interior with trellis border and early type sprays of flowers, flat base. 7 inches long. [For model see Plate 69.] *£50. 0. 0.*

188. An inscribed bell-shaped mug, with ribbed loop handle, painted in a light blue within an arcaded rectangular panel, with a human faced rising sun and inscribed below:

EDW[d] AMOND. WYMONDHAM.

flanked by two larger flower sprays and dated under the foot 1768. 5⅞ inches high. Painter's number '5'.
[This damaged mug is the largest of a matching set of 3, or perhaps in this case of four mugs.] *£110. 0. 0.*

189. The James Fisher teapot, inscribed within a rocaille panel:

IEA[s] FISHER 1769

the reverse painted with a windmill on a mound flanked by trees and with houses at the base of the score, the cover with a smaller version of the same scene and inscribed panel. 4¾ inches high. Painter's number '5'. [No knob to cover and spout damaged.] *£120. 0. 0.*

190. An interesting inscribed bell-shaped mug, with two formal flower sprigs flanking the handle, the remainder of the white body plain and bearing the inscription:

ADD TO KNOWLEDGE
TEMPERANCE
II PETER
IAMES LAST OF
SAXMUNDHAM 1769

the interior of the rim with a lambrequin border in runny blue. 4½ inches high. Painter's number '5'. [Cracked.] *£580. 0. 0.*

191. A fine inscribed large bell mug with bold loop handle and two large flower sprays flanking a light feathery cartouche inscribed:

EDW[d] & MARY
JEX
YARMOUTH

the inside of the rim with a loop and sprig border in runny blue. 6 inches high. Painter's number '5'.
[A matching smaller mug is recorded and originally there was probably a set of three mugs.] *£260. 0. 0.*

Enamel Decoration

192. An inscribed and dated mug of cylindrical shape, with blue zig-zag and green and red entwined floral borders, the puce cartouche inscribed:

ANN CONWAY
1795
A TRIFLE
FROM
LOWESTOFT.

flanked by rose sprigs. 3½ inches high. [Cracked.] [Plate 223.] *£48. 0. 0.*

193. A rare Trifle barrel mug, with blue zig-zag and red and green entwined borders, inscribed:

A TRIFLE
FROM
BUNGAY

within a puce husk and ribbon festoon panel flanked by rose sprays. 3⅞ inches high. *£340. 0. 0.*

194. A fine cylindrical mug inscribed in red:

JOHN ALLCOCK
MAY 10TH
1790

within a puce feathery bordered escutcheon, flanked by sprigs and sprays in Rose tradition, iron-red border inside rim. 4½ inches high. [Plate 212.] *£400. 0. 0.*

195. A rare oblong octagonal spoon-tray of the two bird pattern in Imari palette. 6¼ inches long [Pattern as Plate 144.] *£60. 0. 0.*

196. A very fine coloured birth tablet, with a red line border unusually inscribed in brown:

HENRIETTE
GALL
BORN APRIL 18
1796

the reverse attractively painted with a bunch of flowers in colours tied with a ribbon, within a puce and sepia entwined sprig border, two holes for suspension. Diameter 3 inches. *£370. 0. 0.*

197. A fine bell-shaped mug of small size, with typical loop

handle and loop and dot red border, painted with sprays of flowers by the Tulip painter. 3½ inches high. *£70. 0. 0.*

198. The Calder fluted bowl, with wavy rim and two rows of red and gilt vine meander and festoons, the base of the bowl bearing within a gilt heart shaped panel the inscription:

M AND E
CALDER
NORWICK
1776

[See also items Nos. 58 and 61.] *£240. 0. 0.*

199. The Rev. Robert Potter. A teabowl, coffee cup and saucer, painted with the arms — or, a chevron sable between three mullets pierced gules, below the crest and above the motto 'In Deo Potero' gilt line borders. [See Plate 215.] *£200. 0. 0.*

[It is interesting to see that a cup and saucer from this famous service was sold for £12 in 1938, see item 117, page 243.]

MESSRS. SOTHEBY & CO.., JULY 9th, 1968.

200. A very rare coloured jug with ribbed scroll handle, the lip spout with strainer, the body decorated on a gilt trellis brick-red ground with reserve panels of Chinese figures feeding squirrels in interior. . . 8¼ inches high. [See Plate 189.] *£220. 0. 0.*

201. A rare Lowestoft blue and white basket, the centre delicately printed with a spray of flowers and butterflies, the moulded lattice-work sides applied with rosettes and painted on the inside rim with scrolling foliage, the twisted rope handles with leaf and bud terminals. 8 inches. Crescent mark in blue. *£150. 0. 0.*

Similar to that shown in Plate 133.

MESSRS. CHRISTIES,
OCTOBER 28TH, 1968.

202. A rare Lowestoft blue and white dated mug of bell shape, with scroll handle, inscribed Ann Sawyer 1773, within a typical rococo scroll cartouche. . . . 4½ inches high. Workman's mark 5. *£320. 0. 0.*

[See D.70, page 226.]

MESSRS. SOTHEBY & CO.,
FEBRUARY 4TH, 1969

203. A rare Lowestoft sweetmeat dish, of circular shape, formed into compartments by divisions radiating from a central well, painted in underglaze-blue with a flower in each section, pendent from a scroll border, and the centre with a bridge and pavilion. 7 inch diameter. Painter's number 5. *£160. 0. 0.*

Similar to that shown in Plate 91, see page 205, 'Hors-d'œuvre set'.

204. A rare Lowestoft transfer-printed mug of cylindrical shape printed in blue with figures in an Oriental garden among trees and pagodas, one crossing a bridge, the reverse with a smaller, similar, design, the handle with kick terminal. 5⅞ inches high. *£90. 0 0.*

MESSRS. SOTHEBY & CO.,
FEBRUARY 6th, 1973

205. A rare Lowestoft milk jug of barrel shape with bands of cooping, painted in underglaze-blue. 3 inches high. *£80. 00*

206. A rare Lowestoft saucer-shape plate of Hughes-type moulded in relief with underglaze-blue scenic panels. Diameter 7½ inches. *£80. 00*

207. Lowestoft powder-blue ground coffee-pot of the type shown in Plate 68. Odd cover and crack. 6½ inches high. *£68. 00*

208. A Lowestoft powder-blue bowl with panels of landscape. Diameter 5 inches. *£105. 00*

209. A cream boat of spirally fluted form [as Plate 150] painted with floral garlands. *£85. 00*

210. A rare loving cup (?) similar in form to Plate 153, painted in underglaze-blue. Damaged. *£75. 00*

THE WELL—KNOWN COLLECTION OF
LOWESTOFT PORCELAIN. THE PROPERTY OF
G.W. MIDDLETON ESQ. SOLD BY MESSRS.
SOTHEBY & CO. ON OCTOBER 23rd, 1973

[This section includes only the more important lots.]

211. A very rare Lowestoft veilleuse or Food Warmer with shell handles and satyr masks, painted in underglaze-blue. 6⅜ inches high. Body only. As Plate 104. *£270. 00*

212. A large Lowestoft moulded jug of a standard type. 9 inches high. Slight staining. *£90. 00*

213. A rare egg cup painted in underglaze-blue. 3¼ inches high. Slight crack. *£90. 00*

214. A shallow sauce-boat painted in underglaze-blue — as Plate 124. *£55. 00*

215. A blue and white covered jug or coffee-pot, similar to Plate 135. Handle damaged. *£60. 00*

216. A coffee cup and saucer from the Ludlow service, as Plate 202. Slight crack to saucer. *£120. 00.*

217. A shell-shaped cream boat, as Plate 120, enamelled with flowers. *£105. 00*

218. A rare and attractive inkwell well painted with flowers. Diameter 2¾ inches. *£420. 00*

219. An important and handsome coffee-pot painted by the Tulip painter — as Plate 148. 9 inches high. *£1,200. 00*

220. A rare custard cup and cover painted with simple sprigs. *£115. 00*

221. A typical Lowestoft birth tablet painted in underglaze-blue and inscribed 'Thomas Page, born December 31st 1786'. Slightly cracked. *£500. 00*

222. A blue and white teapot inscribed 'Rob & Mary Godfrey. 1782'. 5½ inches high. *£560. 00*

223. A rare blue and white flask inscribed 'John Toake, Yarmouth 1782'. Slightly damaged. [See Plate 246.] *£1,000. 00*

224. An enamelled mug inscribed:

EB
1793

Slightly damaged. *£300. 00*

Later in this sale other Lowestoft items were sold, including:

225. A rare blue and white cylindrical inkwell. [See Plate 247.] *£300. 00*

226. A rare vinegar (?) bottle with angular handle, as Plate 90. *£100. 00*

BLUE AND WHITE PORCELAINS FROM THE COLLECTION OF THE 2nd VISCOUNT CHANDOS. SOLD BY MESSRS. SOTHEBY & CO. ON APRIL 8th, 1975.

227. An attractive Hughes-type moulded cream or milk jug of the type shown in Plate 72 right. 3½ inches high. Slightly damaged. *£250. 00*

228. A rare octagonal inkwell painted in underglaze-blue. Body crack. [See Plate 248.] *£240. 00*

229. A complete veilleuse painted in underglaze-blue, as Plate 104. Some damage. 10¼ inches high. *£340. 00*

230. A rare and early covered vase (with bird knob) painted in underglaze-blue, as Plate 36. 6¼ inches high. Slight damage but a very nice specimen. *£620. 00*

231. A superb blue and white loving cup or porringer. [See Plate 249.] *£600. 00*

232. A superb, rare and early coffee or chocolate pot and cover painted in underglaze blue. Ex Hunting Collection, as shown in Plate 35. [See sale record 174 where this pot is recorded as being sold for £190 in October 1961.] *£1,350. 00*

233. An attractive and early bell-shape mug well painted with a floral design in underglaze-blue. 6 inches high. c.1760. *£260. 00*

234. An attractive moulded cider (?) mug of the type shown in Plate 66, painted in underglaze-blue. 3¾ inches high. c.1763-5. [See Plate 250.] *£560. 00*

THE COLLECTION OF ENGLISH BLUE & WHITE PORCELAIN FORMED BY GILBERT BRADLEY ESQ., SOLD BY MESSRS. CHRISTIE, MANSON & WOODS ON OCTOBER 12th, 1981.

This very varied collection was gathered together by a discriminating collector who rightly paid little regard to damage, purchasing interesting specimens which gave him pleasure. Few examples cost Mr. Bradley over £50, in fact his most expensive purchase was a rare Derby blue and white vase for £150 — this sold for £1,100!

N.B. The prices here given are the 'hammer prices' on top of which the purchaser paid the auctioneer's 'premium' of 10% plus VAT of 15% on the 'premium'.

235. A rare and early patty pan painted in underglaze-blue. Cracked and chipped. *£220. 00*

236. A rare flared beaker painted in underglaze blue. c.1760. Large chip missing from edge. *£320. 00*

237. A rare and early but damaged inkwell painted in underglaze-blue. Ex Hunting Collection. *£650. 00*

238. A typical Lowestoft blue and white bottle or gugglet. Damaged and repaired. *£380. 00*

239. A rare moulded cornucopia-shaped wall-pocket, painted in underglaze-blue. *£400. 00*

240. An attractive and rare barrel-shaped teapot and cover painted in underglaze-blue. c.1765. *£1,000. 00*

241. A moulded Hughes-type octagonal tea-caddy, similar to Plate 64. *£400. 00*

242. A rare saucer-shape dish or plate painted in underglaze-blue with an Oriental type landscape. Cracked. *£220. 00*

243. A good moulded jug, the body painted in underglaze-blue with an Oriental landscape. Damaged. *£440. 00*

244. An early and rare moulded jug, of the type shown in Plate 56. Large crack, chip and repair. *£420. 00*

[N.B. A further example with very unsightly run blue fetched £260.]

THE HENRY LEVINE COLLECTION OF LOWESTOFT PORCELAIN SOLD BY MESSRS. IRELANDS HALL & PALMER IN NORWICH ON NOVEMBER 25th 1982

The late Henry Levine was one of the old school of Lowestoft collectors. He started collecting in 1915 and several pieces sold in 1982 are illustrated in this book, Mr. Levine having supplied the author with photographs of special pieces in his collection. See also page 35 for my general comments on this sale.

N.B. No auctioneer's 'premium' was charged.

Blue and White

245. A rare so-called chestnut basket with pierced cover, of the type shown in Plate 130. *£1,400. 00*

246. A good moulded Hughes type jug painted in underglaze-blue with mock Oriental landscapes, as Plate 57. *£580. 00*

247. A ribbed tea caddy painted with formal floral pattern, as the example included in Plate 142. *£280. 00*

248. A pair of pierced circular baskets of Worcester type, as Plate 134. *£740. 00*

249. A Worcester type salad or junket dish transfer printed in underglaze-blue — as Plate 127. *£310. 00*

250. An open topped coffee (?) jug, printed in underglaze-blue and inscribed 'John Baker, Yarmouth, 1772'. *£640. 00*
Illustrated in Plate 121. Sold for £18.00 at the Colman sale in April 1948, see sale record 130.

251. A rare blue and white 'A Trifle from Lowestoft' inkwell. [Illustrated in Plate 235, left.] *£2,200. 00*

252. A very rare pounce pot inscribed in underglaze-blue 'For my Friend'. [Illustrated in Plate 235, right.] *£1,450. 00*

253. A cylindrical mug painted in underglaze-blue and inscribed 'John and Mary Livock. Lowestoft 1780'. *£1,100. 00*
Cracked. Sold in the Crisp Collection in 1935 for £8.00. Resold in the Hotblack Collection in 1955 for £16.00.

254. A large covered jug and cover decorated in underglaze-blue and inscribed on the front 'John and Sarah Livock, Lowestoft 1787'. *£1,850. 00*
Cracked. [See Plate 27. Sold in the Colman Collection in 1948 for £28.00.]

255. Two toy teabowls simply painted in underglaze-blue and inscribed on the base 'IL 1788' and 'SL 1790'. *£520. 00*
Sold in the Colman Collection in 1948 for £21.00.

The following related teawares decorated with the standard 'Redgrave Root pattern' are illustrated in Plate 146. This small grouping commanded £1,730.00.

256. A typical Redgrave globular teapot and cover. Body crack. *£240. 00*

257. A rare octagonal teapot stand. *£370. 00*

258. A rare spoon tray of elongated octagonal form. Small crack. *£290. 00*

259. A similar spoon tray. *£270. 00*

260. A rare tea canister, no cover. *£310. 00*

261. A small waste bowl of unusual fluted form with wavy edge. *£140. 00*

262. A typical sparrow beak creamer. *£110. 00*

Enamelled

263. A very rare saucer painted in pink monochrome, as Plate 155. *£460. 00*

264. A tea bowl and saucer from the Ludlow service, as Plate 202 and Colour Plate 9. *£520. 00*

265. A rare fluted teapot enamelled in a typical late style. [Illustrated in Plate 232.] *£580. 00*

266. A very good and typical coffee pot enamelled with panels of Oriental figures. [Illustrated in Plate 192.] Cover slightly restored, crack to handle joint. *£700. 00*

267. A unique flask enamelled with flowers and with the initials 'SA' reputedly made for Samuel Aldred. *£850. 00*

268. A rare but typical cylindrical mug, inscribed 'A Trifle from Lowestoft'. 4½ inches high. Cracked. *£760. 00*

269. A squat mug, inscribed 'A Trifle from Lowestoft', the ground decorated with cornflower sprigs. 2¾ inches high. Restored. *£580. 00*

270. A small cylindrical mug inscribed 'M.A.R. 1793', the ground decorated with cornflower sprigs. 3⅛ inches high. Much damaged. *£250. 00*

271. The attractive large presentation mug, inscribed on the front 'D.I. to H. Gillman 1795'. Cracked. 5 inches high. [Illustrated in Plate 226.] *£580. 00*

The following three items of Lowestoft porcelain were included in a general sale of British ceramics conducted by Messrs. Sotheby & Co. on October 4th, 1983. The prices include the auctioneer's 'premium'.

272. A good but rather small enamelled cylindrical mug, inscribed on the front 'A Trifle from Lowestoft'. 3½ inches high. Slight edge chip. *£935.00*

273. A bright and typical cylindrical mug boldly painted by the Tulip painter. 4½ inches high. Restored. *£550.00*

274. Two good moulded sauce boats of the type illustrated in Plate 59. The initials 'I H' and the date '1762' are worked into the mould below each side panel — a feature reasonably consistent on this form of sauce boat. 8½ inches long. *£1,045.00*

Plate 246. *The front and reverse of a Lowestoft porcelain flask, painted in underglaze blue and dated 1782. In 1973 this was sold at auction for £1,000.* Sotheby's.

Plate 247. *A simple but rare Lowestoft inkpot and pen holder painted in underglaze blue. Painter's number '5'. 2⅜ins. high. c.1765. Sold in 1973 for £300.* Author's Collection.

Plate 248. *A rare Lowestoft octagonal form inkpot, amusingly painted in underglaze blue. Cracked. Diameter 3ins. c.1765-70. Sold in 1975 for £240.* Sotheby's.

Plate 249. *A very rare and attractive Lowestoft porringer, painted in underglaze blue. Painter's number '3'. 3¾ins. high. c.1762-5. Sold in 1975 for £600.* Sotheby's.

Plate 250. *A rare relief-moulded cider (?) mug (see also Plate 66) attractively painted in underglaze blue. Painter's number '5'. 3¾ins. high. c.1765-70. Sold in 1975 for £560.* Sotheby's.

APPENDIX III

Fakes and False Attributions

From the middle of the nineteenth century the Lowestoft porcelains, especially the inscribed examples, have been collectable items and a number of fakes or reproductions have been made which can deceive at least the inexperienced collector.

Most reproductions were made in France and are of the standard Continental hard-paste body, quite unlike the relatively warm, friendly, soft-paste porcelain of the true Lowestoft pieces. In an effort to soften the appearance of the hard Continental body, or to produce the effect of age, a covering glaze which was prone to crazing (the breaking up of the glaze to form a network of fine lines) was used on some reproductions. This can be seen in Plate 241, but I have yet to find it on true Lowestoft porcelains.

Several copies of the blue and white mug shown in Plate 82 were made on the Continent and these bear under the base the following inscription, which is also found on a set of three genuine mugs:

Abr^{m} Moore
August 29th
1765

While the shape of the reproductions is quite good, the blue painting has normally 'run' and has an unpleasant 'blotchy' appearance and the glaze has crazed; compare Plates 82 and 241.

The hard-paste Continental copies are often credited to Samson of Paris, but several other firms supplied reproductions of desirable English porcelains to nineteenth and early twentieth century English buyers. One of these Paris manufacturers, Paul Bocquillon, openly advertised Reproductions of Lowestoft, Chelsea, Derby, Worcester and other fashionable porcelains, and an illustrated advertisement of 1914 includes a plate inscribed, 'A Trifle from Lowestoft'. The hard-paste mug illustrated in Plate 240, is probably his work.

I have as yet seen fakes only of the Abr^{m}. Moore mugs, and various pieces inscribed 'A Trifle from Lowestoft', the standard designs of the Lowestoft factory apparently not having been copied, but the ruling high prices may now encourage the reproduction of other objects.

The hard-paste Continental reproductions of the Abraham Moore mugs and the 'Trifles from Lowestoft' should not deceive many collectors, but some who are less experienced may well start building their knowledge of Lowestoft porcelains on faulty foundations, for several non-Lowestoft pieces are illustrated under false colours in standard works of reference. The following list of errors will warn the reader to regard with great caution the attributions of the articles referred to below:

The Ceramic Art of Great Britain, L. Jewitt. 1878, revised edition 1883. Figures 841 and 842 represent Chinese export market porcelains, not true Lowestoft porcelains.

Lowestoft China by W.W.R. Spelman. 1905.
The first fifty-eight Plates in this book illustrate fragments found on the factory site, and this aspect of the book is of the utmost importance. However, subsequent research has indicated that several of the finished objects which Spelman illustrated are not of Lowestoft origin.
Plate LX, centre. Bowl and cup not Lowestoft, probably Bow.
Plate LXII, fig. 5. Teapot, Bow.
Plate LXIII, Plate, Bow.
Plate LXIV, figs. 1, 2, 4 and 5. Not Lowestoft.
Plate LXV, figs. 1-6. Not Lowestoft.
Plate LXVI, figs. 1, 3 and 4. Not Lowestoft.
Plate LXVII, figs. 4, 5 and 6. Not Lowestoft.
Plate LXX. Jug, Liverpool, not Lowestoft.
Plate LXXI. Doubtful.
Plate LXXII, fig. 1. Probably Derby.
Plate LXXIV. Probably Derby, not Lowestoft.
Plate LXXV. Bow, not Lowestoft.
Plate LXXVII, figs. 1, 2 and 3. Not Lowestoft, probably Bow.
Plate LXXVIII, figs. 1, 2 and 3. Not Lowestoft.
Plate LXXIX, fig. 3. Not Lowestoft, probably Bow.
Plate LXXXI. Although this flask is inscribed 'A Trifle from Lowestoft', it is most unlikely that it was made there and the date, 1769, is some twenty years before this New Hall style decoration came into favour.
Plate LXXXIII, figs. 2 and 3. Liverpool and Worcester, not Lowestoft.
Plate LXXXIV, fig. 3. Worcester, not Lowestoft.
Plate LXXXV, fig. 3. Worcester, not Lowestoft.
Plate LXXXVII, figs. 2 and 3. Early Worcester or Bristol, not Lowestoft.
Plate LXXXVIII, figs. 2 and 3. Derby, although the Lowestoft factory produced a similar model, see Plate 42. The attribution of fig. 1 is open to doubt.
Plates XCII-XCVI. Not Lowestoft.
Plate XCVII, figs. 1, 2, 3, 4, 5, 6, 9, 10, 11, 12, 13, 14, 15, 16, 17, are not Lowestoft.

The First Century of English Porcelain by W. Moore Binns. 1906.
Colour Plate opposite page 164. These objects, with one possible exception, are not Lowestoft. Taking the items from left to right, the first mug is Longton Hall, the creamer is early Worcester, as is the central jug. The next creamer might be Lowestoft but this is doubtful, and the sauce boat is Liverpool.

The A.B.C. of XIX Century English Art by J.F. Blacker, not dated but c.1911.
Page 513. Powder blue plate is Bow, not Lowestoft.
Page 521. Covered vase and tankard at top of page are hard-paste Chinese export market porcelains, not Lowestoft. The author noted in his caption that these were doubtful specimens.

Catalogue of the Herbert Allen Collection of English Porcelain. Victoria and Albert Museum publication. 1917.
Plate 85. Items 486, 487 (numbered 877 in the caption in error), 488, 489, 493 are not Lowestoft although the descriptions in the text include qualifications and they are not

definitely claimed as Lowestoft. The stock Museum photograph of these pieces has been reused in other books which claim the objects shown are Lowestoft.

A fluted teabowl and saucer illustrated in Plate 88 (item 507) as New Hall is, however, almost certainly Lowestoft.

The New Keramic Gallery by William Chaffers, 3rd edition of 1926, edited by H.M. Cundall.
Figs. 588 to 590 are of Chinese hard-paste porcelain and of the five articles shown in fig. 591 only the cup shown at the front to the right of the coffee pot is true Lowestoft porcelain.

Old English Porcelain by W.B. Honey, 1931.
Plate 51, centre. This oval dish is Bow, not Lowestoft.

Lowestoft China by A.E. Murton, 1932.
Facing page 16. These two saucers do not appear to be Lowestoft specimens.

English Blue and White Porcelain of the 18th Century, S.W. Fisher, 1947.
Plate 4.g. Probably not Lowestoft.

English Porcelain and Bone China by Bernard and Therle Hughes, 1955.
Plate 29, middle right. This blue and white sauce boat is probably Bow rather than Lowestoft.
Plate 29, bottom left. Teapot and cover probably Worcester or Caughley although the cup shown with this teapot is certainly of Lowestoft make.

The Concise Encyclopaedia of English Pottery and Porcelain by W. Mankowitz and R.G. Haggar, 1957.
Plate 61C. The oval dish in the bottom row is almost certainly not Lowestoft.

English Blue and White Porcelain of the 18th Century, by Dr. B. Watney, 1963.
Plate 82E. Inkwell, probably Derby, not Lowestoft, an error for which I must admit reponsibility.
Plate 84B. Saucer, possibly Derby, not Lowestoft. One cannot be certain, for the ownership or present whereabouts of the example illustrated by Dr. Watney is not given, but the specimens which I have seen bearing the same printed subject did not show the standard Lowestoft characteristics, and I regarded these as Derby.
N.B. The revised 1973 edition corrects these errors by replacing the original illustrations with other objects.

English Ceramics by S.W. Fisher, 1966.
Plate 132. Although this relief-moulded bowl is very similar to Lowestoft examples, it is probably of Bow manufacture.
Plate 133. The bowl on the left of the top shelf is not Lowestoft, nor are the three pieces shown on the lower shelf.
Plate 135. Although I have not handled the teapot, I have never seen this pointed knob on a Lowestoft specimen of this shape. The creamer shown with this teapot is undoubtedly Lowestoft, although the date given in the caption is some twenty years too early.

BIBLIOGRAPHY

In general the nineteenth century reference books such as Jewitt's *Ceramic Art of Great Britain* and the early editions of Chaffers' *Marks and Monograms* are unreliable, as they tend to confuse Chinese export market porcelains with the true Lowestoft wares.

One of the earliest, and most reliable, contributions to the history of the Lowestoft Porcelain Factory was written by Henry C. Casley (part of this early collection, incidentally, is to be seen at the South Quay Museum, at Great Yarmouth) in the form of a Paper, entitled 'Lowestoft China Factory', which is included in *The Proceedings of the Suffolk Institute of Archaeology and Natural History,* Vol. XI, Part 3, 1903.

In 1904, Frederick Arthur Crisp, an early collector of Lowestoft porcelains, published a printed copy of the Lowestoft Church Registers under the title *The Parish Registers of Lowestoft, Suffolk,* containing records of Baptisms and Burials from 1751 to 1812, and marriages from 1752 to 1812. This book, now very rare, being originally privately printed with an edition of only fifty copies, has proved of great help in tracing the history of persons for whom Lowestoft porcelain was originally made and inscribed, also for dating the period of painters employed at the factory (Chapter IV).

In 1905, W.W.R. Spelman published his *Lowestoft China,* a most important contribution, for the first fifty-eight illustrations show factory wasters or parts of the original moulds, which are now housed in the Castle Museum, Norwich. The following illustrations of finished, complete objects are not so helpful, as many errors of attribution occur and the products of most eighteenth century English porcelain factories are to be found under the Lowestoft description, see Appendix III, page 254.

A very limited edition (150 copies) of an interesting, and sound, book was privately printed in 1907, by the late Frederick Arthur Crisp, under the title of *Catalogue of Lowestoft China in the possession of Frederick Arthur Crisp.** This interesting collection is listed, and in many cases illustrated, with details of their provenance, such as:

> Bought 3 February, 1896, of William Rix Seago of Lowestoft. This is the Ink Pot made for Robert Browne, one of the original partners. It was sold to Mr. Seago by his great-grandson, also a Robert Browne, and is referred to in his affidavit as — Ink Pot with initials R.B. 1762. This was the inkpot of the originator and manufacturer of the factory.

This book was closely followed by *Lowestoft China Factory, and the moulds found there in December 1902,* also by Frederick Arthur Crisp. Again, the edition was limited to a mere one hundred and fifty copies, so that this book is now very rare and expensive.

One of the most important contributions to the study of Lowestoft porcelain took the

---

* This 1907 volume is based on a draft dated 1896, and it is interesting to see that the early draft includes several examples of hard-paste Chinese porcelain, but these pieces were deleted before the publication of the 1907 catalogue.

form of a Paper by A.J.B. Kiddell, Esq., read to the English Porcelain Circle (now retitled the English Ceramic Circle) in November 1929. This Paper, after a brief but scholarly introduction, listed all the then known documentary inscribed and dated specimens. This material is to be found in the *Transactions of the English Porcelain Circle*, No. III, 1931. A revised list is given in the present book, in Appendix I.

In 1932, Mr. A.E. Murton published a little book with the title *Lowestoft China*, which, compared with Mr. Kiddell's researches, appears rather 'chatty', but it does include several interesting points and useful illustrations.

Following on from his Paper read to the English Porcelain Circle, the late Mr. A.J.B. Kiddell (then President of the English Ceramic Circle) published two important magazine articles featuring key-documentary specimens in the collection of Mrs. Russell Colman. The first of these, in *The Connoisseur* magazine of September 1937, discussed the pieces decorated in underglaze blue, while the overglaze enamelled examples were featured in the October 1937, issue. The same authority — Mr. Kiddell — contributed a Paper on 'Richard Powles, Lowestoft Painter' to the *Transactions of the English Ceramic Circle,* Vol. 2, No. 7, 1939.

The late D.M. Hunting made three important contributions to our knowledge of Lowestoft porcelain between 1949 and 1951. An article in *The Antique Collector* magazine of December 1949, dealt with miniature or 'toy' pieces, and one in the same magazine dated December 1951, covered the important subject of teapots. Mr. Hunting also contributed an important Paper to the *Transactions of the English Ceramic Circle*, Vol. 3, Part I, 1951, dealing with the very early Lowestoft porcelains. In 1968, Mr. George J. Levine, of Brundall, published a list of *Inscribed Lowestoft Porcelain.* Books published since this present work was first published in 1969 are:

Lowestoft Porcelain in Norwich Castle Museum
Vol. 1. Blue and White and excavated material, by Sheenah Smith (Norfolk Museums Service, 1975).

Early Lowestoft
by Christopher Spencer (Ainsworth and Nelson, 1981).

In addition there are the three important Papers by John Howell:

Transfer-Printed Lowestoft Porcelain
(*Transactions of the English Ceramic Circle*, Vol. 7, part 3, 1970).

Some Notes on the Introduction of Polychrome Decoration at Lowestoft
(*Transactions of the English Ceramic Circle*, Vol. 9, part 3, 1975).

Early Lowestoft
(*Transactions of the English Ceramic Circle*, Vol. 11, part 2, 1982).

I have also published a tape-recorded, general talk on collecting Lowestoft, which is available with a slim booklet of illustrations at £5.00. This is available post-free in the U.K. from Geoffrey Godden, Chinaman, 17-19 Crescent Road, Worthing, West Sussex, BN11 1RL. (Tel. 0903 35958 in office hours).

Most general reference books give some details of the Lowestoft factory but, with two exceptions, these offer little real help to the serious collector. The two important exceptions are Chapter 7 of Dr. Bernard Watney's *English Blue and White Porcelain* (revised 1973 edition) and Mr. G.C. Bolster's contribution to *English Porcelain, 1745-1850*, (1965).

In addition to these serious works, many magazine articles have been written on this interesting subject. In the main these may be classed as superficial but, although they often tend to infuriate the advanced collector, they can have far reaching results. It was one of these articles, for instance, published in 1934, that first aroused my curiosity about the products of this small factory, and which so started a hobby which has held my interest continuously over the years. I can only hope that this book will serve to spread this enjoyment.

For readers who wish to see fine specimens of Lowestoft porcelains, the following collections in Public Museums can be recommended:

Castle Museum, Norwich.
Christchurch Mansion, Ipswich.
Fitzwilliam Museum, Cambridge.
South Quay Museum, Great Yarmouth.
Victoria and Albert Museum, London.

Other museums, including the British Museum, have interesting pieces, but not a truly representative selection of the many styles and types produced at the Lowestoft factory. There is also a collection at the Lowestoft Library.

Most of the pieces here attributed in the captions to the author's collection may be viewed, by appointment, at Worthing.

A CLOSING NOTE TO WOULD-BE COLLECTORS

Although a wealth of pieces is illustrated in this book, this does not mean that Lowestoft porcelains are plentiful; they are decidedly rare, and consequently may well be expensive, especially the inscribed examples. Scarce as the Lowestoft porcelains may be the new collector should not despair. Several very good, interesting collections have been built up in recent years and most collectors have enjoyed their share of lucky 'finds' — because they knew what they were looking for!

All collectors will have stories to tell of bargains picked up in unexpected places. Such finds, of course, give great pleasure but a good, balanced collection cannot be formed of bargains alone. The far-seeing collector intent on the formation of a worthwhile collection should be prepared to pay the market price, for, if he is not able to do this, many fine examples will be missed and the whole collection will suffer.

Looking back over some forty years of collecting Lowestoft china, I find that the best pieces were acquired from dealers who had a knowledge of the goods in which they traded and asked a realistic price. With the passing of years, prices which caused some concern at the time can now be considered to be ridiculously low. By all means take every advantage of bargains when they appear, but do not rely on them for all your pleasure.

It is, of course, extremely difficult to give guidance on what is a fair and realistic price, especially as today the level of price for all antiques seems to increase monthly. A study of the ruling auction sale prices given in Appendix II will make interesting, but perhaps not very helpful, reading. Prices have risen from sums which now appear laughably low to prices which baffle some collectors who remember the ruling prices only ten, or even five years ago, yet all these represent the ruling prices of their day willingly given by collectors and dealers of the period. Even at today's high prices, the early pre-1770 blue and white wares are, in many cases, undervalued in comparison with some of the more fashionable (but to me less interesting) types.

You will probably be asking if the present increase in prices is likely to continue — one cannot, of course, see ahead but, judging by past trends, the prices of interesting, decorative and collectable antiques will continue to increase as more and more people see the reason behind investing spare cash in such objects, rather than see their resources being whittled away by the rising cost of living, over which they appear to have no control. I am not suggesting, of course, that readers should collect Lowestoft porcelain solely for long-term financial gain, for more worthwhile profit will be gained from the satisfaction that such a collection will afford and from the absorbing interest in its formation.

Finally, a word about damage. Most reference books warn the new collector to avoid damaged pieces at all costs. This is good advice if you are a multimillionaire, but the Lowestoft collector would do well to disregard this advice, for two reasons: in the first place, the Lowestoft wares were made for use (with the exception of the very rare figures) and it is reasonable to expect at least minor damage in them. A small chip to the spout of a teapot or an old crack to a jug (such as can be seen in Plate 140) are excusable, although, of course, any damage should be reflected in the price, and it is obviously preferable to buy a perfect example, rather than a damaged one. Today we probably know of only about one or two per cent (if that) of the factory's total production, as much of the remainder must have been damaged in use and most discarded for that reason. The amount of damage that may be expected is seen in the inscribed presentation pieces (listed in Appendix I) for very few are perfect but, being presentation pieces, they were preserved in the family after damage and not discarded as one would an ordinary mug or jug, and today even badly damaged inscribed pieces command a high price on account of their individuality and interest.

My second reason for stating that the new collector should not shun damaged pieces is that they afford the best means of getting to know the different characteristics described in the book; terms such as 'early compact body' or 'late floury body' become self-explanatory once one has handled two damaged saucers and, more important, one can acquire the 'feel' of the ware, an all important accomplishment that cannot be obtained from any book, or by looking through museum display cabinets.

INDEX